D1606511

Retrieving Apologetics

Retrieving Apologetics

Glenn B. Siniscalchi

PICKWICK *Publications* · Eugene, Oregon

RETRIEVING APOLOGETICS

Pickwick Publications
An Imprint of Wipf and Stock Publishers
199 W. 8th Ave., Suite 3
Eugene, OR 97401

www.wipfandstock.com

PAPERBACK ISBN: 978-1-4982-2843-5
HARDCOVER ISBN: 978-1-4982-2845-9

Cataloguing-in-Publication Data

Siniscalchi, Glenn B.

Retrieving Apologetics / Glenn B. Siniscalchi.

vii + 288 p. ; 23 cm. Includes bibliographical references.

ISBN 13: 978-1-4982-2843-5

1. Apologetics. 2. Catholic Church—Apologetic works. 3. Christianity. I. Title.

BT1103 S342 2016

Manufactured in the U.S.A.   01/07/2016

"Fine-Tuning, Atheist Criticism, and the Fifth Way," *Theology and Science*, Vol.
12, No. 1, (February, 2014) 64–77. Center for Theology and the Natural Sciences,
reprinted by permission of Taylor & Francis Ltd, www.tandfonline.com on behalf
of Center for Theology and the Natural Sciences.

Contents

Part Five: Jesus Christ and the Religious Others

Acknowledgments

MOST OF THE RESEARCH for this book was completed for my dissertation at Duquesne University.

I remain grateful to the following scholars who have commented on individual chapters or the entire manuscript: Dale Allison, Marie Baird, Sally Carey, Jeremiah Cowart, Brian Davies, OP, Richard Grebenc, Paul Griffiths, James Iovino, Karita Ivancic, SND, Patrick Madigan, SJ, R.J. Matava, James Menkaus, Gannon Murphy, Maureen O'Brien, Gerald O'Collins, SJ, Nick Palmer, Ana Plumlee, Louise Prochaska, Phil Taraska, Thomas Weinandy, OFM, Jared Wicks, SJ, and George Worgul. Your incisive comments have significantly improved the contents, grammar, and syntax of this book.

I would be remiss if I failed to acknowledge Stephen Bullivant, Alfred Freddoso, Matthew Levering, and Gerald O'Collins, SJ, for writing the endorsements of my work. Thanks for your unfailing support.

Most of all, I want to thank my wife Kathleen for her patience as I spent many hours writing and formatting this book. I dedicate it to her.

Introduction

WHAT IS APOLOGETICS? HISTORICALLY apologetics is the theological discipline that deals with the defense of the historic Christian faith. Given the popes' recent desires to implement the New Evangelization, it is imperative that Catholic theologians and other intellectually engaged laypersons retrieve this vital discipline.[1] Church leaders call for Catholics to be evangelized so they may go forth to evangelize the world. Advocates of the New Evangelization place particular emphasis on re-proposing the gospel to those who have experienced a crisis of faith because of secularization.

The relationship between apologetics and evangelization is intimate. While apologists are focused on ensuring intellectual consent *about* Christ, evangelists are focused on ensuring commitment *to* Christ. One might argue that the New Evangelization will gain momentum when theologians and other Catholics develop the confidence to share the gospel in a compelling way.[2] Apologetical studies can help motivate Catholics to take the missionary mandate (Matt 28:18–20) and interreligious dialogue seriously. This is why the discipline should be resituated in light of Vatican II (1962–65) and other subsequent developments in the life of the Church.

An Apology for Apologetics

Before we situate the role of apologetics in the Church, it would be profitable for us to recount some of the positive reasons why Catholics and other Christians might engage in apologetics. This "apology for apologetics" will

---

1. For a discussion of the New Evangelization, see Fisichella, *The New Evangelization.*

2. Cf. Levada, "Toward a New Apologetics," 661–67; Levada, "A New Apologetics for the Church in the 21st Century," 7–15; Levada, "Giving Reasons for Our Hope," 33–42.

set the stage for understanding the relevant passages in Vatican II (in chapter 1) which can also serve as an impetus for fostering the defense of the faith.

One reason for doing apologetics is that Scripture commands it. In Jude 3, believers are told to "contend for the faith." In Colossians 4:5–6, the apostle Paul warns the Church: "Conduct yourselves wisely toward outsiders, making the most of the opportunity. Let your speech always be gracious, seasoned with salt, so that you know how you should respond to each one." Paul saw his own role as that of an apologist. In Philippians 1:16, he wrote, "I am here for the defense of the gospel." Cardinal Walter Kasper comments: "faith, as understood in the Bible, is not a blind venture, not an irrational feeling, not an uncalculated option and certainly not a *sacrificium intellectus* (sacrifice of the intellect). Rather, faith can and must give a rational account of itself."[3] Many more passages of Scripture could be cited to support a sound biblical basis for apologetics.[4]

Second, common sense also suggests that apologetics is needed. Unlike mere animals, God created human beings with the ability to reason about the world. Therefore, God expects us to use our minds to explain and defend the Catholic faith.[5] Reason also helps individuals to determine what is true, and how to justify one's beliefs. Without reason, there is no justification for holding to any one set of beliefs over and against another set of beliefs. Socrates once said that "the unexamined life is not worth living." The same goes for Catholic faith: the unexamined faith is not worth believing. Since God did not create anyone without a mind, it is normal for individuals to have questions about the claims of the Church.

Third, apologetics helps to inculturate the gospel. Catholics must be able to understand the wider cultural context where they live in order for effective evangelization to take place. The zeitgeist of the modern West can be traced back to the secular philosophies of the Enlightenment. The hallmark of this movement was to free humanity from the "shackles of organized religion." The impact of this movement is still felt in the academy. These philosophies maintain that faith is equivalent to an opinion or personal taste; only that which is observable is worthy of public discussion and debate. Kasper elaborates on the modern cultural malaise: "Especially in a situation like ours today, when everything depends on the Christian faith making the transition to new cultural horizons and a new epoch, there can be no question of the Christian retreating into the realm of private experience.

3. Kasper, *The God of Jesus Christ*, 67.

4. For more on the Scriptural basis of apologetics, see Dulles, *A History of Apologetics*, 1–26.

5. For a discussion on faith, reason, and credibility, see Dulles, *The Assurance of Things Hoped For*, 204–23.

Today, as hardly ever before in the history of Christianity it is essential that the Christian faith emphasize its reasonableness which is accessible to all human beings."[6] If the very concept of truth has come under fire in our culture, then it would only make sense to explain and defend the notion of truth itself before one can explain what is true.

Fourth, the results of apologetics confirm its validity. Sometimes critics of apologetics complain that this enterprise never produces conversions. But this is a serious misreading of Church history. After trying to debunk the historicity of Jesus' resurrection, Frank Morrison became a Catholic after recognizing the historical evidence for the resurrection.[7] C. S. Lewis came to believe in Christ under the influence of apologetics. Lewis was convinced that many of the people he knew in England who believed in God did so because of arguments for God's existence: "nearly everyone I know who has embraced Christianity in adult life has been influenced by what seemed to him to be at least a probable argument for Theism."[8] Augustine became a Catholic because he heard a thoughtful believer debate with a Manichean. The former atheist, Antony Flew, recently became a deist because of newer arguments for God's existence.[9] Although many more examples could be given, the point is that apologetic defenses have triggered conversions (or a change in perspective) in the past.

Here the objection might be raised that "only the Holy Spirit brings persons to Christ, not human arguments." Such a challenge is shortsighted at best and mistaken at worst. It limits what an infinite God can do. It is not the Holy Spirit *or* human reason. Rather, it is the Holy Spirit using persons who use good arguments in defense of the gospel. When believers engage in the apologetic task, it can also create an atmosphere that makes the Catholic faith reasonable to believe in for outsiders (and even for insiders within the Church).

Many theologians and laypersons say that they have engaged in apologetics, but that they are still ineffective in their witness. What is often overlooked is that conversions are gradual and often take time. We simply do not know how or when God will use the things we say in our dialogue with unbelievers and other doubters. The seeds we plant in our interlocutors' minds may sprout a few days down the road. Conversely, it must be stressed that all those who entrust themselves to Christ have reasons for their faith, whether they are aware of those reasons or not. Not having a reason for faith

---

6. Kasper, *The God of Jesus Christ*, 71.

7. Morison, *Who Moved the Stone?*

8. Lewis, *God in the Dock*, 173.

9. Flew, *There is a God.*

is tantamount to saying that one has faith arbitrarily or by accident. Still writing as an atheist, Antony Flew poignantly explains:

> Discussion of this sort is today widely discredited. People with pretensions either to deep wisdom or to worldly sophistication will tell us that everyone knows that you cannot either prove or disprove the existence of God, and the fundamentals of any religion belong to the province of faith rather than of reason. They could not be more wrong. . . . The claim about the provinces of faith and reason is presumably to be construed as implying that it is either impossible or unnecessary to offer any sort of good reasons: either for making a commitment of religious faith, as opposed to refraining from making any such commitment; or for making any one particular commitment rather than any other. If this is the correct interpretation—and unless it is, the claim would seem to lack point—then it must be recognized how enormously damaging to faith this contention is, and how extremely insulting to all persons of faith. For it makes any and every such commitment equally arbitrary and equally frivolous. They are all made, it is being suggested, for no good reason at all; and every one is as utterly unreasonable as every other.[10]

Thus the issue is not whether there are reasons to believe in Catholicism, but what kinds of reasons the believer already has absorbed into his or her Catholic outlook on the world.

No matter what the circumstances, apologists must never make it their goal to win arguments with their dialogue partner. No one in the discussion should be forced into a win-lose situation. Instead, the apologist must develop the skill of making the Catholic faith attractive, being respectful to his or her dialogue partner. *Ideas* need to be presented and challenged, not *persons* as such. As the framers of *Gaudium et Spes* acknowledge:

> Love and good will, to be sure, must in no way render us indifferent to truth and goodness. Indeed love itself impels the disciples of Christ to speak the saving truth to all men. But it is necessary to distinguish between error, which always merits repudiation, and the person in error, who never loses the dignity of being a person even when he is flawed by false or inadequate religious notions. God alone is the judge and searcher of hearts, for that reason He forbids us to make judgments about the internal guilt of anyone.[11]

10. Flew, *God and Philosophy*, 19–20.
11. Vatican II, *Gaudium et Spes*, 28; cf. 92.

One of the most basic components of apologetics is loving and caring for our dialogue partners. This would not mean that Catholics should refuse to make hard truth claims. Rather, the focus must remain on *how* our defense of the faith is made. Apologists must *propose* the truths of faith, but they must never try to *impose* those truths on individuals who refuse to accept them.

It thus follows that an apologetical mind is one that coincides with a heart for Christ. Hiding the truth is not a sign of love, but of fear. If Catholics truly believe that Jesus is Lord, then they will become evangelical about what they believe. Evangelical fervor will have to include the mind and verbal persuasion. *Arguments* can be given for faith. Being *argumentative*, by contrast, is an abuse of apologetics and should always be avoided. Correlatively, apologetics is about *defending* Catholic truth, and should not be seen as a *defensive* posture in reaction to a hostile, secular world.

Moreover, the apologist is not merely concerned with persuading unbelievers, but is also concerned with motivating believers within the Church. Apologetic presentations are excellent opportunities to explain why people ought to become and *remain* Catholic. Thus apologetics is sometimes needed for Catholic Christians to become confident about what they believe.

It is true that apologetics can sometimes make people feel uncomfortable. But perhaps this stems from apprehending the truth about Christ in the discussion. Let us remember the words of John's Gospel (3:19–21):

> And this is the verdict, that the light came into the world, but people preferred darkness to light, because their works were evil. For everyone who does wicked things hates the light and does not come toward the light, so that his works might not be exposed. But whoever lives the truth comes to the light, so that his works may be clearly seen as done in God.

Whether it is the past or the future, the message of Jesus' cross will be countercultural, demanding a radical change of lifestyle. This realization can make both believers and doubters feel uncomfortable. As Avery Dulles explains in defense of apologetics: "If they [accusations made against the validity of apologetics] come from a mentality that . . . shrinks from any kind of confrontation, the criticisms should probably be discounted. Apologetics has to be somewhat controversial; it should be forthrightly defend the settled teaching of the Church."[12] Not only should we always be ready to give a reason for Christian hope (cf. 1 Pet 3:15 and 1:3), we should also be ready for rejection. But, experiencing some rejection is not due to engaging in apologetics, but to the worldview issues at stake.

12. Dulles, "The Rebirth of Apologetics," 20.

A final reason is that believers should engage in apologetics because a blind faith can lead to self-destruction; a reasoned faith can lead to sanctity. Atheist Richard Dawkins once noted that faith "leads people to believe in whatever it is so strongly that in extreme cases they are prepared to kill and die for it without the need for further justification."[13] Dawkins, it should be noted, is partially correct: blind faith can lead one down the path of violence, but a healthy faith will seek to understand the object in which their faith is placed.

When Christians limit the intellectual engagement of faith, this can literally steer them down the path of violence. But Catholic faith is supposed to influence all of human nature, including the mind. It begins with the conviction of the mind and culminates in the eventual consent of the will. Faith that is based on experience at the expense of reason can lead one to embrace heresy and schism. It could also lead to violence. Reason reinforces faith and makes it come alive; fideism[14] ruins the very impetus for faith itself.

Admittedly, a reasoned approach to defending Christianity has its limits. Here I should mention that apologetics and practical relevance are on two sides of the same evangelical coin. Let us now turn to some of the ways in which apologetics and practice depend on one another. First, apologetics can enhance the evangelist's awareness and confidence in proclaiming and explaining Catholic truth. In this respect apologetics safeguards believers from becoming indifferent. Dulles writes: "If we do not consider that it is important for others to hear the Christian proclamation, we inevitably begin to question its importance for ourselves."[15]

Apologetical studies might also play an important role in facilitating conversion, which can lead one to serve the world in action. Discipleship is supposed to be characterized by ongoing conversion. One of the values of doing apologetics is that it can deepen and enrich one's understanding of Catholic truth. Quite naturally, the theoretical side to apologetics and external practice will naturally affect and reinforce one another.

Similarly, a theology that neglects apologetics can destroy the impetus underlying the New Evangelization. If dialogue is understood in the erroneous sense that faith in Jesus is unnecessary or unimportant, and that Christians engage in dialogue only to understand the "religious other," the Great Commission loses its rationale. But evangelization is essential for fulfilling

13. Dawkins, *The Selfish Gene*, 198.

14. Fideism is a theological position that undervalues the role of reason in examining and religious claims. One either believes in Christianity or one does not. On a fideistic premise, there is no reason to accept one set of beliefs over another. Fideism understands faith as a blind leap in the dark.

15. Dulles, "The Rebirth of Apologetics," 20.

the Church's mission. Missionary zeal is a sign of healthy faith, just as its lessening is a sign of a crisis of faith. Part of the reason for the lessening of missionary zeal is due to a reductive understanding of a theology that forgets the importance of apologetics. The Catholic Church is not merely supposed to be inclusive, but is called to be expansive. Conversely, if the Church is not expanding, then one must question whether the Church is fulfilling its mission.

Here one might note that doing apologetics is actually a form of compassion. Conversely, Catholic dialogue with others will incorporate apologetics when appropriate. Disagreements do not have to be completely incompatible for Catholics to become more apologetical. It only requires that Catholics at least think that their beliefs are apparently different from other viewpoints. The apologetic element in dialogue will help to reveal whether these differences are real or only apparent. The same theme works in reverse. If I hold to beliefs that are wrong or misguided, then I certainly would want other persons to point out where I have made mistakes. Good arguments, which are favorable to views that may be contrary to my own, can help me to see my errors.

If we understand what apologetics is in its most basic sense (the positive and negative defense of the gospel in both theoretical and practical forms), then obviously apologetics will be relevant at every time and place in the life of the Church. Even though our culture and theology continues to change, Catholics still live in an era where people need to be convinced that Jesus is Lord. Obviously this involves Catholics making a reasoned defense of the gospel.

Today apologetical engagement should be more diplomatic (rather than combative) and sensitive to the different avenues that each individual might take in response to the gospel. Although Catholicism is already philosophically well positioned to deal with most objections, the more tactical concern of the apologist has to do with the means of engagement. Defending the faith requires more than knowledge. It requires an artful method. Thus, a clever apologist can outmaneuver someone who is more intelligent or has presented better arguments at the moment.

Retrieving Apologetics

Throughout Church history, different apologetic systems have emerged in response to different challenges posed to Church teaching.[16] At times, the

16. For a discussion of the different models and methods of apologetics, as discussed throughout Church history, see Dulles, *A History of Apologetics*.

different approaches have overlapped with each other. The chapters of this book will follow the same order of the classical apologetics. I will expound on this method in what follows. Before embarking on this approach, we need to expound the Church's teaching on apologetics. In chapters 1 and 2, we will explore the teachings of Vatican II and papal encyclicals on apologetics.

There is also an urgent need to discuss the possibility of reasoned defenses of Christianity in the light of the challenges posed by relativists (see chapter 3). Without a defense of objective truth, there would be no cause to provide reasons for faith. Unless Christianity is considered a fundamentally true faith, then there is no reason to argue for or against it. This book distances itself from rationalistic approaches, and instead provides reasons to believe in Catholic Christianity. Each chapter assumes the tentative conclusions established in previous chapters.

"Classical apologetics" is a step-by-step method of defending Catholicism. This tradition is prominent among Catholic thinkers and reaches back to the early Church Fathers. Following Augustine, Anselm, and Thomas Aquinas, classical apologists maintain that each step builds on or at least presupposes more general preconditions necessary for the rational possibility of faith. A classical apologist establishes the existence of God before he or she will present evidence for the deity of Christ. For these apologists, it would not make sense to argue for the divine identity of Christ unless there is a God who can become a human. Unless Jesus was God incarnate, then it would not make sense to also believe that he instituted a certain kind of Church.

For such apologetics the existence of God can be proven without appealing to supernatural faith. Thus chapters 4–6 will resituate the Thomist proofs for God's existence in the light of modern philosophical debates between theists and atheists. After demonstrating the existence of God, the next step in the classical method is concerned with showing that miracles are possible (and maybe even probable?).

After showing the likelihood of miracles, the New Testament writings are shown to be generally trustworthy in what they affirm about Jesus. The next step tries to show that the Catholic Church is the best expression of Christianity. From the time of the Reformation, Catholic apologists argued that the Catholic Church is the Church which best fits the four ecclesial attributes of the Church as expressed in the ancient creeds. This final step was used to demonstrate that Protestants could not be the one, holy, catholic and apostolic Church of Christ because none of these Christian communities could sufficiently characterize the four marks.

One of the strengths of classical approach is that it concentrates on the common points of reference that are necessary for believers to reach unbelievers with the truth of the gospel. This method reaffirms the importance of human reason. Contemporary Catholic advocates of the classical approach may include Peter Kreeft, Ronald Tacelli, and Benedict Ashley.[17] Vatican II also called for a reasoned faith, and reiterates the First Vatican Council's teaching on the existence and natural knowability of God.[18] The Jesuit theologian John Hardon writes:

> Among the satisfying features of the Catholic faith is seeing how providentially, sometimes prophetically, the Church's magisterium anticipates the needs of the future. Who would have thought, as early as 1870, that by 1970 almost one-third of the human race would be under the political domination of an ideology that professedly excludes the existence of a personal God? Yet in 1870 the same Council that elaborated the divine attributes to strengthen the faith of believing Christians also evaluated the position of those who, only vaguely then, were devising to supplant the divine majesty. . . . By the second half the twentieth century, loss of faith in God or indifference to his existence had assumed global proportions. Vatican II took stock of the situation in the longest and most elaborate analysis of atheism in the sixteen hundred years of conciliar history. This fact alone gives some indication of how different are the issues facing the Church today from those that threatened its integrity during the days of Arius, Nestorius, and Pelagius.[19]

Although Vatican II displayed more historical consciousness and cultural awareness than Vatican I, the former also emphasized the validity of permanent truths. *Gaudium et Spes* reaffirmed the twofold order of faith and reason and praised Aquinas's theology as a model for understanding this relationship.[20]

There is also a long and reputable tradition of "evidential" approaches to defending Christianity. Unlike classicists, evidentialists would rather use reported facts. Strictly speaking, in this model there is no specific procedure as in classical apologetics; there is no logically prior and necessary step before one proceeds to the other preconditions for the possibility of faith. Be that as it may, evidentialism can complement the classical approach by providing evidence for the divinity and resurrection of Jesus.

17. Kreeft and Tacelli, *Handbook of Catholic Apologetics*; Ashley, *Choosing a World-View and Value System*.

18. According to the First Vatican Council, God's existence can be known with certainty apart from the influence of special revelation. Hünermann edn, Denzinger, *Enchiridion symbolorum definitionum et declarationum*, 3004.

19. Hardon, *The Catholic Catechism*, 58, 60.

20. Vatican II, *Gaudium et Spes*, 59.

The evidentialist stresses the need to establish scientific, archaeological, sociological, psychological, historical, and even experiential evidence in any combination of ways that might be profitable in improving the overall case for faith. Evidence is one of many strands in the overall web of argument. One of the strengths of this method is that it can use evidence to support the faith, or to refute (or make less probable) the claims of non-Catholic worldviews. It overlaps with classical apologetics by using evidence, but it tends to overlook the classicist's use of philosophy.

Instead of speaking in terms of proof or demonstration, evidentialists would rather provide cumulative case arguments. This realistic perspective is one of the strengths of evidential approaches. Most of the time apologetic arguments should be counted as probable, not conclusive.[21]

Classical apologists, however, quickly point out against the evidentialist that there is no such thing as bare facts to be assessed. Facts and events have ultimate meaning only within and by virtue of the context of the worldview in which they are conceived. Thus evidence gains its meaning only by its immediate and overall context; evidence as such cannot, without begging the question, be used to establish the overall context by which it obtains its very meaning as evidence. It is a vicious circle to argue that a given fact counts as evidence for a broader truth claim unless it can be demonstrated that the former has already occurred within the context of a theistic universe. Meaning is always derived from within an interpretive context. One cannot argue from the data unless there is an implicit philosophical framework already in place. God, as a matter of fact, alone can make miracles possible. That is, only on the prior contention that God exists is a miracle even possible.

After presenting and defending some arguments for the existence of God, it is necessary to discuss the relevant evidence for Jesus' life ministry and resurrection (chapters 8–10). Given the existence of God, it makes sense to think that God will communicate with the human race (chapter 7). Such expectations might be driving the enthusiasm for the current quest for the historical Jesus.

In chapter 8 I discuss the relationship between theology and history in the New Testament, and deduce some established facts about the historical Jesus. I. Howard Marshall writes:

> Why, then, should it be thought odd to offer to twentieth century audiences the historical backing that they need in order to know whether they should commit themselves in faith to the Jesus who is subject of Christian preaching? Modern people

---

21. A noted evidentialist approach resonates with the theological methods of John Haught, *Science and Religion*; Haught, *Is Nature Enough?*

want to know if Jesus really existed. They want to know if he was the kind of person that the Gospels make him out to be. They want to know if he died and rose from the dead. They want to know whether his general manner of life supports the claims made on his behalf by Christians. And they are entitled to receive answers to these questions.[22]

Similarly, many contemporary New Testament historians have ushered in a strong wave of writings defending the historicity of Jesus' resurrection. The main evidence that is usually offered to skeptics consists of (1) a series of post-mortem appearances to individuals, groups, and enemies of Jesus' followers at different times and places under radically different circumstances, (2) the discovery of an open and empty tomb by a group of Jesus' women followers, and (3) the origin of the earliest disciples' belief in the resurrection despite their every predisposition to the contrary (see chapter 9). For the most part, skeptics have taken these reported facts seriously, but have tried to account for them in naturalistic terms. In chapters 10, I will survey the most salient criticisms of the contention that "God raised Jesus from the dead," and address them accordingly.

"Experiential" methodologies appeal to human experiences of God and the Christian community. Unlike the classical apologetics and evidentialism, this system is practical and oriented toward each individual person.[23] The experientialist is acutely aware that the problems that prevent individuals from deeply embracing the gospel are often psychological and emotional, not just intellectual. Apologists must confront these issues and address them as well. One salient aspect of experientialism is an emphasis on holiness and the development of the entire person. One of the strengths of experientialism is that it takes the limits of reason seriously.

Its proponents are numerous in Catholicism and generally follow the line of thought in John Henry Newman and Maurice Blondel.[24] The strength of this approach lies in its popular appeal and is the most common means by which people come to faith. Unlike the intellectualism of the classical apologetics, the stress here is on the heart and lived experience. The experiential apologist is not as concerned with building a systematic, gradual case as in classical apologetics as much as they want to persuade others by speaking with them about their experiences.

22. Marshall, *I Believe in the Historical Jesus*, 83.

23. For a balanced discussion of experience and reason for effective apologetics, see Davison, ed., *Imaginative Apologetics*.

24. Newman, *An Essay in Aid of a Grammar of Assent*; Blondel, *Action (1893)*; Blondel, *The Letter on Apologetics and History and Dogma*.

For all of this method's strengths, it can be shortsighted in some respects (and possibly harmful in others). It downplays the use of evidence and the propositional mode of theology. Though propositional knowledge may be a poor substitute for knowledge of God, it can still serve as a means to foster a personal relationship with God and others. In the absence of hard evidence, experiential approaches remain an inadequate model. Experiences are never self-authenticating, and they must be interpreted through some other philosophical means. For instance, experiences are often unverifiable and must be taken on faith alone by outsiders. In this way, the hardheaded skeptic is unlikely to be persuaded by merely hearing the testimony of believers and how they came to faith. Many skeptics will quickly dismiss the warm experiences of the Church community by easily dismissing them with naturalistic explanations.

Radical experientialists overlook some of the primary sources for doing theology (for example, Scripture, tradition and the magisterium) for the sake of upholding the validity of their unique experiences. Some experientialists are heavily concerned with practical relevance at the expense of including theoretical approaches to defending the faith.

This book is not heavily concerned with exploring the experiential approach to defending Christianity, and would rather emphasize the classical, evidential, and theological approaches which can help shape one's experience. Readers will have to consult other published works to find strictly experiential or existential approaches to defending the gospel and Church teaching.

However, in chapters 11 and 12, I will elaborate upon an argument that is intimately related to the experiential approach. Instead of merely relaying the testimony of believers who elaborate upon the different ways in which Christian faith has changed their lives, I will examine the effects of Catholic faith upon those cultures it has deeply permeated and influenced. Such positive effects can be understood as motives to believe in Christianity.

Although the argument of these chapters is not based upon a phenomenological encounter with ecclesiastical unity and human holiness,[25] I elucidate some of the positive changes that Catholic cultures have left upon the world for the better. Both chapters try to make sense out of the objection: "Does Catholic belief make a difference in the lives of its adherents?" Conversely, whether one is Catholic, Protestant, or Orthodox, many believers can empathize with the deleterious effects that atheism and de-Christianization are having on society.

---

25. Cf. Dulles, *A Church to Believe In*, 41–52; Dulles, "The Church," in Latourelle and O'Collins, eds., *Problems and Perspectives of Fundamental Theology*, 259–73.

If human beings have a need to hear from God, then responding to his message in Jesus Christ should fulfill a need on how human life is meant to be lived. If the distinctive teachings of Catholicism are true, then we should expect to see it make a difference in the lives of those individuals who entrust themselves to Christ and his Church. By tracing the empirical effects of Catholicism upon the world, one is able to provide evidence for the truth of Catholicism itself.

These changes can be highlighted to reinvigorate an almost forgotten argument in the Church known as the *via empirica*. Notwithstanding the positive changes found in cultures that are unaffected by institutional Christianity, the *via empirica* can be defended in a Church on behalf of the Divine Founder. Given the basic truth of Christianity (see the chapters on God's existence and the resurrection of Jesus), it is imperative that theologians show the difference that faith makes in the life of believers, which can be expressed in sociological categories.

The last model might be called "theological apologetics." In this model theologians exposit the fundamental themes of Catholic theology for improving the case for Christianity.[26] In so doing, they hope to correct common misunderstandings of the gospel and the Church's teaching. If an accurate presentation of Catholic belief is immune from the straw man attacks of skeptics, then there is nothing for the apologist to worry about. Theological approaches to apologetics are characterized by the attempt to provide lucid explanations of how tense theological positions should be held together.

In the final chapters of the book (13–15) I expound and defend the "scandal of particularity" in the face of pluralist challenges. Such an endeavor follows necessarily from the conclusions drawn in the previous chapters. If God miraculously raised Jesus from the dead in response to human needs, then the human race has a definitive reference point to live in the way that God designed them to be. Such a response to the "good news" should make a positive impact upon human life, even on the societal level. But here another question might arise: "why hasn't everyone had the opportunity to hear about the good news?" The final chapters are dedicated to providing answers to the relevant questions in this area of apologetics.

Undoubtedly, a significant challenge that many Catholics are facing is holding their belief in Jesus when faced by opposing claims made by other religions. If the Christological beliefs of the Church are fundamentally true, then any beliefs in opposition to them must be false. There can be no denying

26. Cf. Torrell, "New Trends in Fundamental Theology in the Postconciliar Period," in Latourelle and O'Collins, eds., *Problems and Perspectives of Fundamental Theology*, 11–22. Also relevant is Latourelle's very fine essay "A New Image of Fundamental Theology," 37–58.

this obvious fact. If persons can be saved outside of Jesus Christ, then the Church has erred for centuries about her central belief in the one mediator between God and humanity, casting God's sovereignty into serious doubt.

Another belief that is called into question by religious pluralism has to do with the traditional attributes of God. If God is omnibenevolent and omnipotent, then why would he prevent so many individuals and even groups of people from hearing the good news within their earthly lifetime? How could God fault these persons for not accepting his Son and then send them to eternal torment? Perhaps the main problem with many of the challenges is that they are based on fallacious presuppositions or misunderstandings of God's nature and Christ's uniqueness.

PART ONE

The Legitimacy of Apologetics

— 1 —

Conciliar Apologetics and Interreligious Dialogue

ONE MIGHT COMMENCE A vision of apologetics that is faithful to Catholic teaching by analyzing the documents of Vatican II (1962–1965).[1] As Pope Francis has suggested: "because it draws its life from faith, theology cannot consider the magisterium of the Pope and the bishops in communion with him as something extrinsic, a limitation of its freedom, but rather as one of its internal, constitutive dimensions, for the magisterium ensures our contact with the primordial source and thus provides the certainty of attaining to the word of Christ in all its integrity."[2]

Recognizing that Christians cannot adequately understand the mysteries of faith from a single vantage point, many postconciliar theologians have been keen on emphasizing the multidimensional nature of theological understanding since Vatican II. Apologists should also recognize that although one way of defending the gospel might be needed in a certain context, it would be an egregious mistake to take that one system and use it as the exclusive means to reach persons situated within different circumstances. Nonetheless, the contextual nature of apologetic engagement should not be used as an excuse to negate the use of classical apologetic methods.

The Apologetical Dimensions of Vatican II

A commonsense interpretation of the Council indicates that the faithful are called to apologetically engage the world with arguments for the sake of evangelization. The documents repeatedly stress the need for believers to

1. Cf. Gaillardetz, "Do We Need a New(er) Apologetics?" 26–33; O'Collins, "Fundamental Theology: The Continuing Debate," 97–110.

2. Francis, *Lumen Fidei*, 36.

explain and defend the gospel. Although Pope John XXIII originally called for the Council to let some fresh air into the life of the Church, his intention was not to break off from Sacred Tradition. It is not a Council's role to embark on completely new teaching but to substantiate doctrine in a new cultural climate that the Church finds herself in.

According to the First Vatican Council (1869–1870), for instance, God reveals himself in a supernatural manner, conveying truths that go beyond the reach of human reason. This message is accompanied by the outward signs of miracles and prophecies which show the credibility of God's revelation. Once this revelation is given to humanity, it is capable of being penetrated rationally in order for people to gain a greater understanding of it. This apologetical method resembles the classical approach to defending the faith.

Vatican II did not elaborate on any *method* of apologetics in detail. But this does not mean the Council Fathers did not see reasoned defense of the faith as unimportant or as irrelevant. M. John Farrelly points out: "Vatican II gave primacy to the meaning of God and Jesus Christ but also insisted that reason, common human experience, and the historical value of the Gospels support our faith in the existence of God and his revelation through Jesus Christ."[3]

However, there can be no denying that the Council Fathers were concerned to endorse the validity of apologetics. Appealing to the central apologetical passage of the New Testament (1 Pet 3:15), the bishops urged the faithful that "all the disciples of Christ, persevering in prayer and praising God, should present themselves as a living sacrifice, holy and pleasing to God. Everywhere on earth they must bear witness to Christ and give an answer to those who seek an account of that hope of eternal life which is in them."[4] In the *Declaration on Religious Liberty*, the Fathers stated that "the disciple has a grave obligation to Christ, his Master, to grow daily in his knowledge of the truth he has received from him, to be faithful in announcing it, and vigorous in defending it without having recourse to methods which are contrary to the spirit of the Gospel."[5] Though Catholics can win unbelievers over to faith by their lifestyle, this would not mean that arguments should not be included in the attempt to evangelize others.

Thus the task of defending the faith is commended by the bishops, especially as believers become more accountable to God's standards of discipleship. Catholics "are more perfectly bound to the Church by the sacrament of Confirmation, and the Holy Spirit endows them with special strength

---

3. Farrelly, *Belief in God in Our Time*, 46.

4. Vatican II, *Lumen Gentium*, 10.

5. Vatican II, *Dignitatis Humanae*, 14.

so that they are more strictly obliged to spread and defend the faith, both by word and by deed, as true witnesses of Christ."[6] Catholic laypersons are not merely called to *dialogue* with non-Christians, but must *seek to convert them* to the risen Christ.[7] The *Constitution on Divine Revelation* goes so far as to say that we must "fight in defense of the faith."[8] This rhetorical phrase stresses the great lengths which Catholics must go in order to preserve the Church's teaching against the multitude of challenges that confront us today. All believers have the duty to defend the faith, but the task of safeguarding the gospel is officially entrusted to the magisterium.[9]

One of the great themes of *Gaudium et Spes* has to do with reading the signs of the times in order to effectively answer humanity's deepest questions. The document claims that "The Church has always had the duty of scrutinizing the signs of the times and of interpreting them in the light of the gospel. Thus, in language intelligible to each generation, she can respond to the perennial questions which people ask about this present life and the life to come, and about the relationship of the one to the other."[10]

In reading the culture, Catholics are not only called to engage formal outsiders (and insiders) with arguments for faith, they must also learn effective ways to deliver and defend the message. Method and context must therefore be taken into serious consideration: "within the requirements and methods proper to theology, [believers] are invited to seek continually for more suitable ways of communicating doctrine to the people of their times; for the deposit of Faith or the truths are one thing and the manner in which they are enunciated, in the same meaning and understanding, is another."[11]

In sum, the Council shows a serious concern to use arguments and evidence for the sake of implementing an evangelical spirit (especially if the broader circumstances in a dialogue allow for it). Catholics should not force their dialogue partners into a win-lose situation. But Vatican II teaches both practical and theoretical approaches for the sake of evangelizing both the Church and the world.

Specifically, in the dogmatic constitution, *Dei Verbum*, the bishops reiterate the natural knowledge of God.[12] Traditionally, the Church has held that individuals can know that God exists with reason apart from the

---

6. Vatican II, *Lumen Gentium*, 11.

7. Vatican II, *Ad Gentes*, 30, 39–40.

8. Vatican II, *Dei Verbum*, 8.

9. Ibid., 10.

10. Vatican II, *Gaudium et Spes*, 4.

11. Ibid., 62.

12. Vatican II, *Dei Verbum*, 3. Also see Vatican II, *Nostra Aetate*, 2.

influence of divine, authoritative revelation. Correlatively, this means that fideistic approaches are contrary to Catholic teaching. The bishops announce that "God, the beginning and end of all things, can be known with certainty from created reality by the light of human reason." They also teach that "it is through His revelation that those religious truths which are by their nature accessible to human reason can be known by all people with ease, with solid certitude and with no trace of error, even in this present state of the human race."[13] The way in which individuals can reach God's existence is by considering the things that have been made (Ps 19:1–4; Rom 1:18–20). Hence, the primary argument for drawing out one's conviction that God exists will move from effect to Cause, not through an innate awareness of the idea of God (as in the case of the ontological argument).

Natural knowledge of God is an indispensable aspect of Church teaching. It is important for our purpose that the teaching on natural knowledge of God coincides with the classical apologetic method, which begins with the arguments for the existence of God. The Council boldly favors the use of human reason: "the Church has already repudiated and cannot cease repudiating, sorrowfully but as firmly as possible, those poisonous doctrines and actions which contradict reason and the common experience of humanity, and dethrone human beings from their native excellence."[14] The use of argument should not be dismissed in the light of the problem of atheism— whether it is of the critical or practical variety. The Church "courteously invites atheists to examine the Gospel of Christ with an open mind."[15]

Other passages in the Vatican II documents indicate an affinity for evidential approaches to defending the Church. The Council Fathers endorse the use of historical evidence, for example, in *Lumen Gentium*: "The miracles of Jesus also confirm that the Kingdom has already arrived on earth: 'If I cast out devils by the finger of God, then the kingdom of God has come upon you.' Before all things, however, the Kingdom is clearly visible in the very Person of Christ, the Son of God and the Son of Man, who came 'to serve and to give His life as a ransom for many.'"[16] Christ's life is apologetical in the sense that he testifies to the reality of the Kingdom.[17] An historical approach to Jesus' life can therefore help one to perceive the truth about God and his love for humanity.

13. Vatican II, *Dei Verbum*, 6. Cf. Vatican II, *Gaudium et Spes*, 12.

14. Vatican II, *Gaudium et Spes*, 21.

15. Ibid.

16. Vatican II, *Lumen Gentium*, 35.

17. Ibid., 5. Cf. Vatican II, *Dei Verbum*, 4; Vatican II, *Dignitatis Humanae*, 11; Vatican II, *Ad Gentes*, 9.

Seen in this way, Christ's life is itself apologetical. A historical and theological study of the person of Jesus can convince others that his message is indeed trustworthy. For, Christ gave compelling evidence of the truths he preached.[18] The bishops explain: "It is common knowledge that among all the Scriptures, even those of the New Testament, the Gospels have a special preeminence, and rightly so, for they are the principal witness for the life and teaching of the incarnate Word, our savior."[19]

The dogmatic constitution, *Dei Verbum*, affirms and defends the historicity of the Gospels. However, this would not mean that the Gospels are seen as straightforward, historical reports. Rather, they are fundamentally reliable at their core: "Holy Mother Church has firmly and with absolute constancy held, and continues to hold, that the four Gospels just named, whose historical character the Church unhesitatingly asserts, faithfully hand on what Jesus Christ, while living among human beings, really did and taught for their eternal salvation until the day He was taken up into heaven."[20] In corroboration of this point, the bishops announce that the Gospel writers drew from their recollections of the original eyewitnesses' beliefs.[21]

Yet another method of apologetics is centered around the apologetics of human experience. Vatican II, while characterizes the Church in need of constant reform, holds that the Church is always marked with the sign of unity and holiness. In *Lumen Gentium*, we read:

> When we look at the lives of those who have faithfully followed Christ, we are inspired with a new reason for seeking the City that is to come and at the same time we are shown a most safe path by which among the vicissitudes of this world, in keeping with the state in life and condition proper to each of us, we will be able to arrive at perfect union with Christ, that is, perfect holiness. In the lives of those who, sharing in our humanity, are however more perfectly transformed into the image of Christ, God vividly manifests His presence and His face to human beings. He speaks to us in them, and gives us a sign of His Kingdom, to which we are strongly drawn, having so great a cloud of witnesses over us and such a witness to the truth of the Gospel.[22]

It follows that if we encounter a community of believers, we should perceive some traces of that positive influence in categories that even the formal

18. Vatican II, *Gaudium et Spes*, 3.
19. Vatican II, *Dei Verbum*, 18.
20. Ibid., 19.
21. Ibid.
22. Vatican II, *Lumen Gentium*, 60.

outsiders can suitably understand. These traces can also serve as motives of credibility in support of Christianity.

Apologists repeatedly used this kind of argument to convince the world of the truth of Christianity.[23] As a result of its widespread acceptance in the Church, the argument was dogmatically defined at Vatican I. Vatican II followed the theology of Vatican I, but did not call the Church a "moral miracle." Instead it spoke of the Church as a "sign to the nations."[24]

Vatican II asserts that Christianity helps change the world for the better.[25] A historical and sociological study of the Church's influence upon the world might persuade inquirers to believe in Christianity. Conversely, "it must be admitted that the temporal sphere is governed by its own principles, since it is rightly concerned with the interests of this world. But that ominous doctrine which attempts to build a society with no regard whatever for religion, and which attacks and destroys the religious liberty of its citizens, is rightly to be rejected."[26] Although the Catholic faith has had a positive effect upon those cultures where it is situated, philosophies and religions that are antithetical to Christianity tear down the fabric of society.

Vatican II and the Uniqueness of Jesus

One method of doing apologetics focuses on expositing and defending nuanced theologies of the Church's teaching. Apologists need to address the challenges surrounding the particularity of Jesus in a world where many individuals and entire groups have never had the opportunity to hear about Jesus. This challenge has been taken up by many postconciliar theologians.

Catholic teaching holds that the revelation given in Jesus is unique, full, and ultimate. Jesus is the supreme mediator between God and the human race, truly and finally revealed by God. This divine disclosure in Jesus cannot be known by human reason and/or common experience alone, but is primarily believed in faith. According to *Dei Verbum*: "In His goodness and wisdom God chose to reveal Himself and to make known to us the hidden purpose of His will . . . by which through Christ, the Word made flesh, human beings might in the Holy Spirit have access to the Father and come to share in the divine nature." God became a human being so that human persons might come to know and fulfill the purposes for which they were

---

23. Dulles, *A History of Apologetics*, 36, 50, 54, 78–83, 88–89, 95, 105, 119, 136–37, etc.

24. Vatican II, *Lumen Gentium*, 1.

25. Ibid., 35, 46.

26. Ibid., 36.

made: "Through this revelation, therefore, the invisible God . . . out of the abundance of His love speaks to men as friends . . . and lives among them . . . so that He may invite and take them into fellowship with Himself."[27]

Second, God's revelation in Jesus is unique, incomparably beyond any other divine messages and/or revelatory figures. Scripture and the Church affirm that Christ is the supreme mediator between God and man. 1 Timothy 2:5 announces: "There is . . . one mediator between God and the human race." In John 14:6, Jesus says to his apostle Thomas: "I am the way and the truth and the life. No one comes to the Father except through me." Acts 4:12 puts it this way: "There is no salvation through anyone else, nor is there any other name under heaven given to the human race by which we are to be saved." The implication is that Christ's saving revelation is the only one of its kind. If anyone is saved, it is through Christ, regardless of whether the person is aware of Jesus or not. Vatican II consistently upholds the unique mediatorship of Jesus.[28]

Third, the message given to us in Christ is full and complete. Everything that can be given has been given in Christ. In the letter to the Colossians (2:9), Paul wrote: "For in him dwells the whole fullness of the deity bodily, and you share in this fullness in him." The postconciliar document, *Dominus Iesus*, settled what should count as the appropriate interpretation of Sacred Tradition: "in the mystery of Jesus Christ . . . the full revelation of divine truth is given."[29]

Fourth, no other divine revelation is to be expected (except when Jesus Christ returns at the end of time). God's revelation in Christ is final and unsurpassable. This contention is firmly rooted in the New Testament. Paul says that if anyone—even an angel from heaven—preaches "another" gospel message, they will be condemned (Gal 1:6–9). In Jude 3 we hear of "the faith that was once for all handed down to the holy ones." The book of Hebrews says: "In times past, God spoke in partial and various ways to our ancestors through the prophets; in these last days, he spoke to us through a Son, whom he made heir of all things and through whom he created the universe" (1:1–2). These teachings have also been faithfully preserved in *Dei Verbum*: "The Christian dispensation, therefore, as the new and definitive covenant, will never pass away and we now await no further new public revelation."[30]

27. Vatican II, *Dei Verbum*, 2.

28. Vatican II, *Sacrosanctum Concilium*, 48; Vatican II, *Lumen Gentium*, 8, 14, 28.

29. Congregation for the Doctrine of the Faith, *Dominus Iesus*, 5.

30. Vatican II, *Dei Verbum*, 4. Cf. Congregation for the Doctrine of the Faith, *Dominus Iesus*, 15.

The final aspect of Christ's revelation is that it is universal. In other words, Christ is for everyone, not just for those who identify themselves with Catholicism. The gospel should be preached to all nations (Matt 28:16–20). The International Theological Commission affirmed that only "in Jesus can human beings be saved, and therefore Christianity has an evident claim to universality."[31]

Catholic Apologetics and Interreligious Dialogue

One of the more influential concerns of Vatican II was the Church's engagement with interreligious dialogue.[32] Indeed, the Church "rejects nothing that is true and holy"[33] in the world's other religions. Such a realization has resulted in a tension between "dialogue and apologetics" in the postconciliar period. The principles that govern each of these enterprises are different. On the one hand, an individual Catholic is within his or her epistemic rights to engage in apologetics when the circumstances allow for it. On the other hand, that same believer can and must engage in dialogue when different circumstances arise.

Dialogue, it should be added, is not about converting one's dialogue partner. Thus dialogue and apologetics have a different, yet analogous function in the life of an individual Catholic. These activities are not antagonistic to one another, but epitomize the analogical thinking of a mature Catholic who knows when to engage in one and not the other.

The distinctions between the two must be kept in delicate balance and individually pursued when necessary. Here the postconciliar document, *Dialogue and Proclamation*, settled in the light of the Council what may have seemed like two competing enterprises. The Pontifical Council for Interreligious Dialogue confirmed: "There can be no question of choosing one and ignoring or rejecting the other."[34] "Both are legitimate and necessary. They are intimately related, but not interchangeable."[35] Furthermore, that same document insisted that proclamation (which implies the use of argument for the purposes of evangelization) takes *precedence* over dialogue. Proclamation always holds a "permanent priority"[36] over dialogue.

31. International Theological Commission, *Christianity and the World Religions*, 14, 49.

32. Francesco Gioia, ed., *Interreligious Dialogue*.

33. Vatican II, *Nostra Aetate*, 2.

34. Pontifical Council for Interreligious Dialogue, *Dialogue and Proclamation*, 6.

35. Ibid., 77.

36. Ibid., 44.

So although both of these enterprises play their own unique role in certain circumstances in the Church, they "are not on the same level."[37]

To engage in dialogue helps Catholics to understand the religious others, so that evangelists and apologists might eventually take the best avenue to engage them with the good news. The Pontifical Council rightly says that dialogue "remains oriented toward proclamation."[38] This means that dialogue is at the service of evangelization. Proclaiming the good news "remains central"[39] and is the "climax and fullness"[40] of the Church's mission.

A Catholic theologian of interreligious dialogue, Catherine Cornille, agrees that dialogue should not do away with apologetics. For her, apologetics is supposed to take place *within* the context of dialogue:

> The debate over the relationship between dialogue and proclamation also extends to the question of the legitimacy of apologetics. As such, all authentic dialogue involves a two-way process in which each partner is engaged in a process of not only informing but also convincing the other of the truth of his or her own beliefs and practices. As such, all authentic dialogue necessarily contains a missionary and apologetic dimension. The fullness of dialogue may be regarded as a form of mutual proclamation and in which participants alternately adopt the roles of missionary and seeker. While seemingly contradictory, these roles may coexist in a religious attitude capable of balancing humility and conviction.[41]

Cornille's claim needs to be seriously considered more often by her colleagues working in the field of interreligious dialogue. Vatican II urges the faithful to dialogue with members of the other world religions because the presence of the Spirit is found outside the Church,[42] However, the call to enter into dialogue with other religions is equally marked by the concern to evangelize the religious others.[43]

---

37. Ibid., 77.

38. Ibid., 75.

39. Ibid., 75.

40 Ibid., 82.

41. Cornille, *The Im-Possibility of Interreligious Dialogue*, 71–72. Also see Griffiths, *An Apology for Apologetics*; Griffiths "Why We Need Interreligious Polemics," 31–37; Kereszty, *Christianity Among Other Religions*.

42. See, e.g., Clooney, *Hindu God-Christian God*.

43. Vatican II, *Optatium Totius*, 16; Vatican II, *Ad Gentes*, 30. See also 39–40. Cf. Vatican II, *Dignitatis Humanae*, 11.

Thus the Great Commission retains its permanent validity, even though outsiders can still be saved. Nowhere does Vatican II qualify who should (or should not be) evangelized. Gavin D'Costa affirms:

> Mission to all non-Christian people is required. The Council refrained from *explicitly* applying the universal mandate for mission to any one religion in particular within the documents. However, it made clear that all the religions other than Christianity, all the unbaptized, are the focus for Christian mission. This is continuous with previous magisterial teachings.[44]

Conclusion

Some Catholics may resist apologetics because they mistakenly think that the Church broke away from the tradition of apologetics at Vatican II. They do not appreciate the continuity in doctrine and the way in which it is understood and expressed in different circumstances. The history of Catholicism and Christianity testifies to the fact that theologians and philosophers have defended the faith in every age.

Indeed, the Council's vision of apologetics is multifaceted and cannot be reduced to either a theoretical or practical defense of the gospel. Both methods are indispensable and correspond to the dialogical context of evangelists, apologists, and their interlocutors. Yet always the cumulative, step-by-step method of classical apologetics, along with the use of reason and evidence, retains its validity.

44. D'Costa, *Vatican II*, 6.

— 2 —

Papal Apologetics:
From John XXIII to
Pope Francis

Another authoritative motive for doing apologetics can be found in the papal encyclicals. Catholic theologians should clearly explicate papal teachings in these documents to closely approximate "what the Church teaches" for various branches of Catholic theology. This chapter will discuss the popes' teachings on apologetics by analyzing encyclicals from John XXIII's *Ad Petri Cathedram* (1959) to Pope Francis' *Lumen Fidei* (2013). These teachings continue the tradition of the apologetics of Vatican II.

Instead of taking a chronological approach (beginning with John XXIII and ending with Francis' *Lumen Fidei*), I have organized this chapter thematically around the relevant papal teachings on Catholic apologetics in mind. As in the previous chapter, which was dedicated to the apologetic dimensions of Vatican II, the topics covered in this chapter provide further magisterial support for the contents of this book as a whole and form a basis for the remaining chapters.

The Popes as Apologists

According to contemporary papal teaching, the perennial enterprise of defending the faith is entrusted to every Catholic. Everyone in the Church has a significant role to play in the New Evangelization. "Profession of the Christian faith," says John XXIII, "is not intelligible without strong, lively apostolic fervor; in fact, 'everyone is bound to proclaim his faith to others, either to give good example and encouragement to the rest of the faithful, or to check the attacks of unbelievers,' especially in our time, when the universal Church and human society are beset by many difficulties."[1]

Although every Catholic is called to safeguard the truth of revelation, the popes and bishops are the authoritative defenders of Catholic teaching. Paul VI reiterated this longstanding teaching of the Church: "It is only logical, then, for us to follow the magisterium of the Church as a guiding star in carrying on our investigations into this mystery, for the Divine Redeemer has entrusted the safeguarding and the explanation of the written or transmitted word of God to her."[2] The imperative to do apologetics is not extrinsically imposed upon believers by the magisterium, but is a natural consequence of having faith. John Paul II wrote in *Veritatis Splendor*:

> By its nature, faith appeals to reason because it reveals to human beings the truth of his destiny and the way to attain it. Revealed truth, to be sure, surpasses our telling. All our concepts fall short of its ultimately unfathomable grandeur (cf. Eph 3:19). Nonetheless, revealed truth beckons reason—God's gift fashioned for the assimilation of truth—to enter into its light and thereby come to understand in a certain measure what it has believed. Theological science responds to the invitation of truth as it seeks to understand the faith. It thereby aids the People of God in fulfilling the Apostle's command (cf. 1 Pet 3:15) to give an accounting for their hope to those who ask it.[3]

Part of the reason why the popes assign such importance to doing apologetics is that reason has become increasingly separated from faith. This unnecessary divorce can be traced back to Occam's philosophy in the fourteenth century. The separation of faith and reason has resulted in a variety of philosophical positions that are hostile to the Catholic worldview: positivism, scientism, nihilism, atheism, eclecticism, historicism, pragmatism and, of course, relativism. The popes respond to the crisis of relativism by noting that it is paramount to defend the notion of objective truth. By denying objective truth, one will lose sight of all meaning. According to John Paul II, all of these philosophical outlooks—perhaps especially relativism—compel the magisterium to revisit the relationship between faith and reason and to develop practices that join them together.

By forming a distinctly Catholic world and life-view, it becomes easier for Catholics to enculturate their faith in the secular marketplace of ideas. Apologetics, however, is also directed to believers who promote false

---

1. John XXIII, *Princeps Pastorum*, 32.

2. Paul VI, *Mysterium Fidei*, 22.

3. John Paul II, *Veritatis Splendor*, 109; Also see John Paul II, *Fides et Ratio*, 15, 79.

theologies and practices within the Church. Another reason why apologetics is needed is that it can motivate Catholics to take the missionary mandate seriously.

Apologists should not simply resort to reasoned arguments for faith. This would reduce the enterprise of apologetics to a matter of merely persuading the mind to think in Catholic terms. Rather, the *practice* of Christian faith can also serve as a motive of credibility. Thus truth and love are both needed to help draw individuals closer to faith. In the words of Benedict XVI: "Truth needs to be sought, found and expressed within the 'economy' of charity, but charity in its turn needs to be understood, confirmed and practised in the light of truth. In this way, not only do we do a service to charity enlightened by truth, but we also help give credibility to truth, demonstrating its persuasive and authenticating power in the practical setting of social living."[4]

Christian love is to be extended to everyone, regardless of what anyone believes. But it must be kept in mind that love speaks and defends the truth. Truth, by definition, excludes positions that are contrary to it. Love is therefore related to the practical side of apologetics; truth is directed to the theoretical side. Pope Paul VI explains:

> The fact that we are distinct from the world does not mean that we are entirely separated from it. Nor does it mean that we are indifferent to it, afraid of it, or contemptuous of it. When the Church distinguishes itself from humanity, it does so not in order to oppose it, but to come closer to it. A physician who realizes the danger of disease, protects himself and others from it, but at the same time he strives to cure those who have contracted it. The Church does the same thing. It does not regard God's mercy as an exclusive privilege, nor does the greatness of the privilege it enjoys make it feel unconcerned for those who do not share it. On the contrary, it finds in its own salvation an argument for showing more concern and more love for those who live close at hand, or to whom it can go in its endeavor to make all alike share the blessing of salvation.[5]

John Paul II agrees substantially with his predecessor, and adds that "[Jesus] was uncompromisingly stern towards sin, but patient and rich in mercy towards sinners."[6]

---

4. Benedict XVI, *Caritas in Veritate*, 1. Also see paragraph 2.

5. Paul VI, *Ecclesiam Suam*, 63.

6. John Paul II, *Veritatis Splendor*, 95.

Natural Knowledge of God

The reasoned defense of the faith plays a central role in the popes' views of Christian credibility. Without including reason in matters of faith, one inevitably becomes fideistic. On a fideistic premise, the "common points of reference" that believers might be able to share with unbelievers are lost. This is one of the principal reasons why John Paul II reaffirmed the precedence of metaphysics over modern epistemological approaches in his encyclical *Fides et Ratio*. Those who concentrate on epistemology and hermeneutics at the expense of the metaphysical may forget to ask the more radical questions about objective truth, meaning, purpose, and God.

In *Fides et Ratio*, John Paul II affirmed that the truths that can be discovered through either faith or reason have nothing to fear from one another. If there is any genuine conflict between the two, then one of them has obviously erred. The truths that can be known from special revelation are above the truths of natural revelation, but the former can elevate and burnish what can be known apart from supernatural faith. Conversely, when faith and reason are severed from one another, both of them become enfeebled.

Thus, theologians should not skip over the truths of natural revelation, but should become more courageous in providing arguments in defense of the gospel and Catholic teaching. "Nonetheless," writes the pope, "in the light of faith which finds in Jesus Christ this ultimate meaning, I cannot but encourage philosophers—be they Christian or not—to trust in the power of human reason and not to set themselves goals that are too modest in their philosophizing."[7]

One of the natural knowable truths of faith would be the "first principles" of knowledge, most notably the law of non-contradiction, the law of identity, and the law of the excluded middle. Another natural truth would be the ability to apprehend a true understanding of reality:

> Although times change and knowledge increases, it is possible to discern a core of philosophical insight within the history of thought as a whole. Consider, for example, the principles of non-contradiction, finality and causality, as well as the concept of the person as a free and intelligent subject, with the capacity to know God, truth and goodness. Consider as well certain fundamental moral norms which are shared by all. These are among the indications that, beyond different schools of thought, there exists a body of knowledge which may be judged a kind of spiritual heritage of humanity. It is as if we had come upon an *implicit philosophy*, as a result of which all feel that they possess

7. John Paul II, *Fides et Ratio*, 56; see also paragraph 54.

these principles, albeit in a general and unreflective way. Precisely because it is shared in some measure by all, this knowledge should serve as a kind of reference-point for the different philosophical schools. Once reason successfully intuits and formulates the first universal principles of being and correctly draws from them conclusions which are coherent both logically and ethically, then it may be called right reason or, as the ancients called it, *orthós logos, recta ratio*.[8]

These first principles of knowledge establish the preconditions that allow for the possibility of Thomist natural theology. Indeed, to adhere to first principles is to catch a glimpse of God himself.

Consequently, another naturally knowable truth is the existence of God. Our deep yearning for meaning and truth can be fulfilled only by God.[9] Positing the existence of God seems to rectify the fragmentation that inevitably issues from relativism by supplying the phenomenon of existence itself with genuine coherence. When God is taken out of the picture, it inevitably follows that human beings will eventually suffer.

Although Thomas Aquinas' five proofs for the existence of God are never explicitly mentioned in recent encyclicals, the popes affirm with conviction that creation is "not a product of natural forces working, as it were, by blind impulse."[10] Benedict XVI asks the reader: "how could being emerge from nothing, how could intelligence be born from chance?"[11] Thus, God must be "the first and final cause of all created being."[12] In God are possessed the divine attributes that the magisterium has already dogmatically limned at Vatican I: God is merciful, transcendent, hidden, invisible, uncreated, without limit, free and personal, eternal, immutable, omnipotent, holy, almighty, ineffable, undivided, unsearchable, living, true, and absolute.[13] The popes' consistent presentation and understanding of the divine nature

---

8. Ibid., 4.

9. Ibid., 29. Also see John XXIII, *Mater et Magistra*, 212, 214.

10. John XXIII, *Mater et Magistra*, 63. Also see Paul VI, *Humanae Vitae*, 8; John Paul II, *Veritatis Splendor*, 73, 79; Benedict XVI, *Spe Salvi*, 5; Benedict XVI, *Caritas in Veritate*, 29; Francis, *Lumen Fidei*, 34.

11. Benedict XVI, *Caritas in Veritate*, 74.

12. John XXIII, *Mater et Magistra*, 215.

13. References to the traditional divine attributes are scattered throughout the postconciliar encyclicals. See John Paul II *Dives in Misericordia*, 2, 13; John Paul II, *Dominum et Vivificantem*, 37, 54, 67; John Paul II, *Redemptoris Mater*, 37, 50, 51; John Paul II, *Centesimus Annus*, 62; John Paul II, *Veritatis Splendor*, 1, 7, 11, 52; John Paul II, *Evangelium Vitae*, 1; John Paul II, *Fides et Ratio*, 4, 13, 24, 42, 76; Benedict XVI, *Deus Caritas Est*, 37.

should serve as a corrective to certain drifts toward different versions of pan-en-theism and theistic personalism.[14]

The existence of God can also be known by reflecting on the "universal precepts of the natural moral law." Some of these unchanging moral precepts, according to the popes, include human life, dignity, rights and moral duties. Consequently God must be seen as the Grounding Cause of the natural moral law. In *Pacem in Terris* John XXIII affirmed: "The world's Creator has stamped man's inmost being with an order revealed to man by his conscience; and his conscience insists on his preserving it. Men 'show the work of the law written in their hearts. Their conscience bears witness to them.' And how could it be otherwise? All created being reflects the infinite wisdom of God. It reflects it all the more clearly, the higher it stands in the scale of perfection."[15]

Because human reason can discover at least partial truths about God apart from the influence of special revelation, the philosophies of materialism and atheism are unequivocally condemned. Paul VI said that atheism is "the most serious problem of our time. We are firmly convinced that the basic propositions of atheism are utterly false and irreconcilable with the underlying principles of thought. They strike at the genuine and effective foundation for man's acceptance of a rational order in the universe, and introduce into human life a futile kind of dogmatism which far from solving life's difficulties, only degrades it and saddens it."[16]

Christ and the Church: Signs of Credibility

John Paul II summarizes the historicity of God's revelation in Christ and the "signs" that accompany his life and message:

> To assist reason in its effort to understand the mystery there are
> the signs which Revelation itself presents. These serve to lead

14. When I speak of "panentheism" and "theistic personalism," I am speaking of two ways that some modern philosophers have typically conceived of the divine nature. Theistic personalists usually conceive of God as a person, only without the limitations that humans have. This is a radical departure from the conception of God that was offered by Thomas Aquinas. Theistic personalists and panentheists basically reduce God to one among many creatures. For a discussion, see Davies, *An Introduction to the Philosophy of Religion*, 1–20. In this book I distance myself from modern theism and argue against atheism from a pre-modern, Thomist perspective. The God of modern theism is somewhat responsible for the rise of atheism. For confirmation, see Hyman, *A Short History of Atheism*.

15. John XXIII, *Pacem in Terris*, 5.

16. Paul VI, *Ecclesiam Suam*, 100.

the search for truth to new depths, enabling the mind in its autonomous exploration to penetrate within the mystery by use of reason's own methods, of which it is rightly jealous. Yet these signs also urge reason to look beyond their status as signs in order to grasp the deeper meaning which they bear. They contain a hidden truth to which the mind is drawn and which it cannot ignore without destroying the very signs which it is given.[17]

It is only natural for human beings to search for divine clues about human destiny. Other signs of credibility include Jesus' teachings, actions, and miracles. The human search for answers about death, for instance, can be satisfied by the fact of Jesus' resurrection. "As the risen one," says Pope Francis, "Christ is the trustworthy witness, deserving of faith (cf. Rev 1:5; Heb 2:17), and a solid support for our faith."[18]

The popes agree with the apologetic analyses of the Church itself. Catholic theology affirms that Jesus Christ is the "light of the nations:" his presence, work, and message can be apprehended by outsiders through the Church itself. A major apologetic motif has to do with the positive impact of Christianity upon those cultures where the gospel is faithfully lived and taught. In the corpus of apologetical literature this argument was once known as the *via empirica*. Thus the Church, insofar as she remains faithful to the gospel, can serve as sign of credibility.

Paul VI elaborates upon one version of the *via empirica*: "One part of this world, as everyone knows, has in recent years detached itself and broken away from the Christian foundations of its culture, although formerly it had been so imbued with Christianity and had drawn from it such strength and vigor that the people of these nations in many cases owe to Christianity all that is best in their own tradition—a fact that is not always fully appreciated."[19] Sometimes the popes explain the inner-rationale of the *via empirica* by explaining how the Christian faith provides additional moral motivation to change the world for the better.

Related to the *via empirica* is the negative secular objection that Christianity causes violence. Such a challenge needs to be answered by apologists today. Paul VI was well aware of these challenges and urged apologists to distinguish between what is genuinely Christian and what is not.[20] Negatively, the popes explain that the dechristianization of culture will result in widespread confusion and moral decadence. John XXIII warns that, if the

17. John Paul II, *Fides et Ratio*, 13.

18. Francis, *Lumen Fidei*, 17.

19. Paul VI, *Ecclesiam Suam*, 13; see also 14, 42, 51.

20. Ibid., 11.

Church is rejected, "the very foundations of truth, goodness, and civiliza-tion are endangered."[21] John Paul II adds:

> Dechristianization, which weighs heavily upon entire peoples and communities once rich in faith and Christian life, involves not only the loss of faith or in any event its becoming irrelevant for everyday life, but also, and of necessity, *a decline or obscuring of the moral sense*. This comes about both as a result of a loss of awareness of the originality of Gospel morality and as a result of an eclipse of fundamental principles and ethical values them-selves. Today's widespread tendencies towards subjectivism, utilitarianism and relativism appear not merely as pragmatic attitudes or patterns of behaviour, but rather as approaches having a basis in theory and claiming full cultural and social legitimacy.[22]

Catholicism provided an intellectual context that allowed for the sustained emergence of Western civilization. Whether certain cultured despisers acknowledge this or not, many established institutions of the West (for example, in education and healthcare), are direct outcomes of a Catholic Christian frame of mind.

Unity, Holiness, and Love

People are awakened in the faith by the presence of caring individuals in their lives. As someone once said, the number one argument for Christianity is Christians. But the number one argument against Christianity is Chris-tians. The popes do not settle for theoretical defenses of Catholic teaching. Human holiness, love, and unity can also serve as existential motives of credibility. Apologists are called not only to give answers to objections, but to become answer bearers.

For instance, ecumenism, when properly conceived and implemented, should be seen as a movement in apologetics. In *Redemptoris Missio*, John Paul II explains that "mission" should provide the impetus that underlies the search for Christian unity. "The missionary thrust therefore belongs to the very nature of the Christian life, and is also the inspiration behind ecumen-ism: 'that they may all be one . . . so that the world may believe that you have sent me.'"[23]

---

21. John XXIII, *Ad Petri Cathedram*, 8.

22. John Paul II, *Veritatis Splendor*, 106.

23. John Paul II, *Redemptoris Missio*, 1.

Although Christians are not fully one (that is, to the degree that the Catholic Church defines ecclesiastical unity), ecumenists should practice apologetical tactics to attain full, visible unity.[24] For the ecumenical endeavor demands that Catholics familiarize themselves with the teachings of other Christians. Apologetical theology can help one to understand other doctrinal perspectives and understandings which, in turn, can help persuade other Christians to achieve some sort of unity.

> Full communion of course will have to come about through the acceptance of the whole truth into which the Holy Spirit guides Christ's disciples. Hence all forms of reductionism or facile "agreement" must be absolutely avoided. Serious questions must be resolved, for if not, they will reappear at another time, either in the same terms or in a different guise.[25]

Repressing disagreement between Christians and other religions is not healthy for authentic faith, and certainly not with full Catholic faith.

The unity engendered by marriage and family life can serve as a sign of God's love; marriage and family life need to be safeguarded by apologists.[26] Similarly, Western priests and those called to religious life express their love for Christ by living a celibate life. A priestly life, faithfully discharged, can serve as a convincing sign of the greater reality of the Reign of God.[27]

Recent popes have also emphasized the apologetical potential of charity. Benedict XVI, for instance, maintained that Christian charity is the most convincing apologetic for faith:

> Charity, furthermore, cannot be used as a means of engaging in what is nowadays considered proselytism. Love is free; it is not practised as a way of achieving other ends. But this does not mean that charitable activity must somehow leave God and Christ aside. For it is always concerned with the whole man. Often the deepest cause of suffering is the very absence of God. Those who practise charity in the Church's name will never seek to impose the Church's faith upon others. They realize that a pure and generous love is the best witness to the God in whom

24. Cf. Gaillardetz, "Apologetics, Evangelization, and Ecumenism Today," 9–15.

25. John Paul II, *Ut Unum Sint*, 36.

26. For all passages that link married life and Catholic credibility, see Paul VI, *Sacerdotalis Caelibatus*, 57; Paul VI, *Humanae Vitae*, 8, 16, 18, 21, 25–26; John Paul II, *Redemptoris Missio*, 42; John Paul II, *Evangelium Vitae*, 86, 92–93, 99; Benedict XVI, *Caritas in Veritate*, 44, 53.

27. John XXIII, *Ad Petri Cathedram*, 75; John XXIII, *Princeps Pastorum* 14; Paul VI, *Sacerdotalis Caelibatus*, 13, 24, 26, 31, 34, 43, 45–46, 56–57, 79, 91, 98; John Paul II, *Redemptoris Missio*, 45, 70; John Paul II, *Ecclesia de Eucharistia*, 52, 62.

we believe and by whom we are driven to love. A Christian
knows when it is time to speak of God and when it is better to
say nothing and to let love alone speak. He knows that God is
love (cf. 1 Jn 4:8) and that God's presence is felt at the very time
when the only thing we do is to love. He knows—to return to the
questions raised earlier—that disdain for love is disdain for God
and man alike; it is an attempt to do without God. Consequently, the best defence of God and man consists precisely in love. It
is the responsibility of the Church's charitable organizations to
reinforce this awareness in their members, so that by their activity—as well as their words, their silence, their example—they
may be credible witnesses to Christ.[28]

Another example of the "apologetics of love" is displayed by the life and
death of Christian martyrs. John Paul II argued that the martyrs "provide
evidence of a love that has no need of lengthy arguments in order to convince. The martyrs stir in us a profound trust because they give voice to what
we already feel and they declare what we would like to have the strength
to express."[29]

Likewise, Hans Urs von Balthasar argued that love should be the primary means of apologetic persuasion.[30] As with Benedict XVI and John
Paul II, there is something right about this contention. I do not dispute an
apologetics of love. But it must be remembered that if one loves, then he or
she can and should appeal to reason to defend what one believes (especially
if the context allows for such a discussion). An apologetics of love cannot
replace the enterprise of rational apologetics.

Another approach concentrates on the evidential power of holiness.
"This universal presence of the saints," declared John Paul II, "is in fact a
proof of the transcendent power of the Spirit. It is the sign and proof of
God's victory over the forces of evil which divide humanity."[31]

René Latourelle takes great pains to stress the importance of the evidential power of human holiness in his apologetics.[32] As with von Balthasar's
concern with the apologetics of love, it must be stressed, however, that if
one is holy, then he or she should use every means to reach unbelievers
(and lukewarm believers) with the good news. Holiness may be more than

---

28. Benedict XVI, *Deus Caritas Est*, 31.

29. John Paul II, *Fides et Ratio*, 32.

30. Balthasar, *Love Alone is Credible*.

31. John Paul II, *Ut Unum Sint*, 84.

32. Latourelle, *Christ and the Church*.

rational, but is certainly not less than rational. Conversely, if one uses rational argument, this can become a means by which one is sanctified.

Latourelle paints with broad, beautiful strokes by emphasizing the importance of holiness without elaborating too much further upon the need for rational apologetics. Of course, the latter is not always needed, and is dependent on the context of the discussion. If one's interlocutor is open to critical engagement by weighing and assessing the relevant evidence, then this is a sign that Catholics might need to engage them with theoretical apologetics.

Many individuals come to faith through experiential means, but this would not mean that reasoned defenses are irrelevant. Every person is precious in the sight of God. Thus, we would be doing *some* individuals a grave disservice by refusing to engage them with reason, especially if they ask for such reasons. Since there will always be objections and questions posed to Christianity, the perennial enterprise of defending the faith must continue to be endorsed.

Catholic Apologetics and the Theology of Religions

One of the perennial challenges to historic Christianity lies in reconciling the omnibenevolence of God with the particularity of divine revelation. When the challenge is left unaddressed, it can foster doubt in skeptics' minds about the uniqueness of Jesus and the nature of God himself. This can often lead to an attitude of indifference that stems from an uncritical religious pluralism, a concern which John Paul II specifically addressed:

> . . . one of the most serious reasons for the lack of interest in the missionary task is a widespread indifferentism, which, sad to say, is found also among Christians. It is based on incorrect theological perspectives and is characterized by a religious relativism which leads to the belief that "one religion is as good as another." We can add, using the words of Pope Paul VI, that there are also certain "excuses which would impede evangelization. The most insidious of these excuses are certainly the ones which people claim to find support for in such and such a teaching of the Council."[33]

"Indeed," says Paul VI, "honesty compels us to declare openly our conviction that the Christian religion is the one and only true religion, and it

33. John Paul II, *Redemptoris Missio*, 36. Also relevant are the statements in John XXIII, *Ad Petri Cathedram*, 17; Paul VI, *Ecclesiam Suam*, 107; Benedict XVI, *Caritas in Veritate*, 55.

is our hope that it will be acknowledged as such by all who look for God and worship Him."[34] Perhaps the first way that apologists might answer the challenges surrounding the "scandal of particularity" is to first understand the theological parameters that have already been established by the magisterium.

For one thing, the popes maintain that Jesus Christ is the one redeeming mediator between God and humanity. It follows that Christ's revelation is unique, full, ultimate, and definitive. As John Paul II succinctly stated in *Dives in Misericordia*: "this Redemption is the ultimate and definitive revelation of the holiness of God, who is the absolute fullness of perfection: fullness of justice and of love, since justice is based on love, flows from it and tends towards it."[35]

Second, to accept that Jesus is the one true savior does not mean that "formal outsiders" cannot be saved. Rather, the risen Christ makes himself present to everyone in their unique circumstances, including those who are inculpably ignorant of Christ. Here the qualification of the word "inculpable" must be emphasized for understanding Church teaching. To be sure, those who can overcome their ignorance of Christ are held accountable for explicitly accepting the gospel, which is expressed formally as a member of the Catholic Church. The biblical mandate to evangelize the world retains its validity, even though outsiders can receive Jesus and eternal salvation.[36]

Third, because the "formal outsiders" can be saved, a type of revelation must be accessible to them. However, this type of revelation is "always fragmentary and impaired by the limits of our understanding. Faith alone makes it possible to penetrate the mystery in a way that allows us to understand it coherently."[37] By accepting God's revelation in Jesus, Catholics can know something about the "formal outsiders" that the latter do not know about themselves. Given the popes' concern to evangelize the world, it is only natural that some type of interreligious apologetics and evangelization will be endorsed by them. As John Paul II puts matters:

> Nowadays the call to conversion which missionaries address to non-Christians is put into question or passed over in silence. It is seen as an act of "proselytizing"; it is claimed that it is enough to help people to become more human or more faithful to their own religion, that it is enough to build communities capable

34. Paul VI, *Ecclesiam Suam*, 107.

35. John Paul II, *Dives in Misericordia*, 7.

36. For the universal call to evangelize the world—even in the face of the possibility that outsiders can be saved, see John Paul II, *Redemptoris Missio*.

37. John Paul II, *Fides et Ratio*, 13.

of working for justice, freedom, peace and solidarity. What is overlooked is that every person has the right to hear the "Good News" of the God who reveals and gives himself in Christ, so that each one can live out in its fullness his or her proper calling.[38]

Conclusion

In summary, it is strange that apologetics is lowly esteemed in many Catholic circles today. Apologetics is needed more now than ever. The New Testament writers and early Church Fathers were decidedly apologetical, for there was no Christian influence in the surrounding culture yet. Today, the process of secularization continues to erode the foundations of Christian civilization. It is therefore reasonable to contend that modern Catholics should have apologetical concerns akin to the earliest Christians. In a post-Christian context, it seems reasonable that we should have the same approach. An apologetical outlook might make greater inroads into the wider world. Curiously, many Catholics and other Christians question the discipline of apologetics. Such resistance cannot be justified in light of Vatican II and the papal encyclicals which emphasize a place for apologetics.

To inculturate the gospel does not mean that everything in culture is compatible with gospel values. One way to distinguish between gospel values (that is, "what can be incorporated from the surrounding culture") from what comes from "the world" is to remain attentive to the Word of God: "We must return to the study, not of human eloquence of empty rhetoric, but of the genuine art of proclaiming the Word of God."[39] The Holy Spirit will "ensure continuity and identity of understanding in the midst of changing conditions and circumstances."[40] The bishops are charged with reading the signs of the culture to discern what is compatible with Catholic practice and what is not.[41] Laypersons, then, must carefully follow the lead of the magisterium in making a case for faith in the modern world.

---

38. John Paul II, *Redemptoris Missio*, 46.

39. Paul VI, *Ecclesiam Suam*, 90.

40. John Paul II, *Dominum et Vivificantem*, 4.

41. John Paul II, *Redemptoris Missio*, 54.

— 3 —

Faith, Reason, and
Postmodern Relativism

UNTIL THE MIDDLE OF the nineteenth century, almost every mainstream philosopher in the West held to some form or implicit understanding of the correspondence theory of truth.[1] In the correspondence theory, truth is defined as the property of a proposition that corresponds to reality; truth is an objective description of the way the world is. This notion of truth has been reinterpreted in the West. No longer is truth seen as a goal that all persons should know as an end in-and-of-itself; rather, it is usually understood as something completely inseparable from politics, culture, psychology, biology, race, and gender. In the postmodern view of truth, reality and truth are merely determined by individuals, not uniquely discovered by each person.

Although it is difficult to define postmodernism, the movement is characterized by radical and irreducible pluralism; the rejection of unifying metaphysical or religious claims; and suspicion toward binary categories that characterize different regions of thought or ontological realities. Postmodernism is not completely hostile toward the truth claims of Christianity; but, there are many components of postmodernism that are relativistic. According to these relativists, truth, linguistic meaning, moral values, and human nature no longer have (and never had) stable meanings. Since there is no overarching story to guide individuals with this type of relativism in the background, postmodernism is also characterized, in the words of Jean-François Lyotard, by "incredulity toward meta-narratives."[2]

This relativism makes it impossible, in principle, to have a unified view of the world under the banner of Catholic Christian faith. Some theologians

---

1. Aquinas can be considered a proponent of the correspondence theory of truth. See Peterson, *Aquinas*, 89–113.

2. Lyotard, *The Postmodern Condition*, xxiv.

seem to have absorbed the postmodern view of truth when reflecting on revelation. Avery Dulles said: "Theology, for its part, all too often evades the challenge of truth. Falling into fideism or sheer positivism, many theologians limit themselves to sociological, linguistic, and historical studies of the Bible and Church teaching."[3]

As a result of the paradigmatic shift, the unifying claims of the Church can no longer be seen as true and binding on all persons. The implication is that there is no urgent reason to become or remain a Catholic. What is sorely needed is a response to relativism and its impact on retrieving the discipline of apologetics. In order to reinstate the importance of apologetics, I will address the challenge of relativism and show its incoherence. It would not make sense for apologists to present arguments and evidence for the faith, unless the doctrinal positions they think are provable or "more probable than not" are construed as legitimate claims to truth.

Modernity and Metaphysics

Professor Allan Bloom is no stranger to our current cultural malaise. Surveying the landscape of higher education in the 1980s, Bloom wrote:

> There is one thing a professor can be absolutely certain of: almost every student entering the university believes, or says he believes, that truth is relative. If this belief is put to the test, one can count on the students' reaction: they will be uncomprehending. . . . The danger they have been taught to fear from absolutism is not error but intolerance. Relativism is necessary to openness; and this is the virtue, the only virtue, which all primary education for more than fifty years has dedicated itself to inculcating. Openness—and the relativism that makes it the only plausible stance in the face of various claims to truth and various ways of life and kinds of human beings—is the great insight of our times. . . . The study of history and of culture teaches that all the world was made in the past; men always thought they were right, and that led to wars, persecutions, slavery, xenophobia, racism, and chauvinism. The point is not to correct the mistakes and really be right; rather it is not to think you are right at all.[4]

Bloom's contention has lost hardly any of its relevance in today's cultural milieu. The decline of truth not only occurs in the academy, it is found in

---

3. Dulles, "Can Philosophy Be Christian?" in Foster and Koterski, eds., *The Two Wings of Catholic Thought*, 19.

4. Bloom, *The Closing of the American Mind*, 25–26.

popular culture. The denial of objective truth is usually assumed rather than argued for by the ordinary person. Cheap slogans such as "true for you, but not for me" and "to each his own" run rampant in the culture of postmodernity.

Like most revolutions in human thinking, the emergence of relativism did not creep into Western culture overnight, but can be traced back to the fact/value split of Enlightenment philosophers such as Immanuel Kant (1724–1804). He denied that one could know reality as it is. This severance of fact (reality) from meaning (value) made it easier for persons to be leery of truth claims. Whether these claims are pronounced in the name of religion or not, objective truths are generally regarded with suspicion and are interpreted as expressions of subjective preference. John Caputo succinctly states: "Each thing has its own drive or local force—its 'perspective'—and the world is a multiplicity of competing perspectives. Ideas have not 'truth' but 'value,' that is, an effectiveness that is measured by their capacity to enhance life."[5]

The Kantian divorce of fact and meaning eventually culminated in the philosophy of Friedrich Nietzsche (1844–1900), a forerunner and prophet of postmodernism. Nietzsche wrote:

> What then is truth? A mobile army of metaphors, metonyms, and anthropomorphisms—in short, a sum of human relations, which have been enhanced, transposed, and embellished poetically and rhetorically, and which after long use seem firm, canonical, and obligatory to a people; truths are illusions about which one has forgotten that this is what they are; metaphors which are worn out and without sensuous power; coins which have lost their picture and now matter only as metal, no longer as coins.[6]

For Nietzsche, "There are no facts, only interpretations."[7] A fact is something in the real world; an interpretation is how one understands the world. Michel Foucault explained the origins of Nietzsche's reasoning: "Why does Nietzsche challenge the pursuit of the origin (*Ursprung*)? First, because it is an attempt to capture the exact essence of things, . . . because this search assumes the existence of immobile forms that precede the eternal world of accident and succession. . . . However, . . . there is 'something altogether dif-

---

5. Caputo, "Atheism, A/Theology, and the Postmodern Condition," in Martin, ed., *The Cambridge Companion to Atheism*, 270–271.

6. Nietzsche, "Truth and the Extra Moral Sense," in Kaufmann, ed., *The Portable Nietzsche*, 46–47.

7. Nietzsche, *The Will to Power*, 267.

ferent' behind things: not a timeless and essential secret, but the secret that they have no essence."[8] For Nietzsche, the recognition of objects does not arise out of recognizing actual essences in reality.

As an extension of Kant's distinction between the noumenal (the world in and of itself) and the phenomenal worlds (the world as it appears to human observers), many relativists have affirmed that human judgments about the world are first filtered through psychological, cultural and historical contingencies, leaving little room for metaphysics. With this contention in mind, they contend that accurate knowledge of the world becomes impossible. In reference to the idea that persons must refer to universal human nature to make ethical judgments, for example, Richard Rorty claims: "there is nothing deep down inside us except what we have put there ourselves, no criterion that we have not created in the course of creating a practice, no standard of rationality that is not an appeal to such a criterion, no rigorous argumentation that is not obedience to our own conventions."[9]

The rejection of universals also has an impact on the possibility of interpersonal communication. Since words do not have corresponding referents, language itself loses the power to make definitive statements about reality and is no longer capable of persuading others. Written texts no longer refer to reality when metaphysical truths (such as human nature, objective truths, or moral values) are illusory.[10]

Some thinkers allege that texts must be released from an objective message that readers can somehow discover for themselves. In this view, every meaning in texts can be shown to be ambiguous. The original meaning that the author assigned to his or her writing does not limit the reader's understanding of what is written. Every reader is allowed to impose his or her own meaning onto the text. Jacques Derrida explains: "Those who wish to ground solidarity in objectivity . . . have to construe truth as correspondence to reality. . . . By contrast, those who wish to reduce objectivity to solidarity . . . view truth as, in William James' phrase, what is good for us to believe. So they do not need an account of a relation between beliefs and objects called 'correspondence.'"[11]

The second principal way that relativists have attacked the nature of objective truth is derived from yet another angle of Nietzsche's philosophy. Truth is not correspondence with reality, but is reduced to the function of

---

8. Foucault, "Nietzsche, Genealogy, History," in *Language, Counter-Memory, Practice*, 142.

9. Rorty, *Consequences of Pragmatism*, xlii.

10. Rorty, introduction to J. P. Murphy's *Pragmatism*.

11. Rorty, "Solidarity or Objectivity?" in *Objectivity, Relativism, and Truth*, 22.

power relationships.[12] By suppressing the weak in society, the powerful exert their voice over the weak to guarantee that their voice will be heard and influence the world. In this perspective, truth is seen as that which favors the powerful. In sum, one of the negative impacts of postmodernism is that human understanding is so conditioned by historical and cultural contingencies that it becomes impossible to know objective truth. Relativists also contend that truth is the product of the human drive for power, not of reality as such.

Such ideas undermine the conviction that Catholicism is true for everyone, independently of anyone's belief in it. And if Catholicism is not true, then why should believers seek to evangelize others to believe in it? Thus the denial of objective truth undercuts the impetus for participating in the Great Commission (Matt 28:18–20). What means of persuasion could be given if Christianity is merely one of many opinions in the marketplace of ideas? Relativism thus militates against Catholic apologetics, whose practitioners firmly believe that one of the principal reasons why anyone should believe in Christianity is because it is true for everyone.

Enlightenment Rationalism and Traditional Apologetics

Traditionally, Catholic apologists assumed that truth is objective. The knowability of truth was not a concern for them. Rather, they began with establishing God's existence, the human need for God, and then they argued for the historical credibility of Jesus' divinity. All of this culminated in an assessment of which Church best fits the four ecclesial attributes of the Church (that is, "one, holy, catholic, and apostolic"). This step-by-step method made good sense, for it did not seem reasonable to believe that Jesus is the Son of God unless there is a God who can have a Son (who can also institute a Church). This book seeks to reinvigorate the classical apologetics, but also updates it.

The classical apologetic methodology must be supplemented by a concern to defend objective truth. For, the burning issue today is whether anything is objectively true, let alone that it can be known as such. According to Joseph Ratzinger (later Pope Benedict XVI): "Relativism has thus become the central problem for the faith at the present time. . . . The faith cannot be liberated if reason itself does not open up again. If the door to metaphysical cognition remains closed, if the limits of human knowledge set by Kant are

12. Foucault, "Truth and Power," in Gordon, ed., *Power/Knowledge*, 133; Foucault, *Discipline and Punish*, 27–28.

impassable, faith is destined to atrophy: it simply lacks air to breathe."[13] A refurbished method of classical apologetics must begin with the nature and knowability of truth, for arguments and other related evidence for Christianity have long assumed that there is an objective truth that can be known.

The context must be taken into consideration when doing apologetics. As such, some occasions are simply not conducive to engaging in reasoned approaches to defending the faith. But when the opportunity arises for such an interaction, the first place to begin might be with the nature and knowability of reality, especially if one's dialogue partner is skeptical of objective truth. Indeed, the success of the historical evidence for Jesus and for the positive influence of Christianity upon the world depends on the logical precondition of the existence of a theistic God. Moreover, the success of the arguments for God's existence all depend on first principles such as the law of non-contradiction, the law of identity, and the law of the excluded middle. It is precisely the first principles of knowledge that postmodern relativism resists.

Every so often a good work of Catholic rational apologetics can be found. Benedict Ashley's *Choosing a World-View and Value System*[14] engages central issues of credibility with reason and hard evidence. Like many other published works in apologetics, Ashley successfully avoids the pitfalls of Enlightenment rationalism. Unfortunately, however, there is no engagement with first principles which make the project of natural theology and the *demonstratio christiana* reasonable to engage in. Individuals under the influence of relativism will resist Ashley's book because there is no such thing as objective truth, let alone that it could be known as such.

A great reference work is the *Dictionary of Fundamental Theology*, which has dozens of fine articles concerned with the credibility of Christianity.[15] Yet hardly any of the contributors discuss the postmodern critique and its ramifications for apologetics or evangelization. Avery Dulles' standard work on the history of apologetics barely mentions the influence of rational apologetics after Vatican II.[16]

Because the primary lens through which many individuals interpret the world is relativistic, apologists may begin their defense of Christian faith with the notion of truth. However, some theologians resist anything that resembles apologetics, claiming that it smacks of modern epistemology where the canons of reason are upheld at the expense of other forms of knowing.

---

13. Ratzinger, "Relativism," 316.

14. Ashley, *Choosing a World-View and Value System*.

15. Fisichella and Latourelle, *Dictionary of Fundamental Theology*.

16. Dulles, *A History of Apologetics*.

But this is a serious misreading of Enlightenment rationalism and its threat to traditional apologetics.

Most philosophers maintain that modern epistemology began with the academician René Descartes (1596–1650). Descartes held that, unless knowledge is based in reason alone, one does not have true knowledge. Today many philosophers, including postmodernists, have dealt a heavy blow to Descartes' epistemology. Cartesian epistemology is both self-refuting and arbitrary. Reason alone cannot show that reason is the only guide for knowing truth. As a result, Descartes' epistemological theory has been almost universally rejected by contemporary philosophers.

But this does not mean all versions of foundationalism are incoherent. While the postmodern critique has been widely accepted, it does not successfully apply to modified versions of foundationalism which have been gaining in momentum as of late. These versions are more modest, making it difficult for the postmodern critique to succeed. Without some version of first principles (the foundational principles that make knowledge possible), the common ground that is needed for effective communication becomes impossible.

As in Descartes' epistemology, some principles are universally applicable to human knowers and are inherent to reality itself (otherwise, nothing could be known by anyone at any time or place). In modified versions of foundationalism, first principles are either undeniable or are reducible to the undeniable. Without them, nothing at all could be known. It should be noted that, according to the philosopher-theologian, Thomas Aquinas (1225–1274), first principles are simultaneously both metaphysical *and* epistemological. Since Aquinas is a realist, he makes no disjunction between the rational and the real.

Unlike Cartesian foundationalism, modified versions of foundationalism (which are consonant with Aristotelian-Thomistic philosophies) hold that epistemological foundations are necessary for knowledge, but they are not based exclusively in reason apart from the real world. For Aquinas, for instance, first principles are both epistemological and metaphysical. The self-evident principles of foundationalism are true by their very nature. To be shown later on in this chapter, every person uses first principles. To deny them one must engage in self-defeating claims.

Consequently, one of the objections to anti-realist views of truth (philosophies that take up the epistemology of Descartes) is the problem of auto-referentiality: the incapability of relativism to apply its own tenets to its own conceptions of truth. The second argument for the reality of first principles is that there must be an ultimate basis for truth claims, otherwise there would be an infinite regress of reasons for justifying knowledge (which is impossible).

Hence the main problem with Cartesian foundationalism did not consist in its endorsement of first principles, but *in its restrained definition of what could count as a first principle.* One reason why some Catholics scorn the discipline of apologetics is that it relies on reasoned arguments which easily hearken back to Cartesian rationalism. But the meaning of "reason alone can show that God exists" is highly ambiguous. Does the apologist mean that one can achieve some hypothetical state of pure reason apart from human experience (as in Cartesian rationalism), or does the apologist refer to the exercise of reason and experience apart from the influence of special revelation (Aristotle and Aquinas)? The latter stance should not be equated with rationalism. For Thomists, one can demonstrate the existence of God.

From the standpoint of the apologist, the truths of special revelation can never be demonstrated, but can be shown to be more probable than not. Beginning from the "ground up," Catholic apologists can start with first principles and demonstrate the notion of objective truth and the existence of God; beginning from the "top down," they seek resonance with what is already believed about God's revelation.

Not only is the denial of first principles self-refuting, but adherents of anti-realist views of truth cannot live out their views with any sort of consistency. Indeed, relativists present their views not as mere expressions of feeling, but as viewpoints that their readers will comprehend. They also hold that their viewpoints are preferable to competing positions, and that there are both correct and incorrect interpretations of their positions. As a case in point, Derrida smuggled in a realist conception of truth when he said that one of his critics misunderstood what he was saying (in a long, ninety-three page article!).[17]

Understanding the shift from classical foundationalism to modified versions of foundationalism is hugely important for reinstating the use of reason in the defense of Christianity. For the history of apologetics strongly suggests that, when apologists absorb Cartesian foundationalism, it becomes easy for deism and atheism to follow shortly thereafter.[18]

For example, the truths of the faith should never be seen as a stepping stone that builds on top of the conclusions of reason. One of the problems with the older manuals of classical apologetics is that they often gave the

17. Derrida, "Limited, Inc. abs . . . ," in *Glyph*, 2.162–254.

18. Buckley, *At the Origins of Modern Atheism*; Buckley, *Denying and Disclosing God.*

strong impression that individuals *absolutely had to know* the truths of the preambles of faith before they could make an act of faith.

This procedure is guilty of evidentialism. According to evidentialists, beliefs are rational if and only if one has reasons to ground one's belief. As W. K. Clifford memorably put it: "It is wrong always, everywhere, and for anyone, to believe anything upon insufficient evidence."[19] According to evidentialists, we should not believe in God or in Christianity unless we have good reasons to do so. Although theologians might seek reasons for faith, they must recognize that evangelizing others does not depend upon the success of their efforts. If I do not have good reasons to believe in Christianity (say, because I am ignorant of such evidence), then evidentialists would tell me that I should immediately renounce my faith.

By contrast, the Church insists that although one might have evidence to make faith reasonable, such evidence is not absolutely necessary. Only those believers endowed with certain talents and/or callings are called to do rational apologetics. For Aquinas, the preambles of faith (the existence of God, objective truth, and the human soul) are simply those truths that are within the grasp of natural knowledge; they are not absolutely necessary preconditions for the judgment of credibility. However, the arguments for the existence of God (and the evidences for Christianity) are *sufficient* for the justification of Christianity; but they are *not necessary* for such justification.

Thus the ground upon which our faith rests is ultimately found in God's revelation, given to each and every person. As the *Catechism of the Catholic Church* plainly states: "What moves us to believe is not the fact that revealed truths appear as true and intelligible in the light of our natural reason: we believe 'because of the authority of God himself who reveals them, who can neither deceive nor be deceived.'"[20] Elsewhere, we read that "Faith is *certain*. It is more certain than all human knowledge because it is founded on the very word of God who cannot lie."[21]

The arguments for faith may help to confirm one's belief in Christianity, and they may serve as credible signs to unbelievers, but the arguments do not constitute the ground upon which faith stands or falls. Believing in Christ's revelation, which is confirmed by the Holy Spirit, provides one with the certainty of Christian truth, but the reasons for faith always have a tentative character.

---

19. Clifford, "The Ethics of Belief," in Brady, ed., *Readings in the Philosophy of Religion*, 246. Clifford's essay was originally published in his *Lectures and Essays*, and has been reprinted numerous times.

20. *Catechism of the Catholic Church*, 156.

21. Ibid., 157

Sensitive to the dangers of Clifford's evidentialism, many theologians seem to be unaware of the distinction between the classical and modified versions of foundationalism. As a result, they prematurely reject the field of apologetics. For them, it recalls the parasitical origins of atheism that arise from the attempts to defend Christianity. In his classic work on the existence of God, for instance, Hans Küng argued against the dogmatic definitions about the natural knowledge of God (as pronounced at Vatican I). He claimed that there is no "substructure of reason" that all persons can agree with. Küng also said that the "uncertainty of human existence and of reality as a whole"[22] should prevent apologists from reasoning to God's existence from the things that have been made. Though he was right in arguing that there is no single epistemology, this would not mean that there are no first principles.

Roger Haight claimed that the conditioned nature of human reason precludes the possibility that one can demonstrate God's existence through the use of reason: "That God is, that that God is personal and universally gracious, are not assertions that are based on knowing in an ordinary sense and cannot be demonstrated or verified *in any objective way.* . . . In the end there can be no universal power of reason to uncover the shape of transcendent reality because reason itself is historically conditioned" (italics mine).[23] Unfortunately Haight and Küng misunderstand the shift from classical foundationalism to fallibilism (or, they are simply ignorant of it). Accepting the rejection of classical foundationalism, these theologians obviously do not recognize that some sort of foundationalism must be defensible, and that it includes first principles.

It is one thing to say there is objective truth (which is possible because of first principles). But it is quite another to maintain that human knowers can understand the truth absolutely. We are therefore endorsing a critical realism within the parameters set by fallibilist foundationalism, not a naïve realism on the one hand or an unmitigated skepticism on the other. Alister McGrath explains:

> . . . these conclusions must be treated with caution. While there is a proper place for a critique of the Enlightenment's unrealistic aspirations to total objectivity of judgment, postmodernity must be seen as representing an ultimately indefensible alternative. A critical attitude to the Enlightenment on this specific issue does not lead to the problematic conclusion that no degree of objectivity is possible at all, so that all beliefs or interpretations

22. Küng, *Does God Exist?* 533.
23. Haight, *Dynamics of Theology*, 57, 62–63.

can be held with equal merit. The proper response to the Enlightenment's unrealistic aspirations to objectivity is not to
abandon any attempt at critical evaluation of interpretive possibilities, but to encourage a realistic and cautious attempt to
determine which of the various interpretations of nature may be
regarded as the "best explanation," as judged by criteria such as
parsimony, elegance, or explanatory power.[24]

Critiquing a method of *discovering* the truth is a different enterprise
from defining *what* truth is. Thus the Cartesian tradition had it right when
it understood truth as correspondence with reality. For this tradition, truth
is universal, objective, absolute, and exclusive. The nature of truth had been
accepted from the time of Plato and Aristotle and was not new at the time
of the Enlightenment. Where Descartes got it wrong was in the idea that
knowing the truth must be relegated to "reason alone." For there is a significant difference between the nature of truth and the tests used to discover it.
Apologists can agree with the previous Western philosophical tradition with
respect to the nature of truth, not with the latter which emanated from Descartes. Our knowledge of the truth (an epistemological issue) is influenced
by culture, biology, political environment, upbringing, economics, gender,
and so on. But truth itself (a metaphysical reality) is absolute, universal,
objective, exclusive, eternally engaging, systematic, and one.

Postmodernism and the Need
for Catholic *Apologia*

The success of the Thomist proofs for God's existence all depend on first
principles. If the Council Fathers at Vatican I had Aquinas's proofs in mind,
then it would not mean that classical foundationalism was being upheld;
rather, it must mean that another type of foundationalism must be valid.
What the Council taught, in one way or another, is that some knowledge is
universally accessible and/or known by all people. First principles do not
have to be logically self-evident in order for the Thomist proofs to be considered "proofs" in the full sense of that term.

While Aquinas's arguments for God are not logically compelling, they
still prove that God exists. For, certainty in scholastic terminology allows
for different degrees of conviction: logical certainty, moral certainty, virtual
certainty, and so on. "As a lifelong student of Aristotle," Ralph McInerney
urges, "Thomas was convinced that there are sound and cogent proofs of

---

24. McGrath, *The Open Secret*, 155.

God's existence. For Thomas, natural theology is not a possibility. It is a fact. It is the achievement of pagan philosophy."[25]

While there might be good probabilistic arguments for God, Aquinas says, these arguments are entirely too weak—and make believers a laughing-stock to unbelievers.[26] For Aquinas, probabilistic arguments do not make sense unless it is assumed that we live in an ordered universe. And if we live in an ordered universe, then we need a Supreme Orderer who gives it the order that it has. This is precisely what Aquinas argued for in his Fifth Way (the fifth proof for God's existence as expressed in the *Summa Theologiae*). Thus Aquinas's proofs capture an undeniable existential insight. With fallibilist foundationalism in mind, apologists might argue that any worldview that contradicts the fundamental claims about God cannot be true (and so should be rejected). All non-theistic worldviews can be disproven—because theism can be proven with philosophical arguments apart from the influence of special revelation and faith.

Here anti-apologists may retort: "One cannot reason anyone into believing in Christianity." This is certainly true, but a couple of things must be kept in mind. Such a contention may forget that God can use human reason to reach doubters or even formal outsiders to faith. God can work through the intellect to lend credibility to the decision of faith. Anything less would be fideistic. In the words of Brian Hebblethwaite:

> It is surely a mistake to regard the logic of theological rationality as something wholly internal to the perspective of faith. Torrence, and Barth too, are entirely persuasive in their insistence on theological rationality being responsive to the unique nature of theology's object. But the supposition that theological thinking has its own logic only available within the relation of grace and faith . . . makes theology, natural or revealed, undiscussable, immune to criticism, and unsusceptible of being pondered hypothetically.[27]

Many theologians are correct when they claim that faith has its own unique rationality which is unavailable to unbelievers. But this does not mean that theological claims should not be evaluated by Catholics and their critics. Faith is not a blind leap in the dark without reason. Yet reason will not *demand* faith, for unbelievers can always come up with different excuses as to why the faith is false or irrelevant. When considering the relevant reasons for faith, apologists must never give the impression that faith is based

25. McInerney, *Characters in Search of Their Author*, 66.

26. Aquinas, *Summa Contra Gentiles*, 1.9.

27. Hebblethwaite, *In Defence of Christianity*, 59.

strictly on one's discovery of the preambles to faith. Rather, the Christian faith is based on revelation. Faith, however, can be supported and reinforced by reason.

As a result, apologists will now have to resort, for the most part, to a cumulative case for Catholic faith, not demonstration (though God's existence can still be proven in the non-mathematical sense of the term). Apart from the *preambula fidei*, however, apologists have to work with probabilistic arguments in support of Christianity, which marshalls the best evidence we currently have in, say, science, history and philosophy. When apologists argue for the plausibility of Catholicism, they cannot defend the faith as true unless they presuppose first principles which are not limited or relative to cultural, historical, or other social contingencies. Unless first principles exist and can be known by all, the Catholic worldview would have to remain insulated. Such a position is fideistic, and implies that there is no reason why anyone should have faith.

Some Christian doctrines can be temporarily bracketed off from the entire picture of Christian faith and seen as explanatory hypotheses that account for a wide variety of features, including history, the cosmos, and the nature of humanity. Yet we would still be within our epistemic rights to argue that the total Catholic worldview can outstrip rival hypotheses because of its explanatory power, comprehensiveness, plausibility, logical consistency, livability, and so forth.

Some theologians are now beginning to utilize the newer approach to apologetics in reaction to the evidentialist challenge. As a reaction to modernism, postmodernism resonates well with the provisional nature of knowledge advanced by modified versions of foundationalism (and vice versa). Believers can retain their presuppositions when comparing and contrasting their views with other competing claims. The final assessment is decided by the *Weltanschauung* that resonates and makes the most sense out of the agreed upon evidence.

In Defense of the Correspondence Theory of Truth

In the correspondence view (or, as others might call it, a "realist conception of truth"), minds are either knowing or ignorant; propositions are either true or false; and reality is either real or imaginary. Truth pertains to those propositions that accurately reflect reality. So, when a proposition (i.e., a belief, thought, statement) corresponds to reality, then the proposition is said to be true. When the proposition does not correspond to reality, then the proposition is said to be false (or, depending on the content of the proposition, it may be partially true or partially false). When a mind assents to a true proposition, then a person has knowledge of the truth.

A proposition, moreover, needs to be distinguished from a sentence. A proposition is what a sentence either affirms or denies. Here we might say that a proposition is what a sentence means. Questions, imperatives, exclamations, requests, and entreaties are not propositions, but presuppose the truth of at least one proposition which successfully refers to reality. For example, the imperative command, "do not allow abortions!," is not a proposition, but presupposes the proposition that "abortion is wrong." The proposition "abortion is wrong" corresponds to reality in the moral realm. Propositions, moreover, can be controversial, trivial, obscure, frightening, or comforting. Yet none of these features of propositions refute a correspondence theory of truth. Although the significance or subjective effect of a proposition might be person-relative, this does not mean the truth or falsity of the proposition (or the correspondence theory itself) should be doubted.

Hence, the nature of a proposition needs to be distinguished from the effects it has on persons. Divine revelation is not only personal but is propositional, but it comes to persons in various forms, and it has many different effects on individuals. The propositional model reminds us that one Mind can in fact communicate with human minds. Without a propositional view, the cognitive content that is necessary for interpersonal communication is rendered impossible.

Similarly, a proposition is not the same thing as a *perspective*. Everyone has perspectives about what they *think* is the truth. Perspectives can be biased, prejudiced, ignorant, and uninformed, but this is not the same thing as saying that truth itself is relative. Rather, a perspective is always a perspective on or about something or someone, independent and outside of the percipient's viewpoint. Perspectives are either successful or unsuccessful in their attempt to capture reality. Taken to the extreme, perspectivalism is self-stultifying, for it assumes that perspectivalism is true—and that all other views in competition with it are false.

Thus truth itself must be distinguished from what is true, how one arrives at the truth, and the effects that truth might have on persons. In no way is metaphysical objectivity incompatible with epistemological subjectivity. Our epistemological thrust toward the truth is loaded with all sorts of factors which influence us as limited knowers—level of intelligence, background beliefs, education, gender, motivation, personal interests, upbringing, genetics, and so forth. All true propositions have a few common characteristics. First, truth is exclusive and antithetical. For every true article of reason or of faith, any other viewpoint which opposes it will be false.

So, truth is, by definition, antithetical and definitive. Anything that opposes the truth is incorrect.

Theologians should recognize that although human beings are unable to state the truth exhaustively, the goal of every Catholic teacher should be exactitude. All truths are absolute (truth applies to everyone, at all times and everywhere) and objective (if something is true then it is true for everyone regardless if anyone believes in it or knows it or not). Truth is also unified and systematic (truth is one; truth will never contradict another truth). It is always an end in-and-of-itself; it is never a mere means to an end.

There are at least two positive arguments in support of a correspondence theory. First, the theory has commonsense appeal. Before one comes to the philosophical task of understanding the world, one already has a common-sense notion of what truth is. Therefore its pre-analytic justification gives individuals something with which to start. When most people speak of truth, they usually refer to "what is the case." Second, those who endorse arguments against the correspondence theory seem to presuppose it in their own presentations against it. In short, the correspondence theory of truth seems rationally inescapable. To say or imply that "a true statement does not correspond to reality" one must hold, in one way or another, that this describes reality.

Advocates of critical realism recognize that we are always in the process of trying to achieve a fuller perspective on the truth. Belief in the universal lordship of Jesus does not entail that we can prove this truth. Believers participate in the give and take of argument and evidence both for and against faith. In any case, genuine respect for the mysteries of faith might prompt one to understand more fully what is believed, attempting to reach people with arguments for the gospel.

Addressing Challenges to the Correspondence Theory

In this section we address major arguments against a correspondence theory that come from the standpoint of philosophical theology. These objections are often used to undercut the need for apologetics.

(1) The first objection is that *the correspondence theory of truth is not found in Church teaching or in the Bible*. It has never been the primary intention of Church teaching, however, to enunciate a particular theory of truth. When councils or popes pronounce on certain theological matters, they simply assume that the doctrines are true.

The main biblical terms for truth are *emet* and *aletheia*. Although these terms are broadly understood and multifaceted, the biblical writers assumed that the actions and teachings they referred to were aspects of reality: faithfulness, rectitude, and so on. Clearly, the Scriptural authors assumed that what they were saying in regard to salvation depended on reality.[28] In post-biblical tradition, "in addition to the use of the notion of truth derived from Greek philosophy [i.e., truth as correspondence], we find in some of the fathers and in the liturgy a resumption and development of the biblical conception of truth, but sometimes with a stronger emphasis on its doctrinal aspect. Generally speaking, truth designates the Christian faith, i.e., the divine revelation as it has been handed down in the church."[29]

(2) The next objection says *that the correspondence theory is unable to account for the mysteries of faith*. This objection is often influenced by Eastern religious thought. In this view, all religions are seen as inadequate pointers to what is ultimately inexpressible. The ultimate mystery of God exceeds the use of human logic and/or philosophy.

However, Catholics should understand the incomprehensibility of God in a way that preserves some knowledge of the divine. On the one hand, Catholics are not totally agnostic about the divine. It is not under dispute that the truth about God goes beyond conceptual and linguistic categories of speech. Truth is more than rational; it is personal, moral, dynamic, and life-changing. There is always room to explore further the fullness of truth. Absolute truth does not mean that our understanding of it is absolute. On the other hand, although truth goes above and beyond reason, our grasp of it is definitely not irrational. While the "otherness" of God evades both cognitive and linguistic categories, this does not mean all language is incapable of referring to God.

One cannot say that language does not apply to God unless one applies certain concepts to God in the first place. Take the statement "no linguistic categories or conceptions can apply meaningfully to God." One would need to know something meaningful, positive, and true about God in order to know that nothing linguistic or conceptual applies to him; thus theologians cannot know what God is *not* unless they already know something of what God *is*.[30]

In sum, one must know something meaningful (and positive) about the term "God" in order to employ the *via negativa*. Otherwise one could

28. Levering, *Scripture and Metaphysics*.

29. de la Potterie, "Truth," in Fisichella and Latourelle, eds., *Dictionary of Fundamental Theology*, 1133.

30. Aquinas, *Summa Theologiae*, 1.13.2

not distinguish God from created entities. The primary issue is not whether we can apply certain concepts to God, but how we pour meaning into those concepts. The way meaning is poured into these concepts is negative. God's essence *is* to exist. Therefore, agnosticism is not to be equated with the affirmation that God is incomprehensible.

(3) Some relativists respond: *first principles are merely expressions of Aristotelian logic*—constructions of Western thought which are not applicable to other cultures (or religious understandings).

In reply to this common objection, one can point to the objector's confusion about the nature of propositional truth and how this relates to the linguistic style and/or thought patterns used to express a proposition. Consequently, there is a difference between cultural expressions and the underlying logic which undergirds every person's thinking. Mentioned earlier, a proposition is not the same thing as a sentence. Thus the relativity of sentences should not count as a refutation of the correspondence theory of truth. How our language applies terms is often relative, but this would not entail dropping the correspondence theory. Philosopher John Searle observes:

> We arbitrarily define the word "cat" in such and such a way; and only relative to such and such definitions can we say, "That's a cat." But once we have made the definitions and once we have applied the concepts relative to the system of definitions, whether or not something satisfies our definition is no longer arbitrary or relative. That we use the word "cat" the way we do is up to us; that there is an object that exists independently of that use, and satisfies that use, is a plain matter of (absolute, intrinsic, mind independent) fact.[31]

In effect, denying that the relative selection of terms prevents persons from saying that something can be objectively true makes no more sense than saying that we cannot satisfy our craving for a dessert because there are many kinds of desserts.

Here it might be noted that a *rejection* of the correspondence theory does not amount to convincingly *refuting* it. One cannot refute first principles without employing them in the process. Saying that "first principles merely express Aristotelian logic" must also affirm first principles. So if the objection itself is true, then it must be false. Any justification of the assertion that "first principles are merely the expressions of Aristotelian logic" would, in one way or another, have to employ first principles.

---

31. Searle, *The Construction of Social Reality*, 166.

(4) Still other critics insist that *truth is uninformative and uninteresting in the correspondence theory*. Objective truth is static, abstract, cold, and impersonal. In this position truth is not found in propositions, but in persons alone. These critics argue that truth is more of a humane, not an objective, concept, and does not lie in propositions.

We can set aside the obviously self-refuting nature of the contention (because the objector is using a proposition that is designed to convince his or her listeners) and demonstrate that, even if the point is granted, this would still not count as an argument against the correspondence theory. Truth may go *beyond* the propositional, but it is not *against* the propositional. At most this objection goes against the possibility of knowing completely the nature of truth. Truth is formally distinct from what is true.

In the case of the apologist, there are some specific truths that are already held. On the one hand, one can make arguments from the "bottom up" on the basis of first principles and arrive at some undeniable conclusions: namely, that truth is objective, that God exists, that human beings are more than just material stuff. These truths are based upon first principles. This approach is confident about our mutually shared assumptions about human nature and self-evident first principles. This would be a more traditional apologetic methodology. Perhaps the truth that something exists is uninformative and abstract, but we can also know with certainty that God exists, and that an anti-realist view of truth is false. Perhaps these truths are "uninteresting," but then again this contention is clearly person-relative and does not apply to everyone!

On the other hand, it is perfectly acceptable to begin with fundamental Christian truths and then compare them with competing perspectives. Apologists can claim that some things are true, and then attempt to rationally argue for these truths. Everyone must begin somewhere; *all* people interpret reality in a way that is consistent with their underlying presuppositions. No believers are left with a floating, uninformative conception of truth, but presuppose the truths of faith. There is no reason to deny that truth can be a channel by which individuals come to better understand and experience God. Personal encounter with the divine simply cannot take place in a cognitive vacuum, but assumes that some things are true.

Such a "top-down" approach asks which worldview and value system resonates and thus make the most sense out of the agreed upon evidence. Even if this approach begins with a Catholic worldview, this would not have to mean that the good news is irrational or that the evidence in favor of the Catholic faith cannot be trusted. Perhaps the gospel is true and the evidence is trustworthy. As C. S. Lewis wrote: "I believe in Christianity as I believe that the Sun has risen—not only because I see it, but because of it,

I see everything else."[32] Apologists have no choice but to begin with their theological presuppositions. This is no different from anyone else (atheists, agnostics, and other religionists) coming at the debate from within their perspectives. It is possible that Christians know the truth about God *because* of faith. What is then needed to help persons to determine the truth would still be the careful weighing and assessing of evidence from the various perspectives to the best of our abilities.

(5) *A fifth objection to our use of the correspondence theory maintains that absolute truth prevents inculturation and human individuality.* However, there is a difference between the nature of truth and the various ways in which individuals and groups of people arrive at the truth and express it. There is a difference between the nature of truth and the effect it has on individuals. Truth, as we have seen in our worldview, is not parochial, partial, and provincial. It allows for creative cultural expression and individuality so long as the Catholic worldview is firmly believed and faithfully lived out. Certain cultures can make the gospel message more conducive for reception within that particular culture. Receiving God's truth does not flatten us out in blind obedience to Christ, but liberates persons to become who they were meant to be. Affirming the objective truth of Catholicism carves out space for the development of individual spiritual gifts, callings, and personality types in the risen Christ.

Catholics might argue that we would expect the one true faith to be able to affect all people, regardless of the culture they inhabit. When missionaries endeavor to present the timeless truths of the gospel to persons who have been previously unaffected by the Catholic worldview, they are not starting from nothing, but are convinced that, because every human being is made in the image of God, there are many truths (including the gospel) that all persons can understand. As John Paul II declared:

> In proclaiming Christ to non-Christians, the missionary is convinced that through the working of the Spirit, there already exists in individuals and peoples an expectation, even if an unconscious one, of knowing the truth about God, about man, and about how we are to be set free from sin and death. The missionary's enthusiasm in proclaiming Christ comes from the conviction that he is responding to that expectation, and so he does not become discouraged or cease his witness even when he is called to manifest his faith in an environment that is hostile or indifferent.[33]

32. Lewis, "Is Theology Poetry?" in *Essay Collection and Other Short Pieces*, 21.
33. John Paul II, *Redemptoris Missio*, 45.

If the gospel message is true, then we would expect it to resonate with every person, at least eventually. *Gaudium et Spes* states: "Moreover, since in virtue of her mission and nature she is bound to no particular form of human culture, nor to any political, economic, or social system, the Church by her very universality can be a very close bond between diverse human communities and nations, provided these trust her and truly acknowledge her right to true freedom in fulfilling her mission."[34] Although human minds are subject to the fluidity of semantics and the syntax of different languages and thought patterns, there are some universal constants—such as first principles, fallibilist foundationalism, and the referential nature of propositions. It is noteworthy that Vatican II teaches that the Church should focus on what unites (rather than divides) us as a human race.[35]

Apologists will now want to emphasize the success of missionary activity across the many cultures of the world (to bolster their claims about Christ). This is an argument that we shall develop in this book. The catholicity of the Church testifies to the fact that people from different cultural and religious backgrounds can come to understand the same basic gospel message, and that it changes individuals and even whole societies for the better.

(6) Sixth, *some claim that either/or thinking can lead to violence.* Apart from the fact that either/or thinking is rationally inescapable (i.e., the law of non-contradiction), it must be stressed that first principles do not lead persons to become violent, but that certain understandings and applications of what is thought to be true can steer persons down the path of violence. Christians who hold that everything should be conceived in one shade of black and white may unknowingly harbor bad attitudes and justify violence that is opposed to healthy forms of faith and evangelism.

So I am not saying that we should renounce hard truth claims, but that certain interpretations of them need to be jettisoned. In a reductive understanding of truth it becomes easy for Christians to view outsiders as enemies who deserve to be punished because they think differently from believers. Charles Kimball points out: "When particular understandings become rigidly fixed, and uncritically appropriated as absolute truths, well-meaning people can and often do paint themselves into a corner from which they must assume a defensive or even offensive posture."[36]

Responsible Catholic thinking does not do away with absolutes, but allows for a variety of interpretations within an orthodox spectrum. Truth leads

---

34. Vatican II, *Gaudium et Spes*, 42.

35. Ibid., 61.

36. Kimball, *When Religion Becomes Evil*, 46. See Dennett, *Breaking the Spell*, 51, 251, 295.

to a symphony of voices in unity, not stagnant uniformity. One-sided approaches to faith can lead one to become irrational and combative. But, when Christians limit the intellectual engagement of faith, this can make them prone to become violent. For example, David Koresh and Jim Jones ordered the women in their groups to have sex with them. These women bypassed the voice of common sense and conscience and, in blind faith, did what they were told—all in the name of "faith." When reason and faith are divorced from one another, this can lead persons to violent and bizarre behavior.

Richard Dawkins may define faith as "blind trust, in the absence of evidence, even in the teeth of evidence,"[37] but Catholic faith is all about responsible thinking, personal freedom, and common sense. Faith is a rational step into the light, demanding responsible thinking; it is not a credulous leap in the dark. Reasons can be given for faith; no truth of reason will ever contradict the truths of revelation and vice versa.

It should be stressed that accepting Catholic faith involves high stakes in the life of discipleship; it demands that we become confrontational with the secular world's ways of doing things. Catholics simply cannot rest content in a world streaming with error and many forms of injustice. Apologists must remain person sensitive and culturally aware within the confines of truth-centered dialogue and debate with those who do not share distinctively Catholic beliefs.

According to Vatican II, the study of other world religions should help Catholics to learn how to appreciate the truths and refute errors in other faiths: "Let them [seminarians] also be introduced to a knowledge of other religions which are more widespread in individual regions, so that they may acknowledge more correctly what truth and goodness these religions, in God's providence, possess, and so that they may learn to refute their errors and be able to communicate the full light of truth to those who do not have it."[38] In *Ad Gentes*, the Fathers state: "Moreover let them take care that apostolic activity be not limited to those only who have already been converted. A fair proportion of personnel and funds should be assigned to the evangelization of non-Christians."[39] Dialogue is not a definitive substitute for apologetics and evangelization.

---

37. Dawkins, *The Selfish Gene*, 198. See also 330.

38. Vatican II, *Optatium Totius*, 16. Cf. Vatican II, *Dignitatis Humanae*, 11.

39. Vatican II, *Ad Gentes*, 30. See also 39–40.

Conclusion

Many relativists do not define truth as an objective description of reality. With the relativist view in mind, the Church's central claims can no longer be seen as binding on all persons. Rather, the Catholic worldview is reinterpreted in terms of opinion. Indirectly this shift makes the enterprise of apologetics unfashionable. Thus the need to reinstate dialogue and debate has been neglected. In this chapter I argued that reason and evidence is at least useful in making the beliefs of Catholics more credible than competing claims. For the hardheaded skeptic who is willing to think through the reasons for and against the gospel, the use of argument for the purposes of evangelization remains indispensable.

C. S. Lewis captured this insight in the *Screwtape Letters*. In the story the senior demon of hell, Screwtape, instructs a lower ranking demon on how to dissuade persons' from taking the role of reason and evidence in the life of Christian faith. For in so doing, skeptics and other lukewarm believers will be less convinced of Christianity. After all, says Screwtape to his disciple in training: "Your man has been accustomed, ever since he was a boy, to have a dozen incompatible philosophies dancing about together inside his head. He doesn't think of doctrines as primarily 'true' or 'false', but as 'academic' or 'practical', 'outworn' or 'contemporary', 'conventional' or 'ruthless'. Jargon, not argument, is your best ally in keeping him from the Church."[40] Screwtape knew that clear thinking was on the side of the Church.

---

40. Lewis, *The Screwtape Letters*, 8.

PART TWO

The Existence of God

— 4 —

Knowing That God Exists:
Retrieving the Teaching of *Dei Filius*

CATHOLIC THEOLOGY TRADITIONALLY HELD that God's existence can be known with certainty apart from the influence of authoritative, divine revelation. This longstanding belief reached a high point at the First Vatican Council on 24 April 1870 when, in response to the prevailing trends of traditionalism, rationalism, and fideism,[1] the Council Fathers steered a middle course in response to these extreme positions, declaring that God's existence can be known with certainty through the natural light of human reason.

Many Catholic theologians and philosophers vigorously defended the Council's teaching well into the middle of the twentieth century. But after the Second Vatican Council, theologians began to neglect it, and, in some cases, argued that it was irrelevant or even problematic for faith. According to Denys Turner: "most theologians today do not so much think that the existence of God cannot be proved as seem altogether to have given up thinking about the issues involved, and simply assume—probably on unexamined arguments from Kant—the impossibility of it."[2]

Despite many protests to the contrary, the Council's teaching on natural knowledge of God should be retrieved for a postconciliar apologetics. We turn to a defense of the Council's teaching on God, and then answer contemporary objections that have been raised against it.

---

1. While rationalists insist that reason is a sufficient means to discover religious truth, fideists hold that reason is irrelevant in matters of religion, arguing that faith is the only way to know that there is a God. Emanating from the French thinker F. R. de Lammenais, traditionalists maintain that knowledge of God is based on believing the prelapsarian message that was given to Adam and Eve, and subsequently preserved in Jewish and Christian oral traditions.

2. Turner, *Faith, Reason and the Existence of God*, ix. Cf. 3, 6.

Knowing That God Exists

Thomist philosophers agree that the natural knowledge of God is not necessarily philosophical. It can be pre-philosophical. Professional philosophers are not at an advantage over ordinary persons when it comes to knowing that there is a God. Walter Kasper explains: "Thomas says the same thing in a more substantive way. . . . This element of the unconditioned in the conditioned is not first brought home to us by a complicated proof; it is grasped unthematically in every knowledge of the conditioned as conditioned. When thus understood, the cosmological argument is in the final analysis simply reflecting this primordial knowledge; it is an explanation of the astonishment felt at the wonder of being."[3] Ordinary persons do not have the time, energy, or resources to study the arguments for and against the existence of God. But this does not prevent them from knowing that there is a God. And this is why, at the end of each of the Five Ways, Aquinas says with confidence: "and this is the God that all people speak of."

In the view of Aquinas, faith sees the importance of using reason. Within the context of faith, therefore, one can know with certainty that God exists. To deny that God's existence can be proven as an article of faith not only gets something wrong about faith, it also gets something wrong about reason. However, faith does not stretch the shape of reason in a direction that is unnatural to it, but strengthens and clarifies one's natural knowledge of God.

Here it should be noted that, although Christian faith might be the way through which individuals come to know that God exists, *discovery* is not the same thing as *justification*. Outsiders to the faith can indeed perceive the force of the arguments for the existence of God. As Turner notes, the idea that faith leads one to reason is not "some pretentious, cross-disciplinary claim to a merely arbitrary epistemic hegemony of faith as if, say, equivalently, a microbiologist were on grounds of some need of microbiological theory absurdly to require the mathematician to come up with a particular mathematical result regardless of whether it could be defended on mathematical grounds."[4]

The nature of God was also discussed and defended at the Council. Commenting on the conciliar declaration, John Hardon said that the divine attributes were not chosen incidentally, but were defined deliberately for the purposes of safeguarding the faithful: "Fifteen internal attributes of God, independent of his role as Creator, are enumerated. These are not mere expressions of piety and still less were they chosen at random." He

---

3. Kasper, *The God of Jesus Christ*, 103.

4. Turner, *Faith, Reason and the Existence of God*, 4.

continues: "They represent so many affirmations about the Godhead as the genius of unbelief had raised to the surface. In the century since this divine litany was assembled and, more than ever today, it serves as a check list of faith in a being without whose existence no other premise of Christianity has meaning."[5] By referring to the divine intellect and will, the Council excluded an impersonal pantheism and deism. The idea that God is distinct from the world excludes all of the many types of pan-en-theism. The infinity of God means that God possesses every perfection without limitation.

The Metaphysical Argument

Let us now reflect upon the pre-philosophical intuition of God in the form of a philosophical argument. Many scholars maintain that behind Aquinas' five proofs there is one basic form of argument. Each of the Five Ways begins with a different starting point (i.e., change, causality, contingency, perfection, and final causality), but they all presuppose the existence-essence distinction spelled out in one of Aquinas' earlier and more influential tracts, the *De Ente et Essentia*. Commonly known as the *intellectus essentiae* argument, I will defend a contemporary version of this argument in this chapter.

One of the argument's strengths is that it establishes a being whose essence and existence are identical. Its essence is to exist. While each of the Five Ways, as arguments *simpliciter*, do not entail all the traditional attributes of God, within their broader philosophical context they lead to nothing less than that.[6] That metaphysical context is provided in a more immediate sense in the *De Ente*.

Although many atheists are unwilling to grant the truth of Thomas' arguments, some agree that his proofs remain one of the best resources for justifying belief in God. At the very least, they argue, the argument has epistemic value for theism. According to these atheists, it may fail as a proof, but theists are given ample epistemic justification for holding that God exists.[7]

Premise 1: At least one potential being exists. It is impossible to allege that nothing exists without implicitly conceding truth in the process of denying it. If someone denies that something exists, they are saying something significant. Otherwise, why listen to the person? The proposition "nothing

---

5. Hardon, *The Catholic Catechism*, 55.

6. For a scholarly treatment of the Five Ways, as understood within Aquinas' historical context, see Wippel, *The Metaphysical Thought of Thomas Aquinas*, 442–500; Feser, *Aquinas*, 62–130.

7. Mackie, *The Miracle of Theism*, 89; Rowe, *The Cosmological Argument*, 249–269. See Flew, *God and Philosophy*, 102.

exists" is self-defeating. While it is logically possible that nothing exists, it is actually undeniable that something exists.

Since the statement "at least one potential being exists" is not logically necessary, the argument does not proceed on the assumption that we are proving logically the existence of God. When Aquinas speaks of demonstrating God's existence, he does not speak of proving God in the sense of a logical proof. It is logically possible that nothing ever existed—including the universe and God—but it is undeniable that something does exist. Logic cannot show that something exists, only that it is possible for something to exist. When I say that a *potential* being exists, I mean that a being exists that does not have to exist. It is possible that a potential existent does not have to exist. This conclusion is an undeniable fact of experience. A potential being is a being that did not have to come into existence, but nevertheless exists without ultimate necessity.

We will now argue for the existence of a *potential* being. First, beings must either be necessary, possible (potential) or impossible. Philosophically speaking, this exhausts all options. We can set aside the existence of an impossible being (for an impossible being is not), and also the notion that the beings that currently exist are necessary beings. A necessary being is a being that cannot fail to exist. The nonexistence of a necessary being is a contradiction in terms. If there is a necessary being, then it exists out of necessity. A necessary being is equivalent to a purely actual being with no potential. An actual being with no potential must have many attributes: immutability (not able to be changed), simplicity (not divisible), eternality (not in time), infinity (not limited), etc. The beings that currently exist, however, are beings in space and time.

As a simple being, a necessary being cannot be partly anything. Nor can there be more than one such actual being. For if there were more than one purely actual being, then there would have to be something which distinguishes the one purely actual existent from the other. There would have to be something that the one has which the other lacks, but this cannot be the case if both of them are unlimited. More importantly, an actual being must be uncaused. On the basis of sense experience, it is clear that the beings that exist are not actual beings without further potential. Those things that exist are changing, moving in space and time, and have the capacity for additional causal change. They are not wholly simple, immaterial, and immutable.

Positing the existence of potential beings is an undeniable fact of existence. Many atheists do not dispute the first premise. Atheist Richard Gale notes, "These are commonplace observational facts that only a complete skeptic about our senses would want to challenge."[8] In reference to the Five Ways, Graham Oppy agrees with the first premise: "the first prem-ise in the argument seems unproblematic: there are many beings that are 'contingent.'"[9]

Premise 2: The existence of every potential being is actualized by an-other. Whatever has the potential for nonexistence is not a purely actual being. A potential being is not a purely actual being; hence it must be caused or preserved in existence by something other than itself. No potentiality can actualize itself. Therefore, there must be some actuality apart from it that can account for its potential existence. For if any potential being exists, then it does not have to exist. When I speak of the actualization of potential be-ings, I am referring to the transition that takes place in a being from potenti-ality to actuality (all the while retaining its potential for additional change).

The change that takes place is a sustaining cause, not a cause in the temporal sense of becoming. Nicholas Everitt seems to accept the causal premise: "in all our experiences of series of events, we have never expe-rienced an event which did not depend on a predecessor, and if we try to think of what an event might depend on other than a predecessor, no an-swer comes to mind."[10]

The second premise is evident, given the aforementioned definition of change. Change means to pass from a state of potentiality to a state of actu-ality. Although rocks do not have the potential to express emotion, persons have that potential. When this potential is actualized in people, then they change in feeling. A being that changes must have some potential for that change. Otherwise this change could never be actualized. No potential for being a certain way can actualize itself. For, potentiality is not actual. The essence of a potential object cannot be what brings it into existence, for considered in itself, potentiality is the mere essence of something, not an actual existent. Thus potentiality itself cannot cause anything.

When an actual being has potential, then it must be caused by some-thing other than itself. Since the potential being cannot be prior to itself in order to cause its own existence, then something else must have been in existence to bring it into existence. Moreover, it goes without saying that such a happening is not self-causation. The sheer potential to be something cannot account for something achieving that potential. The possibility for

8. Gale, "The Failure of Classical Theistic Arguments," in Martin, ed., *The Cam-bridge Companion to Atheism*, 90.

9. Oppy, *Arguing About Gods*, 104.

10. Everitt, *The Non-Existence of God*, 67.

existence does not account for existence. Sheer potentiality (essence) is formally distinct from actuality (existence).

Only something that actually exists can account for the existence of something else. John Shook observes: "Premise 2 and variations on its theme (such as 'every effect must have a cause') appear to make sound common sense. Intellectual curiosity and scientific methodology spring from this basic theme, which appears to be essential to the normal functioning of our brains . . . if something unusual catches our attention, or if we just focus our attention, we can ask and often answer the 'why?' question which our mind so easily arouses."[11]

Conversely, out of nothing, nothing comes. Likewise, if a potential being is not preserved in existence by another, then it would immediately go out of existence. No matter how many potential beings there might be, they are unable to remain in existence without something actualizing them. To say that potential beings can exist without a cause is equivalent to holding that potential beings can come into existence out of nothing without a cause. But nothing is the complete absence of being; nothing has no causal power.

Every potential being is either self-caused, caused to exist by another, or uncaused. This triple classification exhausts all of our options. Potential beings cannot cause themselves; they would have to precede themselves which is impossible. Neither can potential beings be uncaused. If they were uncaused, then they would be the ultimate ground of being. Hence we conclude that all potential beings must be caused by another. The type of causality involved in this view is conserving causality. It is concerned with the causes in the here-and-now, not with originating causes in the temporal sense of origin.

Premise 3: An infinite amount of potential beings (which have been caused by another) is not possible. A chain of causes wherein every potential being is preserved in existence by an actually infinite amount of other potential beings is impossible. Either the series of all potential beings is sufficient to account for itself or it is not. But the series cannot account for itself. For if each being in the series of caused beings is itself caused, then adding all of them together will not alter the fact that each of them are still in need of a cause. If each part in the entire series of potential beings is potential, then the entire sum of these beings will still remain potential. If someone chooses to make the series longer, this will not turn the sum of potential beings into a fully actual set of beings which are able to account for themselves.

By saying that a potential being can merely account for some other potential existent is tantamount to saying that one paratrooper whose

11. Shook, *The God Debates*, 134.

parachute does not open can prevent another paratrooper from falling to the ground (i.e., another paratrooper whose chute will not open either). When one adds falling paratroopers by grabbing hold of other falling paratroopers, this will only compound the problem, not lessen it. If there were no first cause then there would be no final effect. But there is an effect; therefore there cannot be an infinite regress.

No effect has within itself the power to cause something else. Rather, it must be an actual being working in and through each potential being which causes them to be what they are. Arguing for an infinite amount of causes is possible is tantamount to saying that every single potential being has come from nothing. Not a single potential being has any real ground for its own existence, but depends on something else to account for it. The only being that can actualize another into a state of potentiality and actuality must be an actual being without potential. Only a being of pure actuality with no potential is capable of preserving the existence of another.

Conclusion: The only being which can cause a potential being in existence is an actual being. Therefore, at least one first actualizer exists. The first actualizer's essence is to exist. This conclusion follows inescapably on the basis of each previous premise. We know that if something exists, then it must exist necessarily or depends on something else for its existence. Something exists. This being is not a necessary existent. Unlike a necessary being, its nonexistence is a real possibility. Its nonexistence, moreover, has already been (say, before it existed in the form it which it now appears).

Since a potential being's nonexistence is a possibility, it exists as a composite of actuality and potency. It remains actual because it exists, and it has potential for additional change. And we see it changing. Every being that is a composite of actuality and potentiality is caused to exist by another. Therefore, a first actualizer must be responsible for sustaining each and every potential being in existence in the here and now. The nature of the first actualizer is different from potential being(s).

2nd Conclusion: The nature of a first actualizer must be necessary, one, good, eternal, infinite, immaterial, simple, immutable, omnipresent, and omnipotent. Given the nature of the first actualizer, there cannot be more than one of them. The nature of this being is what all people mean when they speak of God. We might also add that this being is not sensible, for potential beings are known through human senses and the first actualizer is known only by negating what is already known about potential beings. This conclusion, says Aquinas, is what all people mean when they speak of God. Since a purely actual being has no potential, it cannot change; it is immutable.

Moreover, the necessary uncaused cause must be nonspatial (infinite) and atemporal (eternal). Since time and space involve a change of position and time, an actual being cannot exist in space or time. It lies beyond space-time and thus properly transcends both of them. According to Oppy, "If the existence of the physical universe depends upon something else, then—at the very least—there are possible worlds in which there is no physical universe because that something else is different in some way. Moreover, if there is neither space nor time 'beyond' the physical universe, then the 'something else' upon which the existence of the physical universe depends can be neither spatial nor temporal."[12] Oppy invokes a necessary existent as responsible for potential beings, even though he does not think it is God. Nonetheless, his point is well taken. Everitt also seems to agree with this conclusion: "The only way in which the resort to a creator will block an infinite regress of super-creator, super-super-creator, and so on, is if the creator can have a different *kind* of existence from the universe."[13]

A necessary being must also be indivisible, or simple. If the necessary, unchanging, timeless, and spaceless being were composed of parts, then it would be capable of decomposition. But an actual existent does not have any potential for anything, including decomposition. We conclude: a pure, actual being must be utterly simple. A being that is pure act must also be infinite in power. Having the power to keep things in a state of potential existence, it can have no limitation in any respect. Therefore, the actual being must be infinite in power. A necessary existent is uncaused; its essence is to exist. The fact that essence and existence converge also provides support for its simplicity. All potential beings have existence inasmuch as they must participate in the existence of the actual being. Without the actual being, all potential beings could not exist and be what they currently are.

Lastly, an actual existent must be good. Nonexistence is neither good nor evil, for it is not. But if something exists, then it is good. In Aquinas' metaphysics, goodness and existence are convertible categories. If something exists, then this is a good quality, not an evil one. Evil is not a substance, but the very privation of being. Thus existence is equivalent to what is good, and nonexistence is not anything. It is confusing to say that if a purely actual being exists, then it could be an evil God or some other being. Oppy is incorrect when he says that the most that could be said about the conclusion is that a first actualizer exists—a first existent cause that is "not itself in a process of change."[14]

---

12. Oppy, *Arguing About Gods*, 106.

13. Everitt, *The Non-Existence of God*, 71.

14. Oppy, *Arguing About Gods*, 103.

Thomas Aquinas and Atheism

Let us now turn to the major critiques of Thomas Aquinas' argument. (1) The first objection is that *Aquinas arbitrarily models reality*.[15] Some critics have argued that the way Thomists model reality is arbitrary, a loaded metaphysics that is certainly not necessary. For these critics, reality can be explained and described from other legitimate perspectives.

By contrast, Thomists want to argue that the object that exists must be either a potential being or an actual being. Only potential beings and an actual being exists. Or, just actual being exists. Philosophically speaking, this exhausts all of our options. Jacques Maritain noted:

> In order to recognize in the philosophic proofs of the existence of God, notably in the five ways of St. Thomas, [and] their full demonstrative value, it is not necessary to be a philosopher trained in the school of Aristotle and Thomas Aquinas, nor even to be a philosopher by profession. What is prerequisite is to perceive and adhere firmly to the primary truths which Thomist philosophy attempts more successfully than any other to justify. . . . But in the East as in the West it is by no means the only philosophy to recognize and to cultivate these primary truths. Indeed, the very fact of their primacy prevents them from being the monopoly of any one system; they precede every system. They are part and parcel of what has been called the natural philosophy of the human intelligence. . . . They are grasped by common sense before being the object of philosophic consideration.[16]

Apart from referring to actuality and potentiality, there is no third category of being. Nor is there such a thing as a sheer potentiality. Sheer potentiality is not an actual being, but the mere capacity for something to exist in a certain way. The Thomist way of understanding the world is derived from undeniable human experience. We do not superimpose the categories of potentiality and actuality onto reality. These categories are used to describe the world the way it really is.[17]

(2) Petitio Principii *and the First Premise*. Another response to the first premise is that it begs the question in favor of God's existence. But this argument is philosophically naïve. If such an objection implies intuitively that if something exists then God must exist, and some person recognizes

15. Smith, *Atheism*, 251; see also Flew, *God and Philosophy*, 91.

16. Maritain, *Approaches to God*, 16–18.

17. For a defense of Thomist metaphysics, see Wippel, *The Metaphysical Thought of Thomas Aquinas*; Ashley, *The Way Toward Wisdom*.

the soundness of the proof, this would be a quick short-cut through the argument. Such an intuition would make the point of the argument without going through the sequence of each premise.

But if the objector means that the argument cannot be made unless the natural theologian was already convinced in her mind that there is a God before she even sits down to lay out the premises of the argument, then we must admit that this is psychologically true, but it is nevertheless a trivial objection. Nobody formulates an argument unless they intend to demonstrate the likelihood of a conclusion. But this should not be considered a case of circular reasoning because the major premise does not state that God exists.

(3) *The Causal Principle is an Illusion.* Under the influence of David Hume, many contemporary atheists have argued that the causal principle is illusory. Thus the causal premise cannot be taken seriously. Yet, Thomas' argument is not based on empirical observation, but on metaphysical necessity. Causality is not based on conceptual (or definitional) necessity as in the Leibnizian cosmological argument, but is based on the existential insight that nothing can be brought into existence without a cause. As the atheist philosopher J. J. C. Smart rightly acknowledges, the Humean critique of causality has no relevance to Thomas' argument.[18]

According to Hume, all metaphysical reasoning is unreliable. But Hume's skepticism has been vulnerable to serious criticisms. For Hume, meaningful propositions are empirical or analytical. He claims that the empirical has content but tells us nothing about metaphysical reality, such as God. Like the principle of empirical verifiability based on Hume's two kinds of propositions, this is a self-destructive proposition. For the statement that "only analytic or empirical propositions are meaningful" is not itself an analytic (true by definition) or empirical statement. Hence, by its own criteria, Hume's claim is meaningless. But if one allows that such statements are meaningless, then why cannot metaphysical statements about causality be meaningful?

If a potential being exists, then it must be caused to exist by another. The only kind of being that is not caused by another is an uncaused being. Since an actual being is not the same thing as a potential being, the latter must have a cause. No less a critic of theism than Graham Oppy tentatively says: "it seems quite uncontroversial to accept that some things have causes."[19]

---

18. Smart and Haldane, *Atheism and Theism*, 163–64.

19. Oppy, *Arguing About Gods*, 100.

Other atheists have claimed that Thomists need to explain how the actual being causes/preserves each and every potential being. Thomists respond: since we cannot grasp what an actual being is, but only what it is not, we cannot know *how* an actual being causes potential being. We know that the first cause exists and is responsible for potential existents, but we cannot comprehend *how* it exists, let alone *how* it might cause or preserve finite beings. We can apprehend the change in causality, but not fully comprehend it. The asymmetric character of the relation between actual being and all potential beings cannot be emphasized enough.

(4) *Chance Explains the Second Premise.* Still others claim that the causal premise is dubious because the world might be explained as a result of chance. However, chance refers to an event which is incapable of being predicted in advance. Events of this sort are due to our ignorance of all the causal factors involved. A tsunami that kills millions of people might seem like a chance event to innocent bystanders, but if scientists had all the relevant knowledge required to predict its occurrence, then we would indeed be able to save lives before the tragedy happens.

A second meaning of chance is due to the intersecting lines of different causal chains. Sometimes when two forces collide an unforeseen consequence occurs and we call it a chance event. This is precisely what happens in natural selection. Third, we can also talk of chance in quantum physics. At this level, scientists speak in cautious terms, usually in terms of probabilities rather than strict cause-effect relations.

None of these examples would overthrow the truth of existential causality. In each case of the causal principle being at work there are causes needed for an effect. Some explain chance as that which happens spontaneously without a cause. But it is impossible to ascribe chance with a power to do anything. There is simply no such thing as a chance cause. Chance is merely a word to cover up our ignorance. So even in the case of quantum indeterminacy, a cause is still at work.

(5) *Thomism and Medieval (Outdated) Science.* Some Thomists have been accused of presupposing an antiquated scientific view of the world. As Anthony Kenny alleged, Aquinas' arguments depend on his false medieval view of the world.[20] As such, Aquinas' arguments cannot be trusted because of this obvious flaw. Others have assumed the same stance as Kenny. Mackie picked up on Kenny's criticism and said that Thomas' arguments rest on a false scientific view of the world.[21]

20. Kenny, *The Five Ways.*
21. Mackie, *The Miracle of Theism,* 87.

But many Thomists contend that changing scientific views are irrelevant to Aquinas' argument. For Aquinas' argument is a *metaphysical* argument, not a scientific one. This argument from science applies only with Aquinas' *use of illustrations to establish the truth of the premises*, not to the arguments *per se*. Science does not determine the truth of the premises. We might conclude: the argument from bad science can now be laid to rest; for it does not understand the point of Aquinas' argument. As the former atheist, Antony Flew, said: "Once it is appreciated, with some difficulty, . . . it will become clear that this argument . . . is safely beyond the reach of science."[22]

(6) *Issues Related to Infinite Regresses.* Atheist writer B. C. Johnson offers a criticism of the third premise of the Thomist argument. He writes: "Compare a row of dominoes endlessly long . . . which has always been toppling a domino at a time. One could ask what began the dominoes' movement in the first place. But this is just to assume that there was a first place."[23] Thus some atheists have argued that Thomists must assume the first uncaused member of the causal series.

But Aquinas' argument does not depend on a question-begging argument in support of the limited regress. Aquinas allows for the possibility of an infinite regress in the temporal sense of becoming, but this should not become an excuse to avoid inquiring why the series itself exists. This explains why Johnson's objection misses the point. Therefore it is unnecessary to claim that Thomists beg the question in support of a finite regress of potential beings.

More atheists would rather illustrate the possibility of an infinite regress. For instance, Mackie uses an illustration where an infinite regress would be possible: endless motion around a circle. But this illustration merely gives psychological insight into the nature of an infinite regress. And this illustration is no substitute for argument. The circle must have already been drawn or created within a finite, limited world. So it does not help atheists to posit illustrations when they are dis-analogous to the problem at hand. Pseudo-examples of infinity can at most count as an abstract or potential infinite, not as an actual infinity in the structure of the concrete world.

"In all our experience," Everitt concedes, "chains are *always* of finite length, and if they are suspended vertically, they are *always* supported by something that is not itself a chain or another link in a chain. A chain might be hanging from a nail in the wall, it might be held aloft by a person, and so on."[24] Whereas common sense leads one to accept a limited amount of

22. Flew, *God and Philosophy*, 88.

23. Johnson, *The Atheist Debator's Handbook*, 69.

24. Everitt, *The Non-Existence of God*, 67.

potential beings, infinite regresses are counterintuitive. Until atheists can successfully argue for an infinite regress (and not merely provide illustrations or provide examples of potential infinities), then their case should not be accepted. For the atheist, an infinite series must be, counter-intuitively speaking, a brute fact.

(7) *The Universe is the First Actualizer.* Still other critics have argued that even if there are potential beings, the fundamental elements of the universe are the necessary beings. J. L. Mackie asks: "Why, for example, might there not be a permanent stock of matter whose essence did not involve existence but which did not derive its existence from anything else?"[25] In this view the ultimate sub-atomic particles which compose the universe just exist, being dependent on nothing.

Notice that there is no denial of the principle of causality or a first actualizer in saying that the universe is responsible for the "potential parts of the universe." The critic acknowledges that the first cause is responsible for the here-and-now existence of potential beings. Therefore the first actualizer is not just another "potential being." While accepting each of the previous premises, the atheist prematurely concludes that the actual being is the universe itself.

Some atheists argue that the notion of a cause applies only within the sphere of time and space. They claim that the cause is outside the realm of sense experience; it would be nonsensical to claim to understand it. Despite the commonsense appeal of Aquinas, Everitt concludes that such a "deeper reality" is unknowable: "Our background expectations about the nature of physical chains of links are therefore very different from our background assumptions about causes in general, and we cannot assume that what seems obvious with the former will also apply to the latter."[26]

But Everitt's objection does not amount to much. In the Thomist argument, the premises employ the concept of cause within the time-space continuum, but at the conclusion the meaning assigned to the cause is negated. Since an actually infinite amount of essentially hierarchical, sustaining causes is impossible, we have no choice but to resort to a cause that is uncaused. Otherwise we are left with another limited being. Or, we are left with every potential thing coming into existence from nothing without a cause.

Though on the level of experience it can be difficult or even impossible to pinpoint what is doing the causing, this does not mean that potential beings can exist without an extrinsic Cause (i.e., a Cause that has the divine attributes). In the *De Ente* argument, there are no intermediate potential

25. Mackie, *The Miracle of Theism*, 91.
26. Everitt, *The Non-Existence of God*, 67.

beings that serve as an ultimate cause. If a potential being exists, then an actual being exists. The latter works in and through each potential being in an essentially ordered series (not an accidental series) of beings. In the absence of the actualizer, there can be no potential beings. When we try to understand the nature of the actualizer, we realize that human language can only make valid predications of its essence, not express it fully. Thus the actual being is not finite, not limited, etc.

Other atheists maintain that the universe is the first actualizer, because that would be a simpler explanation than invoking God to account for it. As Douglas Krueger claims: "This explanation is simpler than the explanation that god *and* the universe exist. The simpler view is more likely to be true than its rival since the 'universe only' model assumes less than the other model."[27] Whenever it is possible we should use the principle of parsimony to get rid of unnecessary causes.

By contrast, while atheism is theoretically simpler than theism (numerically speaking), it is ultimately a simplistic explanation; thus atheism should not be preferred over the universe *and* God. Otherwise we would be left with a more difficult phenomenon to explain, one begging for explanation: potential beings which cannot be explained by an infinite regress. "God and potential being(s)' turns out to be the simplest way to account for potential beings.

(8) The next objection is *Who Made God?* Richard Dawkins holds that Aquinas "makes the entirely unwarranted assumption that God himself is immune to the regress."[28] But the frequently asked question "who or what caused God?" is usually guided by the refusal to accept the impossibility of an infinite regress or by a false understanding of existential causality. Unlike the principle of sufficient reason, the causal principle does not state that "everything must have a cause." Rather, every potential being must have a cause, or every finite, limited, changing being must have a cause. If God is eternal, then he is uncaused. It would be silly then to ask "What caused God?"

Thus the questioner who asks "Who made God?" commits a categorical fallacy. They eliminate from the outset any possibility that the ultimate cause of potential beings might be God. It is like asking "who caused the being who is, by definition, uncaused?" As a result, Thomists have not given much attention to this objection, and rightfully so.

(9) *Not Enough Attributes of the First Actualizer to Consider it "God."* Many atheists insist that unless most or all the divine attributes can be demonstrated, then the first actualizer cannot be equated with God. In response,

27. Krueger, *What is Atheism?* 151.

28. Dawkins, *The God Delusion*, 100.

Thomists have relied on the distinction between formal and material objects of knowledge. Persons can recognize the same object in different formal respects. The God of the cosmological argument is the same God as the God of Christianity, but the former cannot be known *as* the Triune God until one has faith *in* him. Philosophers cannot prove everything there is to know about God. The success of this atheist criticism depends upon what the atheist is looking for.

However, most of the divine attributes flow directly from the second conclusion of Aquinas' argument. Once a being of pure act is shown to exist, the divine attributes come cascading down, one right after the other. Since existence as such is unlimited unless conjoined with a limiting essence, then a being whose essence is existence will exemplify all perfections infinitely. God will be infinite in his goodness, knowledge and power, as well as in other attributes.

Once the essence of the argument is correctly understood, the final conclusion is extended by additional arguments to demonstrate that the first actualizer is one, simple, immaterial, immutable, omnipotent, eternal, and so on. If the first cause's essence is to exist, then it contains all the perfections that there can be. As Thomas goes on to say after the conclusion of the Five Ways, "All perfections existing in creatures divided and multiplied, pre-exist in God unitedly."[29]

(10) *The First Actualizer has Contradictory Attributes.* Other atheists argue that the attributes are incompatible with one another. Richard Gale represents this argument: "The most telling objection that can be lodged against the cosmological argument is that it is impossible for such a being to exist, thereby showing that this argument's conclusion is necessarily false."[30] No matter how compelling Aquinas' argument might seem to be, its conclusion cannot be true. For the attributes of the first actualizer contradict one another.

But this objection is fallacious for a variety of reasons.[31] On the face of it, there is nothing logically contradictory in the existence of an actual being. Since we know what a potential being is, we can just as easily conceptualize a non-potential being. We know what an actual being is not. Necessity denotes that a purely actual being is not dependent on anything else for its existence; immutability is another way of saying that it does not change. All

---

29. Aquinas, *Summa Theologiae*, 1.13.5.

30. Gale, *On the Nature and Existence of God*, 238.

31. The best published work on the coherence of the divine attributes remains Garrigou-Lagrange, *God*.

the attributes stem from experiencing the nature of the world and drawing conclusions based upon it.

Knowledge of God is derived from negating what is known about the world. The negative terms used to speak about God do not mean that we are left with nothing. Positive information about God is derived from applying the principle of causality. He is a being because all potential beings depend on him for their existence. He is pure actuality because he is the first cause of lesser actualities. We can prove that the first actualizer exists, not what he is. Though divine attributes are deduced, they all refer to the one being whose essence is to exist. He is one being, but many things can be said about him. There is only one being to which these attributes apply.

(11) *There Might be Many Actualizers*. But what if there are many actual beings, each of which is uncaused? However, even if the argument were granted, it would not be a favorable conclusion for atheism. Surely the atheist does not want many Gods!

Nonetheless, Thomists have always had the resources to combat this problem. If an infinite being exists, then there cannot be more than one of them. As Norris Clarke said: "This is a quick and easy step, admitted by just about all metaphysicians, I believe, once the existence of an absolutely infinite being is granted."[32] If there were more than one actual, unlimited being, then there would have to be something that distinguishes the one from the other(s). But there is no way for an infinite being to differ from another unless there is some potential for differentiation inherent in each of them. Actual being has no limitations. Hence there can only be one infinite actualizer.

Conclusion

Of all modern documents of the Catholic Church, *Dei Filius* stands as a prophetic voice in the midst of a bewildering amount of intellectual and pastoral challenges now facing the Church. In a graphic passage on atheism and unbelief, Walter Kasper writes:

> Modern atheism [which stems from the philosophies of the Enlightenment] has put theology in a difficult position. Of particular importance here is mass atheism, a phenomenon unparalleled in past history; it regards the practical, if not theoretical denial of God or at least indifference to belief in God as being by far the most plausible attitude to take. As a result, theology has been stripped of its power to speak to people and to communicate with them. There are now no generally accepted images,

32. Clarke, *The One and the Many*, 221.

symbols, concepts, or categories with which it can make itself understood. The crisis in the presuppositions for understanding talk about God is the real crisis of present day theology. To put the matter in more Scholastic terms; the crisis of contemporary theology arises from the loss of the *preambula fidei*, that is, of the presuppositions which faith needs if it is to be possible as faith and if it is to be able to make itself intelligible as faith. The quandary becomes clear when we consider the various ways in which theology comes to grips with modern atheism.[33]

Part of the reason why theoretical and practical atheisms are gaining such strong headway in the West comes from the ongoing separation of faith and reason. Not only do many Catholic theologians and philosophers depreciate or at least neglect Vatican I's teaching on natural knowledge of God, but also many atheists continue to challenge it as well.

Although these criticisms are developed in sophisticated forms, each of them fails to capture the essence of Aquinas' natural theology. Neither side of the theist-atheist debate shows any signs of weariness, but Thomists continue to have the philosophical capital that is needed to answer the relevant criticisms and show the inherent weaknesses in them.

33. Kasper, *The God of Jesus Christ*, 47.

— 5 —

Thomas Aquinas and
the Moral Argument

THE MORAL ARGUMENT FOR the existence of God is one of the central arguments being discussed in the burgeoning field of natural theology. The debate is almost exclusively represented by divine command theorists (those who maintain that God alone is locus of moral values) and atheistic moral realists (those who maintain that objective moral truths can exist in the absence of God). Atheist philosophers typically appeal to human nature to determine what is moral. But in so doing, they prematurely conclude that there is no need for God to account for moral norms. Divine command theorists respond to the atheists: in order to retain moral objectivity, we must act in response to moral values or divine commands which lie beyond human nature. Otherwise, they say, we would be left with ethical relativism, subjectivism, and nihilism.

Following Thomas Aquinas' formulation of participation metaphysics, I contend that both of these positions have significant insights, and both of them falter in other respects. Aquinas' Fourth Way bridges the gap between atheists and divine command theorists when discussing the moral argument. In agreement with the atheists, Thomists maintain that basic moral norms are grounded in human nature. But this reference point presupposes the existence of a Divine Lawgiver. Otherwise, it would not make sense for atheists to refer to *human nature* as the basis for basic moral norms.

In response to divine command theorists (and this would include proponents of the newer, modified version of the theory), Thomists insist that human nature is a necessary condition, but definitely not a sufficient condition, for objective morality. God is necessary as the ultimate ground of objective moral norms which are grounded in human nature.

Although Aquinas did not directly offer a moral argument for God's existence anywhere in his corpus, his fourth proof for the existence of God as expressed in the *Summa Theologiae* might be recast in a way that resolves the tensions in this debate. As it now stands, the debate presents us with a false dichotomy between the divine command theory and atheist moral realism. A more technical version of Aquinas' Fourth Way will be presented to show how overcoming the tensions in the debate this might be accomplished.

Atheist Moral Realism and Modified Divine Commands

Almost all atheist moral realists agree that morality is not strictly based on popular opinion or cultural convention. Erik Wielenberg, for instance, contends that there are some acts that are intrinsically good even if they do not lead to anything of value: "If there are activities available to us during our lifetimes that are intrinsically valuable, then our lives can have internal meaning even if God does not exist. Even if there is no supernatural commander to assign purposes to our lives . . . I submit that there are such activities."[1]

Individuals do not have to believe in God to know and act in response to moral principles. Wielenberg says: "The foundation of morality is a set of axiomatic necessary moral truths. No being, natural or supernatural, is responsible for the truth of or has control over these ethical truths."[2] Consequently, not only can we know that moral truths exist without belief in God (as revealed in Christ or through some other supernatural disclosure), but we should also be able to know and abide by them even if nobody recognizes them as such.[3] Atheist philosopher Paul Kurtz agrees: "I would argue that certain moral principles of morality are true regardless of their origin, and generally they are warranted independent of their religious foundations or lack of them."[4]

These basic moral norms are properly basic beliefs. These are beliefs that all normally functioning individuals should have. The "first principles" of morality constitutes the starting points for moral knowledge: "Claims about what is intrinsically good are the axioms of ethical theory; they are

---

1. Wielenberg, *Value and Virtue in a Godless Universe*, 34.

2. Ibid., 66.

3. Ibid., 64.

4. Kurtz, *Forbidden Fruit*, 15. Cf. 30, 31.

the starting points, the first principles. As such, they are unlikely to be the sort of things that can be *proved*. Nevertheless, it is perfectly consistent to say that some activities are intrinsically valuable—and that we *know* what some of these are."[5] Many atheist philosophers who are moral realists agree about this philosophical framework for ethics: basic moral truths exist, and they can be known. Ordinary language and common sense assume that morality is objective.

They differ from one another in the details. Some atheists are moral Platonists. In this view moral truths reside in some ephemeral world apart from the material world. Still others reject the Platonic approach and maintain that human nature is sufficient for persons to discover and act upon moral principles. In either case, God is not included in the overall picture. For many atheists, basic moral principles are objective and knowable by all properly functioning individuals without having to invoke some deeper metaphysical foundation.

But, according to proponents of the divine command theory, many problems attend to the atheist view. As J. P. Moreland and William Craig argue:

> What does it mean to say, for example, that the moral value *justice* just exists? It is hard to know what to make of this. It is clear what is meant when it is said that a person is just; but it is bewildering when it is said that in the absence of any people *justice* itself exists. Moral values seem to exist as properties of persons, not as mere abstractions—or at any rate, it is hard to know what it is for a moral value to exist as a mere abstraction. Atheistic moral realists seem to lack any adequate foundation in reality for moral values but just leave them floating in an unintelligible way.[6]

Atheists need to explain how impersonal moral "abstractions" can exist in the absence of any personal beings. On a theist account, moral truths reflect the nature of a personal God.

Second, even if moral precepts existed in some ethereal realm, it is difficult to see how they could have any morally binding power on human beings. Craig and Moreland continue:

> Suppose that values like mercy, justice, love, forbearance, and the like just exist. How does that result in any moral obligations for me? Why would I have a moral duty, say, to be merciful? Who or what lays such an obligation on me? As the ethicist

5. Ibid., 35.

6. Craig and Moreland, *Philosophical Foundations for a Christian Worldview*, 492.

Richard Taylor points out, "A duty is something that is owed. . . . But something can be owed only to some person or persons. There can be no such thing as duty in isolation." God makes sense of moral obligation because his commands constitute for us our moral duties. Taylor writes, "Our moral obligations can . . . be understood as those that are imposed by God. . . . But what if this higher than human lawgiver is no longer taken into account? Does the concept of a moral obligation still make sense? . . . [T]he concept of moral obligation [is] unintelligible apart from the idea of God. The words remain, but their meaning is gone."[7]

If we feel guilty for violating moral rules, there is probably a person to whom we are responsible to do the right thing. If no human person existed, then objective moral truth would still matter. Thus there must be Someone who grounds moral truth. Given the traditional definition of what a person is, we should conclude that he or she has intellect and will.

Other moral philosophers exploit the inadequacies of holding consistently to atheism and objective morality. Here the argument is that atheists cannot adequately explain a naturalistic understanding of the world which produces human beings who can act and respond to moral truths. The fabric of reality must be structured in such a way as to allow organisms to evolve to the point of recognizing these moral truths.

Without a structured universe, atheists could never begin to make intelligible statements, let alone intelligible arguments against theism. Structure, it may be added, is another form of teleology. Moreover, teleology implies the existence of a Designer. In this way, it is argued, atheist moral realists must implicitly borrow from a theistic premise to formulate the arguments that they do.

In the same vein, Elizabeth Anscombe argued in a well-known article that modern ethical positions (such as atheist moral realism) continue to borrow from Christian ethical systems. Such positions, she argued, once made complete sense: it was once recognized by Christian societies for so long as morality was directly rooted in God's nature.[8] No more questions needed to be asked about who or what grounds moral truth!

To conclude, it is fantastically unlikely that a nonconscious, immaterial, impersonal, valueless, and materialistic process could produce objective moral principles and persons and situate both of them in such a way that the former can be structured and known by valueless persons who can know

7. Ibid., 493.
8. Anscombe, "Modern Moral Philosophy," 1–19.

and act in response to them. Wielenberg sees the implications: "And if, as I believe, there is no God, then it is in some sense an accident that we have the moral properties that we do."[9] In what seems like a desperate attempt to justify a response to these kinds of criticisms from divine command theorists, Wielenberg says that valuable truths can "sometimes" spring from the greater context of utter valuelessness.[10] But it is difficult to see how value can "sometimes" arise out of utter valuelessness. If something is valueless it has no potential for producing value. If the universe has the potential to produce something valuable, then the universe is not ultimately valueless.

The fourth and final argument is that there are many atheists who have admitted the intrinsic connection between objective morality and God. Correlatively, they say that atheism cannot account for objective morality. Bertrand Russell claimed to stand on the "firm foundation of unyielding despair."[11] He wrote that "The whole subject of ethics arises from the pressure of the community on the individual."[12] J. L. Mackie recognized that objective moral principles would indeed be "queer" in a naturalistic universe. If they exist, then he argued that they would furnish the Christian theist with a defensible argument for God's existence: "If . . . there are . . . objective values, they make the existence of a god more probable than it would have been without them. Thus we have . . . a defensible argument from morality to the existence of a god."[13] Richard Dawkins added: "The universe we observe has precisely the properties we should expect if there is, at bottom, no design, no purpose, no evil and no good, nothing but blind pitiless indifference."[14] Many more citations could be provided. The point is that many atheists, both past and present, have seen the intrinsic connection between objective morality and the existence of God.

In summary, many divine command theorists contend that moral values, duties and accountability nicely resonate with a personal, theist universe, not with an atheist one. Conversely, it is unlikely that objective moral principles can exist as traditionally defined in a naturalist universe. Since objective morality seems undeniable (some actions are good; others are evil), one ought to maintain that God is responsible for these features of morality.

9. Wielenberg, "In Defense of Non-Natural, Non-Theistic Moral Realism," 40.

10. Ibid., 40.

11. Russell, *Why I Am Not a Christian*, 107.

12. Russell, *Human Society in Ethics and Politics*, 124.

13. Mackie, *The Miracle of Theism*, 115–16.

14. Dawkins, *River Out of Eden*, 132–33.

Advantages of Thomist Natural Law

The debate on the moral argument is usually represented by two viewpoints. Paul Kurtz frames the debate: "There are two opposing approaches to morality and ethics that have been in constant conflict in human culture. The first is best exemplified by Jesus, Moses, and Mohammed, who declared that moral principles are divinely inspired and who enunciated them without any effort at rational definition or justification. The second is typified by Socrates, who sought to use reason to define and justify his ethical ideals and continually subjected them to critical scrutiny."[15] Although Thomists are rarely involved in the debate on the moral argument, one does not have to endorse either of these extreme positions in arguing for God's existence. The notion of participation metaphysics splits the horns of the dilemma in the debate.

Divine command theorists have some of the resources to combat atheist moral realism. Without a transcendent and personal anchor, one cannot have objective moral values, duties, and accountability. To be more precise, their arguments do not demonstrate the existence of God, but are formulated as a conditional case. William Craig casts the following argument: (1) If God does not exist, objective moral values and duties do not exist; (2) objective moral values and duties do exist; (3) therefore, God exists.[16] Craig also seeks to increase the plausibility of premise 1 by arguing that objective morality is unlikely in a naturalist universe. He hopes to make a connection between objective moral values and God's existence.

Thomists may roughly agree with Craig's conditional claim, but for them it can be recast in way that demonstrates the existence of a theistic God. The best expressions of the divine command theory and the natural law argument form a structural unity.

Other atheists have said that Craig's argument begs the issue in favor of theism. Wielenberg claimed that atheists do not have to explain why there is objective morality because the theist's argument begs the question: "Craig claims that nihilism is false only if there is a single ultimate standard of value. This is mere question begging; my view posits no such single standard and yet is incompatible with nihilism."[17] This complaint is at the heart of Wielenberg's case: divine command theists unnecessarily require atheists to explain their ethical foundations.

---

15. Kurtz, *Forbidden Fruit*, 46.

16. Craig, *Reasonable Faith*, 172.

17. Wielenberg, "In Defense of Non-Natural, Non-Theistic Moral Realism," 39.

But the Thomist view does not fall prey to Wielenberg's challenges. In the Thomist view, participation metaphysics is seen as the necessary ingredient to tease out an explicit connection between objective moral principles and God. Thomists claim to demonstrate the existence of God on the basis of objective moral norms—a God with all the traditional divine attributes. Moreover, the Thomist argument does not make a conditional claim for a vague "personal and transcendent anchor of morality." One does not have to know the eternal law prior to acquiring knowledge of an essence of something. If this were not the case, then in principle an atheist or an agnostic could not acquire knowledge of human nature.

Similarly, many divine command theorists have argued that individuals do not have to believe in God or ascribe to a particular religion to account for objective moral norms. Natural lawyers gladly welcome this clarification by divine command theorists. From a historical standpoint, the atheist criticism (namely, divine command theorists hold that "morality depends on religion") holds true of the traditional divine command theory proposed by Brunner, Barth, and other theologians who were pessimistic about human nature and what can be known about God apart from special revelation. But newer versions of the divine command theory have moved one step closer to Thomas' view by distinguishing between nature and grace. The traditional divine command theory was closely linked with fideism.

On modified versions of the divine command theory moral principles are known by everyone. Divine revelation brings these basic moral principles to fulfillment by helping individuals to know what is good and right more clearly. In no way does God's revelation in Christ suppress what persons already know about morality, but brings moral truth to completion.[18]

Another strength of the newer divine command theory is that it avoids strong versions of divine voluntarism. Far from being arbitrary, moral values flow from God's essentially unchanging nature. God is, by definition, loving, just, and good. This moves yet another step closer to traditional Thomism. Craig Boyd has observed: "But this theory of the good—as a value—smacks of natural law assumptions concerning what we can know and the limits on what God can command."[19]

Divine command theorists have also successfully argued that individuals cannot consistently hold objective moral values in the absence of God's existence. As Craig puts it: "If there is no God, then what's so special about human beings? They're just accidental by-products of nature which have evolved relatively recently on an infinitesimal speck of dust called the

18. Pinckaers, *The Sources of Christian Ethics*, 127, 182.
19. Boyd, *A Shared Morality*, 142.

planet Earth, lost somewhere in a hostile and mindless universe, and which are doomed to perish individually and collectively in a relatively short time. On the atheistic view, some action, say rape, may not be socially advantageous and so in the course of human development has become taboo."[20] Natural law theorists stand alongside Craig's vivid contentions about an atheist universe: a world without God is a world without objective morality, meaning and purpose.

To conclude, contemporary divine command theorists have successfully exposed the problems of atheistic moral Platonism, and have challenged the dubious contention that objective morality can be consistently defended in a world without God. One of the principal weaknesses of the modified version of the divine command theory is that it does not consider the normative value of human nature when responding to atheistic accounts that do not draw inspiration from Plato.

Thomist natural lawyers grant to divine command theorists that atheists want to "eat their cake and have it too." But a more comprehensive argument that includes the normative value of human nature might help atheists reconsider their position.

Thomist Natural Law and the "Fourth Way"

Atheists rightly acknowledge that the human virtues can be attained without believing in the Christian God. Aquinas would not disagree with their contention. All persons have been made in the image of God and are able to attain the human virtues. All persons, according the Angelic Doctor, are endowed with human rights, dignity, conscience, moral responsibility, and the capacity to recognize moral right and wrong. As Ralph McInerney put it: "The natural law, as St. Paul remarks, is inscribed in our hearts. But knowing natural law does not entail knowing St. Paul."[21] As of result of this subtle distinction, many philosophers have mistakenly argued that there are versions of natural law theory which do not include God. But this contention is clearly mistaken. One does not have to believe in God to follow basic moral truth. It is quite another thing to say that, given the existence of objective norms, which are grounded in human nature, God must exist.

Thomists will also admit that atheists can formulate a system of ethics without immediate reference to divine revelation or to the Church's moral teachings. We should not be surprised to see atheists at least concede that

20. Craig, *Reasonable Faith*, 175.

21. McInerney, "Thomistic Natural Law and Aristotelian Philosophy," in Goyette, Latcovic, and Myers, eds., *St. Thomas Aquinas and the Natural Law Tradition*, 38.

human life is worthwhile insofar as people perform intrinsically good acts. Not only is it possible to outline such an ethical framework, but our atheist dialogue partners have been able to do it. Both atheists and theists argue that basic moral truths are objective (moral absolutism) and knowable (moral realism).

Perhaps the best example of a basic moral truth is the first principle of morality: "do good and avoid evil."[22] First principles of morality are good actions to perform in and of themselves. These actions are not good to perform as a mere means to an end. Second, the first principles prescribe behavior; they do not merely describe behavior. Only free agents are required to abide by them. Third, first principles are not temporally conditioned truths, but are applicable in all times and places. They also universal, having binding power on every person. These norms are also non-conventional; they are not based on mere human apprehension of the moral realm, but hold whether anybody believes in them or not. Lastly, objective moral norms are discovered—not completely invented. Atheists would most likely have no problem with these characteristics of moral norms. The "moral realism" in their system is not in dispute.

Now, the following argument can be formulated by drawing from Thomas's writings on participation. This argument is a more technical version of the Fourth Way.[23] Thomists have emphasized that participation is the key element to understanding Thomas' metaphysics.[24]

First, Thomas notes that all perfections (proper actions of creatures) are not predicated substantially, but only by participation. Humans do not have being or goodness by nature, but only by participation. If humans had being by nature, then we would always have to exist.

Secondly, whenever something has a perfection by participation, then ultimately that perfection must come from something that has that perfection by essence. The term participation is a technical term taken from the Neo-Platonists, and it refers to whenever something shares in a perfection that something else has by nature. For example, water is not hot by nature, and hence heating something is not its proper action. Fire is hot by nature, and heating something is its proper action. If water is heated by a fire, then it is able to perform the proper action of the fire: heating something. Water is hot by participation and hence shares in the perfection of the fire. Because

---

22. Aquinas, *Summa Theologiae*, 1–2.94.2.

23. Expositions of the Fourth Way can be found in Gilson, *The Christian Philosophy of Saint Thomas Aquinas*, 70–74; Wippel, *The Metaphysical Thought of Thomas Aquinas*, 469–79.

24. Rziha, *Perfecting Human Actions*, 6–28.

water is not hot by nature, if it has heat, then this heat can necessarily be traced back to something that is hot by nature: some type of fire.

Thirdly, the life of virtue (or moral goodness or any other perfection in the moral life) cannot be predicated of humans substantially (not all humans act morally) but only by participation. The highly virtuous individual participates in the eternal law more than less virtuous persons. There are different degrees of participation.[25] Hence, there must be something that is virtuous by nature which is the cause of all other virtue. That which is virtuous by nature is God (using the term virtuous analogically). In Thomas' own words: "there must be something which is to all beings the cause of their being, goodness and every other perfection." Thomas adds: "and this we call God." This argument does not require any sort of divine command theory and can be applied to any moral law. A law is a perfection because it rationally orders something to its proper end.

Since law is a dictate of reason, it is not of the substance of humans but a participated perfection. Since it is in humans by participation, it must ultimately come from something that is law by nature: the eternal law, or God. This argument applies whether or not the law is determined by natural law (which participates in the eternal law) or is divinely revealed. Theologian John Rziha says:

> The ability of humans to rationally direct themselves to an end, at first glance, can appear to make humans autonomous in the sense that they are independent from God. However, rationality does not make humans independent from God, but rather allows humans to rationally participate in divine direction. Human reason, like all created realities, is what it is because of its relation to its divine cause. Because all effects participate in their cause, human reason has a divine foundation: it exists by participation in God's own knowledge and grows by greater participation in this knowledge. It is only because humans participate in God's knowledge that they are able to direct themselves as human agents.[26]

Some of the advantages of the Thomist argument over the divine command theory can now be adduced. First, Thomists begins with the first principle of morality and demonstrate the existence of God on that basis. A Being whose essence is to exist is shown to be responsible for the existence of morally good persons. Aquinas did not first ask his readers to accept the existence of God before understanding the concept of natural law (as with

25. Ibid., 74, 114–15.
26. Ibid., 184–85. Cf. 258–59, 264.

the case of Craig's divine command theory). Rather, he asked them to consider the possibility of goods in the real world.

Once it has been shown that a self-subsistent Being exists, it is commonplace for Thomists to show that this Being is the same God as the God of traditional theism. Divine command theorists are unable to arrive at the same conclusion on the basis of their moral argument. With regard for each of the Five Ways, Aquinas considered each of them to be distinct and demonstrative proofs for the existence of God: "There are five ways in which one can prove that there is a God."

Yet another advantage of the natural law argument is that it avoids the arbitrariness problem. Both Robert Adams and William Craig have argued that God is necessarily loving and just, and that God would not command evil atrocities. While such arbitrary commands are logically possible, they claim, these commands are never actualized by God.

This argument begs the question, because in order to have an internally consistent position they must abandon any independently meaningful standard of goodness apart from the assumption of a certain sort of God. When Craig says "if theism is true, then we have sound foundation for morality," he should admit that "theism" can be a loaded term, at least by those who do not share his theist perspective. Norman Kretzmann exposed this problem in one of his writings in defense of natural law. He argued against "theological subjectivism," a form of the divine command theory, by exposing the problem when divine command theorists assert that God is the good in the absence of relying on some natural law doctrine:

> But do not suppose that the adherent of theological subjectivism can extricate himself from this terminal embarrassment with a pious rejoinder that God is good and can be relied on not to approve of moral evil. The only standard of moral goodness supplied by theological subjectivism is God's approval; and so say within the context of theological subjectivism that God is good comes to nothing more than that God approves of himself—which is easy to grant but impossible to derive any reassurance from.[27]

Kretzmann's point is hugely important. For atheists are quick to ask divine command theists: how do we know that God is the Good on a divine command account? Thus atheist urge their dialogue partners to think more deeply about the independent reason for holding, by definition, that God is equivalent to the Good. To be sure, God and the Good are formally distinct notions. This independent reason, moreover, must come from a place that atheists already recognize. Why, then, include God in the picture? Atheists

27. Kretzmann, "Abraham, Isaac, and Euthyphro," in Stump et al., *Harmartia*, 35.

press the divine command theorist even further: atheism is a simpler world-view than theism. Atheist Kai Nielson poignantly comments:

> It isn't that man judges God—that is indeed blasphemy—but what is true is that no reality, no force or being or world ground, no matter how powerful or eternal, would be called "God" unless that reality were taken to be good by the agent making that judgment. That is to say, before we can appropriately use the word "God"—given the meaning it has in Jewish, Christian, and Moslem discourse—to characterize that reality—e.g., that being, force, or world ground—we must already have made a judgment about its goodness. This shows that our concept of goodness and our criteria for goodness are prior to and not dependent on our belief in the existence of some "world ground" or "transcendent being." Since this is so, no one can get one's exemplar, one's model for what one ought to be and do, from simply knowing that a totally unlimited being exists who created all other beings and was not created himself.[28]

Divine command theorists should not dodge the issue at this point and simply pass the ball back to atheists by asking them to explain how atheism is compatible with objective morality. Rather, divine command theorists should take the question seriously and admit that they do not have the resources to answer it. This question cannot be dismissed as a matter of moral epistemology or semantics, but is closely linked to the word "theism" (an ontological reality) in the first premise.

Not all theists should be dismayed at this point. Atheists incapable of accounting for objective morality, but Thomists can give a sufficient answer to Nielson. The goodness of which the natural lawyer speaks depends on an objective basis of goodness that persons can understand apart from recognizing that God is ultimately responsible for limited goods. In the natural law view, both God and human nature are needed for morality. As one considers the nature of limited goods, one is led to inevitably conclude that a good God exists. The existence of God emerges as a conclusion to an argument by recognizing that limited moral goods exist. While God's goodness is different from human goodness, Thomists have long recognized the continuity and similarity between the two.

We must understand the nature of the God who is thought to issue divine commands. But the only way that we can know whether this God is a God worthy of worship is if we have a preliminary understanding of limited goods. Alisdair McIntyre wrote: "Any account of divine commands

28. Nielson, *Ethics Without God*, 31.

as foundational to morality, as antecedent to and partially or wholly definitive of justice, such as we are offered in one version by Occam [a traditional account of the divine command theory], in another by Adams [modified versions of the divine command theory], has to fail."[29] Divine command theorists do not have the luxury of arguing from the world of experience to a certain conception of God. Our conception of human goodness will determine how we understand the manner in which God is said to be good.

In Thomist philosophy, God is the creator and ruler of human nature; he determines what behaviors will contribute to human flourishing in light of their final, ultimate end. If the basic precepts of the law were to change, then God would have to change human nature. The moral instructions in divine revelation are not arbitrarily given by God, imposed upon persons. Law is not so much about external statutes as much as it is about an interior dimension which exhibits God's ordering of the creation and human nature. The law is not at odds with human nature as it is in Kant and other rule based systems. Divine revelation is communicated because it helps persons to become who they were meant to be. In other words, God issues revelatory commands on the basis of the way in which the world and human beings are already constituted and made by him.

A Thomist Response to Atheistic Objectors

Here I address different criticisms in the atheist literature that seek to challenge theistic ethical positions. Most of these criticisms do not apply to Aquinas' fourth proof.

(1) The first argument that might be raised against the proof is that *atheists are just as moral as theists*.[30] This contention does not count as a defeater and misses the point of Aquinas' argument. The central issue in this debate has to do with explaining who or what can account for moral ontology, not how moral truth is lived out. A Thomist may enter the debate and argue that atheists are unable to account for moral ontology in a naturalist universe, and that objective morality can be used in a starting premise in a demonstrative argument for God's existence.

Perhaps atheists have thought that the theists held that atheists are immoral because traditional proponents of the divine command theory have typically formulated their position in that way. Fideism, deontology, and religious exclusivism commonly stood alongside of the older divine

29. McIntyre, "Which God Ought We to Obey and Why," 364.

30. Nielson, *Ethics Without God*, 15, 101–2; Sinnott-Armstrong, *Morality Without God?* 22–23.

command theory. Even worse, divine command theorists argued that one could not be moral unless one had faith in the Christian God.

Natural law theorists have long acknowledged that the human virtues can be practiced without special revelation or faith. Regardless of whether somebody believes in God or not, all persons can desire and succeed in being virtuous. According to Aquinas: "All desire the final end, because all desire their perfection, which is what the final end signifies," even when all "do not agree about the content of that final end."[31]

(2) Second, some atheists argue that *different religions propose contradictory accounts of morality.*[32] Unfortunately for this objection, it has nothing to do with taking moral ontology seriously. As a Catholic natural lawyer, I submit that not all ethical views proposed by the different religions of the world are correct. And I maintain that the Fourth Way can prove that God exists. To put this in other words, contradictory views within the different religious traditions would not mean that God does not exist or that God is not necessary to ground morality. The debate should be focused on moral ontology, not on religious diversity, applied ethics, moral epistemology, or even moral semantics.

(3) Other atheists may ask: *How do individuals recognize a divine command?*[33] This argument might hold some water against divine command theories, but it does not succeed against natural law. Divine voluntarists hold that only those who entrust themselves in faith to the Christian God (read: what the Bible says about morality) can know what God commands. But on the natural law view, all persons can know and respond to the basic precepts of the moral law.

Further, and more importantly, this objection is concerned with moral epistemology (how we know what is moral), not with moral ontology. How we recognize a divine command (or special instructions given to humanity from God) is a different issue than accounting for moral ontology itself.

(4) The next argument is that *Old Testament moral injunctions are contradictory.*[34] Even if this argument is true, it would have nothing to do with explaining what accounts for objective morality. At most it would refute a certain understanding of biblical inerrancy or a lopsided understanding of

31. Aquinas, *Summa Theologiae*, 1–2.1.17.

32. Kurtz, *Forbidden Fruit*, 13–14, 62–63; Nielson, *Ethics Without God*, 100; Paul Kurtz, "The Kurtz/Craig Debate," in Garcia and King, eds., *Is Goodness Without God Good Enough?* 27, 34, 39.

33. Sinnott-Armstrong, *Morality Without God?* 122–23, 136–37; Sinnott-Armstrong, "Why Traditional Theism Cannot Provide an Adequate Foundation for Morality," in Garcia and King, eds., *Is Goodness Without God Good Enough?* 108.

34. Kurtz, *Forbidden Fruit*, 57.

biblical inspiration. Second, this challenge is directed at Jewish-Christian theology, not at the Fourth Way which is part and parcel of the philosophical preambles of faith.

Closely linked with the aforementioned objection is that *theistic ethics lead to violence*. Sometimes atheists maintain that the Old Testament commands believers to be violent. Again, even if this argument were true, it would have nothing to do with successfully explaining what accounts for basic moral principles. At most it would count as an undercutting defeater of the holiness of the Church, a restricted understanding of biblical inerrancy, or one-sided interpretations of the Scriptures. Misinterpretations of the Bible can facilitate violent religious acts.[35] This violence can occur when the literalist method of biblical interpretation is used at the expense of other methods. Be that as it may, this hermeneutical debate has nothing to do with the moral argument which precedes theological reflection.

(5) Fifth, *the theistic account is unable to develop its views on morality*.[36] However, the natural law does not claim to be a comprehensive theory of morality. Instead it must be complemented by other normative systems, such as virtue ethics. Combining natural law and virtue ethics enables the natural law theorist to assess each moral situation as it arises.

Formally speaking, the first precepts of the moral law are unconditional, universal and unchanging. However, other features of living the moral life will adjust according to how the good is perceived by individuals in different circumstances. While the natural law prescribes certain actions to be done, virtue ethics is more agent-centered, concentrating on the kind of person one is becoming. These two ethical systems do not oppose one another, but are mutually reinforcing and necessary for morality. For Aquinas, it is reasonable (natural law) to be virtuous (virtue ethics). The virtues ought to be pursued and developed, and vices ought to be avoided.

It follows that the virtuous person is disposed to abide by the precepts of the moral law; continuous observance of its precepts will help one to become virtuous. A proponent of virtue ethics still presupposes the validity of moral norms (or, the striving toward the good). For if the virtue ethicist does not presuppose the objectivity of moral norms, then the virtues could not be seen as anything other than a mere skill or habit. But this is not how virtue ethicists typically think about the virtues.

In a reductive view of the virtues one could develop the "skill" of torturing innocent persons, and still call it "virtuous." Intuitively speaking, we know that torture is not virtuous, but is objectively evil and not in need of

---

35. O'Collins, *Rethinking Fundamental Theology*, 216–64.
36. Kurtz, *Forbidden Fruit*, 33, 45, 53.

justification to explain why it is evil. Lastly, even if natural lawyers were unable to develop their views on morality, this would not mean that individuals should not try to account for the basic moral truths that exist.

(6) Sixth, *moral absolutism does not take circumstances into consideration for assessing moral dilemmas.*[37] This objections seems to imply that endorsing unconditional imperatives disallows exceptional moral cases, and that the endorsement of unconditional imperatives leads to intolerance. Influenced by Immanuel Kant, some ethicists have relied almost exclusively on moral obligations at the expense of other sources of morality. According to Servais Pinckaers: "Originating in the manuals intended for the education of the clergy, this idea of morality spread to the people during recent centuries through homilies and catechisms. It created an image of the priest as one who taught what we should and should not do, with the accent on sins to be avoided."[38]

Pinckaers argues that within this intellectual climate "justice hardened and assumed two contrary aspects: defense of subjective rights on the one hand and, on the other, societal pressure in the name of the law, with the force of obligation and threat of constraint. These were quickly resented as forms of oppression."[39] Unlike modern proponents of natural law, the neo-scholastic theologians and jurists did not hold that all precepts could be known by any rational person. They did not authentically represent the thought of Aquinas. Both experience and reason are included in his understanding of natural law:

> When set forth in terms of precepts, natural law is presented to us externally and communicates to our reason and conscience moral demands that restrict our freedom with the force of obligation. But make no mistake: this law is not the work of a will external and foreign to us. Precisely because it is the expression of our natural inclinations, especially the spiritual ones, this law penetrates to the heart of our freedom and personality to show us the demands of truth and goodness. These guide us in the development of freedom through actions of excellence. Thus natural law is an inner law. It is the direct work of the One who has created us to image him in our spiritual nature and our free, rational will. The exigencies of natural law have their source both in God and in our human nature.[40]

37. Nielson, *Ethics Without God*, 160, 193, 206; Kurtz, "The Kurtz/Craig Debate," 28–29.

38. Pinckaers, *The Sources of Christian Ethics*, 17.

39. Ibid., 39.

40. Ibid., 452.

Exceptions to the rule should not be used as an excuse to abrogate the notion of moral absolutes. Jean Porter observes: "Hence, the natural law more broadly understood does include specific moral norms as well as a fundamental capacity for moral judgment, although there is considerable room for both legitimate variation and sinful distortion at the level of particular norms."[41]

More importantly, even if some natural law thinkers did not take circumstances into consideration for assessing moral situations, this would have nothing to do with accounting for those timeless moral truths which are grounded in human nature. As we have already seen, atheist moral realists also accept the existence and knowability of objective moral truths.

(7) Likewise, the idea that *theological ethics destroys moral motivation because it is authoritarian*[42] is misplaced. Thomists recognize that, although first principles are insufficient for developing a complete moral theory, they must be complemented by secondary precepts of the natural law, the virtues, and a developed interior life. Formally stated, the first principle of morality cannot (and simply does not) prescribe any particular, concrete action. Experience is needed to complement one's search for the good.

Thomas himself distinguishes the first principles of morality and the different ways they are applied to new circumstances and situations. For Aquinas, the virtues are needed to make a correct moral assessment in difficult scenarios. Aquinas says, "the natural law is altogether unchangeable in its first principles. But in its secondary principles, which . . . are certain detailed proximate conclusions drawn from the first principles, the natural law is not changed so that what it prescribes be not right in most cases. But it may be changed in some particular cases of rare occurrence, through some special causes hindering the observance of such precepts."[43] Aquinas has a particular example in mind: the inapplicability of returning a borrowed item when it is known by the recipient that it will be used to harm or kill another.

Natural law theorists have always stressed the need for careful reasoning, assessing each situation as it arises. The law cannot be upset or destroyed, but it can change by new extensions, applications, and human encounters with new situations and circumstances. The unchanging law of nature and its implementation should be distinguished. More to the point, even if the first principle of morality is "authoritarian" and binding on all

---

41. Porter, *Nature as Reason*, 14. Cf. 289.

42. Kurtz, *Forbidden Fruit*, 71; Nielson, *Ethics Without God*, 53, 73, 90, 188; Sinnott-Armstrong, *Morality Without God?* 110, 119.

43. Aquinas, *Summa Theologiae*, 1–2.94.6.

persons, this would not mean that one should not try to explain the moral ontology of the first principle.

(8) The atheists may continue with another related objection: *divine rewards and punishments are not good motives for helping individuals to become moral.*[44] Like many other atheist arguments, this claim does not challenge the moral argument, but against certain understandings of divine revelation. Hence this criticism is irrelevant to whether or not the moral argument constitutes a sound piece of reasoning. Further, the critic seems to be assuming that God is an arbitrary deity, not the locus of goodness itself. For, according to natural lawyers and virtue ethicists, the good is something to be done because it is worthwhile as an end-in-itself.

(9) *If an action harms another, the atheists say, then it is wrong and not in need of further justification.*[45] Now, this argument is certainly correct in one sense (i.e., if an action harms another, then it is wrong), but it misses the general thrust of the Fourth Way. For one thing, the harm-based account is unable to tell what actions are right, only the ones that are wrong. Surely this makes the "harm-based account" shortsighted.

Second, this view still does not explain the peculiar fact of the first principle of morality. Undoubtedly, the first principle does not need *justification* on a harm-based account, but it does not follow that it does not stand in need of an *explanation*. Given the metaphysical schema of Aquinas, it follows inescapably that moral principles are explained by the existence of God.

(10) *Other atheists may argue that evolution is all that is needed to account for morality.* But evolution explains how we come to *discover* those moral precepts, *not that we invent* those precepts.[46] The reasoning of these atheists exemplifies the genetic fallacy. At most it proves that our subjective apprehension of morality has biologically evolved, not that moral precepts are illusory or ungrounded in human nature.

Moreover, this chapter recognizes that atheist accounts of morality are objective. It is not concerned about responding to atheists who are subjectivists, nihilists, or relativists, but is directed toward those atheists who recognize the cognitive content of moral truth. Unlike divine command theorists, atheist moral realists have recognized the connection between

44. Nielson, *Ethics Without God*, 54, 126; Sinnott-Armstrong, *Morality Without God?* 46–47.

45. Sinnott-Armstrong, *Morality Without God?* 57, 68, 74, 117, 128.

46. Thomist natural law is compatible with biological evolution; see Boyd, "Thomistic Natural Law and the Limits of Evolutionary Psychology," in Clayton and Schloss, eds., *Evolution and Ethics*, 221–38; Ashley, "The Anthropological Foundations of the Natural Law," in Goyette, Latcovic, and Myers, eds., *Saint Thomas Aquinas and the Natural Law Tradition*, 3–16.

human nature and morality. Following a moral precept is closely linked with cooperating with human nature. When somebody freely chooses an action that corresponds with their nature, they end up doing something purposive—something with future direction (because nature is driven toward a final goal).

Moreover, many atheists recognize that evolution is insufficient for understanding and living the moral life. Walter Sinnott-Armstrong says: "Morality is like physics and mathematics in this respect (though not in many other respects, of course). What evolves are only moral *beliefs* and *attitudes*, not moral *facts* or *truths*. When T Rex ruled, there were no free agents to rape or be raped, but it was still true that free agents ought not to rape other free agents. This moral principle can be true even at times when it does not apply to anyone because nobody could break it."[47] Sinnott-Armstrong makes this argument in response to Christians who think that evolution is incompatible with objective morality.

It has been said that mores should be distinguished from morals. Science can only describe human behavior, not prescribe what actions should be done. According to Mark Murphy, hardly any ethicists today accept "the sociobiological account of morality. And it is obvious why most moral philosophers do not accept this wrongheaded view. If we start only with the facts of evolution—we will never be able to cross the gap simply from a story about how our species in fact evolved to any claims about what we genuinely have reason to favor or promote."[48]

Conclusion

A crucial grasp of Aquinas' metaphysics is necessary for understanding his particular views on sub-disciplines in philosophy such as natural law morality and the philosophy of God. Today many ethicists want to speak about morality without having to assume the metaphysical. Nowhere is this omission of the metaphysical more evident than in the writings of contemporary atheist philosophers and their primary competitors, the divine command theorists.

Thomists can bridge the gap between these two opposing views through their reliance on participation metaphysics. Of course, atheist moralists prematurely conclude that God's existence is not necessary for moral principles. Instead all that is needed is human nature and careful reasoning.

47. Sinnott-Armstrong, *Morality Without God?* 92–93.

48. Murphy, "Theism, Atheism, and the Explanation of Moral Value," in Garcia and King, eds., *Is Goodness Without God Good Enough?* 122.

On the other hand, divine command theorists have not paid enough attention to human nature. Aquinas' Fourth Way can be reformulated to exploit the connection between human nature, objective morality, and the existence of God.

— 6 —

Fine Tuning, Atheist Criticism, and the Fifth Way

PHYSICAL COSMOLOGY IS ONE of the newest and fastest growing fields of science, taking hold of the public imagination at an astronomical rate. Why is this? Cosmologists tackle questions related to the origin of the universe and the fundamental laws of nature. Thus the cosmologist's concerns are often linked to the big questions of human existence: Why are we here? Where did we come from? Philosophers have capitalized upon the fine tuning constants and quantities to formulate a newer teleological argument for God's existence.[1] As a result of this convergence of philosophy and science, the fine-tuning argument has become common in the natural theologian's battery of arguments for God. One can easily get the impression that cosmic design or a dysteleological view of the world are the only two options to take in the current atheism-theism debate.

Like the modern watchmaker argument formulated by William Paley, the argument from fine-tuning should not be confused with Thomas Aquinas' fifth proof for the existence of God. While the former is based on efficient causality, the latter is based upon final causality. As in the case of the moral argument, some atheist criticisms are relevant to the modern philosophical approach to God, but they do not affect Aquinas. After briefly expounding the fine-tuning argument, I will argue that Aquinas' Fifth Way offers a more convincing proof for God—one that evades the most common atheist criticisms leveled against modern design arguments.

---

1. Manson, *God and Design*; Holder, *God, the Universe and Everything.*

The Fine-Tuning Argument for God's Existence

Since the early 1970s scientists have been stunned by the discovery of the delicate balance of initial conditions given at the initial moment of the big bang for the emergence of life in our universe. A slight deviation from any of these values and quantities would have radically altered the fabric of the reality, preventing the emergence of all carbon based life as we currently understand it. As such, we now know that life-prohibiting universes are vastly more probable than life-permitting ones. Not only must each of the fine-tuning constants must be precisely fine-tuned, but the ratios in between these constants be finely-tuned. Since we live on a planet that is already teeming with biological life, the natural theologian argues that the phenomenon of fine-tuning cries out for an extraordinary explanation. Advocates of cosmic design typically cast the argument in the following way: (1) The fine-tuning constants are due to either physical necessity or chance or design; (2) The constants are not due to physical necessity or chance; (3) Therefore, they must be due to design.[2]

These natural theologians are concerned with arguing to design (and not arguing from the very fact of design). For them, the conclusion of the argument entails the existence of a designer. The first premise seems to include all the available options. Notice that in this version of the argument there is an inference to design. Design is considered the tidiest explanation of the fine tuning constants. Other forms of the argument do not take any set of objective criteria that might involve taking inferences seriously. Instead they are content with the fine-tuning constants and quantities resonating with the existence of God—at least more than it would in a mindless, atheist universe. In the second premise the natural theologian seeks to demolish the scientific hypotheses of necessity (i.e., the universe had to exist in a certain way) and chance (i.e., the world we inhabit is one of an infinite number of universes), leaving room only for cosmic design.

Without the fine-tuning constants, the origin of life and its subsequent evolution on earth could not occur. As the theoretical astrophysicist Paul Davies observes,

> The severe mauling meted out to the design argument by Hume, Darwin and others resulted in its being more or less completely abandoned by theologians. It is all the more curious, therefore, that it has been resurrected in recent years by a number of scientists. In its new form the argument is directed not to the

2. Craig, *Reasonable Faith*, 161.

material objects of the universe as such, but to the underlying laws, where it is immune from Darwinian attack.[3]

Thus the notion of cosmic design has come roaring back in the scientific community, at least among theologically minded physicists. Let us now turn to a defense of the second premise.

First, physical necessity is not a likely candidate to adequately explain the fine-tuning constants. In this view the constants and quantities must have the values they do. Once the "Theory of Everything" (T.O.E.) has been formulated, scientists will discover that the universe had to be the way it is. However, one of the central problems with this hypothesis is that many theorists hold that the structure of the universe could have been otherwise. More importantly, the discovery of the T.O.E. would not do away with the need for design, but simply push the issue of fine-tuning back one step: what fine-tuned the grand unified theory to enable the lesser laws of the universe to be the way they are? So the central problem with the T.O.E. would not, and indeed cannot, do away with the question of fine-tuning. Even if the T.O.E. is discovered, it would not eliminate the need to explain the rationality of the universe. Rather it would extol the significance of rationality, pushing the need for explanation back one further step.

Secondly, if there are necessary facts about the universe that must be accepted without reason (so-called "brute facts"), then rationality breaks down and the world is absurd. In other words, what need would there be to do science if there is a grand unified theory? As Davies goes on to say: "It is difficult to be convinced that there are any necessary things in nature. Certainly all the physical objects we encounter in the world, and the events that befall them, depend in some way on the rest of the world, and so must be considered contingent. Furthermore, if something is necessarily what it is, then it must always be what it is: it cannot change."[4] This explains why some theorists have argued that God himself might be the final "Theory of Everything," or why everything in the world has to be the way it is.[5]

On the other side of the first premise is the chance hypothesis. These theorists have argued that "chance" best explains the fine-tuning by invoking the multiverse hypothesis. These objectors often envisage a fluctuation of energy, in accordance with basic quantum theory at the beginning of time, which produces successively all sorts of universes, undercutting the need for an intentional agent.

---

3. Davies, The Mind of God, 203.

4. Ibid., 162–63.

5. Ibid., 171.

But the chance view is problematic for several reasons. Chance is often posited in conjunction with the acausal interpretation of the indeterminacy principle. In this interpretation of the principle, the motion of sub-atomic particles is ontologically without a cause, leaving reality ultimately chaotic and unpredictable. But indeterminacy is an epistemic, and not an ontological, issue. As Robert Russell muses: "We speak of this kind of chance when we do not know, or prefer to ignore, the underlying causal factors—while believing they are there in principle. We could in principle give a complete causal—i.e., deterministic—description of natural processes from the cells to galaxies; we chose a statistical description merely out of convenience."[6] We cannot rule out the existence of causal influences that are currently undetectable. If chance were really a description of ontological reality, then it would inescapably follow that science itself would break down. For science assumes the orderliness of nature.

Closely linked to an acausal view of the indeterminacy principle is the world ensemble, the idea that there are many parallel universes in different dimensions mirroring our own world. Our time-space continuum blistered off one of these unobservable universes. Our world just happens to exist with the properties necessary for life. Although the multiverse hypothesis seems to fly in the face of Occam's razor, unobservable universes are carefully posited in terms of what is already known about our universe. Even with this inductive procedure in mind, many theorists have held that the multiverse remains highly speculative. So speculative, in fact, that theorizing about them will only get more confusing and abstract. As John Polkinghorne writes: "People try to trick out a 'many universe' account in sort of pseudo-scientific terms, but that is pseudo-science. It is a metaphysical guess that there might be many universes with different laws and circumstances."[7]

Nevertheless, even if there were other universes, this would not mean that our universe was not designed. So long as there are not an infinite number of universes, the multiverse does not support the chance hypothesis. Arthur Peacocke explains: "any argument for theism based on 'anthropic' considerations may be conducted independently of the question of whether or not this is the only universe."[8] It is perfectly consistent to believe in an ensemble of universes and a designer. Because every universe would be governed by a different set of physical laws, a designer would still be needed to explain the fine-tuning to account for each of them.

6. Russell, "Does the 'God Who Acts' Really Act in Nature?" in Peters, ed., *Science and Theology*, 85.

7. Polkinghorne, *Serious Talk*, 7; cf. 70.

8. Peacocke, *Theology for a Scientific Age*, 109.

As long as there are a limited amount of universes, design still needs to be reinstated. For, positing an infinite number of universes seems equivalent to the theologian positing God. Davies suggests: "The glaring contradiction with the cosmic selection theory is that it requires an infinity of unseen universes just to explain the one we do see. In this respect it is scarcely an improvement on theism, with its hypothesis of an unseen God."[9]

Yet another problem with the multiverse theory is that there must be at least one "many universes generator" that is responsible for breaking universes off one another. What enables the generator to exist in a certain way to make these baby universes? The answer would have to be a grand designer or some other designed mechanism. As Davies puts it, "this theory [the multiverse] must still presuppose the concept of law, and begs the question of where those laws come from, and how they 'attach' themselves to universe in an 'eternal way.'"[10] By way of summary, we might conclude that the multiverse does not contravene the need for design, but merely pushes it back one step. Although the laws of physics are radically different in these other universes, this would only mean that they need some deeper explanation.

By eliminating the first two options of law and chance, the inference to cosmic design becomes the best candidate for explaining the fine-tuning constants. Because of the inadequacies of the first two options, the modern natural theologian usually opts for the design hypothesis. As the Princeton physicist, Freemon Dyson, memorably said, "As we look into the universe and identify the many accidents of physics and astronomy that have worked together to our benefit, it almost seems as if the universe must in some sense have known that we were coming."[11]

The Designer and Atheist Criticism

Now if something is designed, this means that it was deliberately put together by an intelligent agent. The word "intelligent" is derived from two Latin words, the preposition *inter*, meaning "between," and *lego*, which means "to bring together." According to its etymology, therefore, a designer is an agent who can intelligently bring together and choose between competing

9. Davies, "Is the Universe Absurd?" in Peters, ed., *Theology and Science*, 74.

10. Davies, "The Unreasonable Effectiveness of Science," in Templeton, ed., *Evidence of Purpose*, 53. Elsewhere, Davies, *The Mind of God*, 222, writes: "we still require the same basic structure of the laws in all these universes in order to make sense of the theory."

11. Dyson, "Energy in the Universe," 59.

alternatives. A designer by definition has intelligence. Considering that the laws exhibit design, the designer's fidelity in creating and sustaining the universe in being seems to be upheld.

Not only must the designer of the laws serve as a grounding cause of the laws of the universe, but there must be some kind of analogous relationship between his rationality and the intelligibility of the cosmos. The ground that is responsible for the symmetry of the laws serves as a precondition for cosmologists to rationally investigate the universe. The Creator and creation are both seen as rational. One might argue that if the deep seated congruence of the rationality present in the world find some sort of an explanation, it must lie in some more profound reason. Such a reason would be provided by the rationality of the designer.

With this astonishing conclusion in mind, many atheists have challenged the conclusion of the designer as a theistic God. As it now stands, they argue, we know next to nothing about the designer, let alone that there is only one of them (or how the designer sustains the laws). These atheistic challenges, while unappreciative of what has been concluded, seem to make sense. The designer might not lead one to accept theism (or, to be more precise, to accept a pre-modern theism). Perhaps there are many unknowable designers that are responsible for the laws.

Richard Dawkins adds yet another challenge. He argues that even if a designer exists, then who or what designed him?[12] Since complexity can only be explained by greater complexity, then the designer must also be designed. Though Davies has no theological axe to grind, he agrees with Dawkins' contention: "Simply declaring that God made the world and selected a judicious set of laws offers no real explanation at all. It invites the question of who, or what, made God. Unless one can say why God exists, and how God goes about imposing an order on nature, the explanation is vacuous. Since one corollary of the tenet of *creatio ex nihilo* is that God could have made a different universe, the problem of why God made this universe is acute."[13]

If God's choice to make a certain set of laws within the universe is arbitrary, are we left with cosmic absurdity? On the other hand, if the choice is determined by God's personal nature, then what would determine his nature to make such a choice? While this challenge serves as a backhanded complement to the success of the argument, it also seems that the atheist has exposed a significant weakness in it. Although the atheist critic of cosmic design has unwittingly accepted the notion of design when casting this

12. Dawkins, *The God Delusion*, 109, 120–21, 125, 141, 143, 147, 149, 153, 158.
13. Davies, "Is the Universe Absurd?" 75.

specific complaint against the design argument, she leaves us with another unresolvable challenge: what designed the designer?

Perhaps the most fatal objection is that the cosmic design argument commits the "god of the gaps" fallacy. Since the argument is formulated as a probabilistic case for God, the natural theologian argues that God is the best explanation of the fine-tuning constants. But atheists are quick to point out that such a conclusion is hasty and that science itself proceeds on the assumption that natural causes are always to be preferred over theological ones. Davies observes:

> The central objection to invoking such a being to account for the ingenious form of the universe is the completely ad hoc nature of the explanation. Unless there is some other reason to believe in the Great Designer, then merely declaring, "God did it!" tells us nothing at all. It simply plugs one gap—the mystery of cosmic bio-friendliness—with another—the mystery of an unknown intelligent designer. So we are no further forward.[14]

It is not within the province of science to detect "design" in nature. Science dismisses the notion of formal and final causes and is not concerned with them. Theists might wish to see design in the universe, but the scientist is methodologically constrained to seek natural explanations alone.

The Fifth Way as an Alternative

The modern teleological argument and Aquinas' Fifth Way are similar in that they begin with the ordered structure of nature. Perhaps the greatest strength of the fine-tuning argument is that it generally avoids the abstract philosophical discussions that have characterized the field of natural theology. Today many people are suspicious of philosophy and would rather listen to the voice of science. Notwithstanding the common caricature of science as a "definitive voice," Thomas Aquinas has the resources to combat the challenges of atheists who often play down or ignore the significance of the Fifth Way because of the predominant use of modern design arguments.

Dawkins, for instance, equates the Fifth Way with the modern design argument.[15] Since Aquinas' argument has been exploded because of Darwin's theory of evolution, he affirms that the Fifth Way does not succeed. Consequently, Dawkins' conflation of the two arguments has prevented him from taking Aquinas' proofs more seriously.

14. Davies, *The Cosmic Jackpot*, 200.
15. Dawkins, *The God Delusion*, 79.

One of the main reasons why Thomists ignore modern design arguments is that the argument may deny the soundness of Thomistic metaphysics. The inspiration of the modern teleological argument can be traced back to the philosophy of thinkers such as Bacon, Galileo, Descartes, Hobbes, Boyle, and Locke who devised mechanistic conceptions of material reality. While these thinkers successfully refuted Aristotle's *physics* ("the earth is at the center of the universe"), they unfortunately equated this refutation with a denial of his *metaphysics* (for example, the act-potency distinction). Thus, it follows that any refutation of Thomist metaphysics must come from within the sphere of philosophy, not from science.

Proponents of modern design arguments claim that the particles which constitute the material universe should be understood upon the model of human artifacts. Each part of the artifact has no tendency to perform a specific function in and of itself, but when placed in conjunction with other nonpurposive parts, the final outcome must be given a purpose by an outside designer. As in the case of Paley's watch, each metal part that constitutes the timepiece has no intrinsic tendency to function as part of a watch. Here it is at least possible that the watch could have evolved through random, unpurposive processes. On the latter view, there is no such thing as final causes. Material substances are instead reconceived as microscopic particles, devoid of goal-directedness. But one thing that has remained constant throughout the history of the debate on the modern design argument is the rejection of final causes.

Today many philosophers have embraced a mechanistic view of the world for understanding the nature of scientific explanations. But they differ on whether an outside designer should be invoked for the seeming contrivance of material realities. Natural theologians who follow the lead of Paley have appealed to the existence of an outside designer. Of course, atheists reject that option and instead favor of naturalist explanations. Atheists have also appealed to methodological naturalism in science and believe that the theist prematurely fills in the gap of currently undetectable naturalist causes. Neither camp, however, agrees that the Thomist notion of final causes is inherent to nature. On the contemporary scene, Thomists might be the only theists who deny the "intelligent design" approach in natural theology. Instead the Thomist endorses the goal-directedness of nature as a viable alternative. Let us now turn to a contemporary summary and defense of the Fifth Way.

(1) *Irreducible teleology is immanent to the natural order. Every agent, including natural agents, act for a particular end.* Like the starting point in Thomas' other proofs for God, this premise is said to be evident to human senses. Thomist philosopher John Wippel comments: "In support of this

claim Thomas reasons that it follows from the fact that they always or at least usually (*frequentius*) act in the same way in order to attain that which is best. This shows that they reach their respective end(s) not by chance but by intention."[16] Incidental exceptions due to chance do not lessen the fact that natural beings almost always act in a certain way rather than another. If an agent did not have an end, then there would be no reason for it to act in one way rather than another.

Notice that the focus is not merely on sentient beings, but refers to all beings in creation. Even unintelligent objects act in certain ways because of the final cause immanent to them. "Therefore and a fortiori," Wippel says, "Thomas concludes that natural agents need not deliberate and that nonetheless, they tend to their ends."[17] No agent acts in one way rather than another unless it is already in act. That is why every agent, regardless as to whether it is sentient or not, is determined to exist in a certain way. Thomas does not assume that some things look as if they had been designed or put together by an outside designer, but that all agents act in a certain way even though they do not necessarily know what they are doing.

The reason why premise one is significant is that it shows that things do not happen by chance. For example, every time one combines baking soda and vinegar the mixture fizzles. Vinegar acts in this particular way when it is combined with baking soda. Even before the baking soda is added to the vinegar, it has the predisposition to fizzle rather than acting in some other way.

(2) *But natural agents must be directed to their end by another.* The only alternative to saying that agents are not directed by another is to attribute the cause to chance. But chance merely refers to events which cannot be predicted in advance. We do not know all causal factors involved: "Moreover, we should note that Thomas, following Aristotle, does not regard chance as a being or *per se* but only *per accidens*. Chance is simply our way of referring to a situation in which independently operating causes intersect or collide without any of the particular agents foreseeing that the occurrence will happen."[18]

To give an example of what Aquinas means by chance: a tsunami that kills millions of people might seem like a chance event to innocent bystanders, but if scientists had all the relevant knowledge required to predict its occurrence, then we would be able to save lives before the tragedy happens. A second way to understand chance stems from understanding

16. Wippel, *The Metaphysical Thought of Thomas Aquinas*, 480.

17. Ibid., 481.

18. Ibid., 483.

the intersecting lines of different causal chains. Sometimes when two forces collide an unforeseen consequence occurs, and we call it chance. This is precisely what happens in the process of natural selection. As Wippel says: "If one accepts this explanation of chance events, mere chance can hardly account for the regular and beneficial activity of natural agents, whether we regard that activity as beneficial only for the agents themselves, or also for nature taken as a whole."[19]

If A did not point to or was directed toward B as its natural cause, then there would be no way to say that A could naturally cause B rather some other effect. Notice that this contention would hold true even if there were nothing in creation other than sub-atomic particles without living organisms. Since the particles would not choose for themselves which way to act, their actions must be chosen in advance for them by an extrinsic cause. Unless an intelligence is responsible for the specific actions of the particle (including the way that it exists), then there would be no reason for it to exist in one way rather than another.

(3a) *Therefore, natural agents are directed to their end by an Intelligence.* Aquinas does not refer to irreducibly complex objects that can be explained by either design or chance. He does not affirm that the "scales tip" in favor of the design hypothesis either. No probabilities or analogies are considered by him:

> Aquinas is not saying "Arrows are complex objects made by intelligent beings, and certain natural objects are also complex; so, by analogy, we can infer that they were made by an intelligent being too." Nor is he even saying "Arrows reach their mark because an intelligent being makes them do so; therefore, by analogy, we can infer that anything that aims at a certain end must be made to do so by an intelligent being"—as if the argument were an extremely feeble inductive generalization at all, nor an argument from analogy, nor an argument to the "best explanation." Instead Aquinas' claim is a very strong one; he is saying that an unintelligent object *cannot* move toward an end—unless directed by an intelligence. This is a metaphysical assertion, not an exercise in empirical hypothesis formation.[20]

The goal-directedness of material substances is accounted for by an Uncaused Intelligence. Since noncognitive agents do not explicitly know their own ends, "the only way of accounting for the ability of an end to influence

---

19. Ibid.

20. Feser, "Teleology," 157.

such an agent is to appeal to an inclination which is impressed upon that agent by some intelligent being."[21]

There might be a potential relation between vinegar and baking soda before they come into contact. The only way for the vinegar to have this relation to the action of fizzling is if it exists in some prior intelligence. The relation between two items that does not yet exist in reality cannot reside in material objects, but only in thought. As Norris Clarke explains: "Such a presence, as the term of a relation to a not-yet-existent-future, cannot itself be that of a *real being*. Hence it must be present in some mode of *mental being*, or idea, even though it is not necessarily recognized as such by the immediate agent in which it resides, i.e., in all non conscious agents. . . . The ordering of means to achieve a not-yet-existent end is in fact one of the defining characteristics of intelligence itself."[22] Inanimate objects that do not have knowledge cannot be directed toward an end unless there is some intelligence directing the object in one way rather than another. Final causation can only be made intelligible by a Supreme Intelligence. Therefore final causation in the natural order is made intelligible by an outside Intelligence that directs natural objects to their respective ends.

(3b) *The nature of the Intelligence must be one, simple, unlimited, immutable, eternal, omnipotent, and omniscient.* Earlier I have shown that all the traditional attributes of God follow from the Thomist proofs for God. Feser rightly adds: "When this notion is itself unpacked, all the divine attributes follow. Hence the suggestion that the ordering intellect might be a very powerful but still finite designer (often raised against the 'design argument') or even as an extraterrestrial (as ID [intelligent design] theorists sometimes allow) is also ruled out. The Fifth Way, when worked out, is intended to get us all the way to the God of classical theism."[23]

Advantages of the Fifth Way

In this final section I show the advantages of Aquinas' Fifth Way over modern teleological arguments for God's existence.

For instance, the first strength of the Fifth Way is that it demonstrates the existence of God, not settling for some mere probable argument for a "God hypothesis." In this way, the Fifth Way completely avoids the scientifically based charge known as the "god of the gaps." For Aquinas, probable or improbable arguments do not make sense unless we live in an intelligible

21. Wippel, *The Metaphysical Thought of Thomas Aquinas*, 484.

22. Clarke, *The One and the Many*, 204.

23. Feser, "Teleology," 159.

world with final causes. The terms "probable" and "improbable" only make sense in an ordered universe.[24]

Second, unlike the modern teleological argument, the Fifth Way says something significant about the nature of the First Cause. As Thomas Crean observes: "[intelligent design arguments] would not be equivalent to St. Thomas' fifth way. They can't lead us directly to God. They lead us to a designer, but they don't prove that this designer is God. The designer could be a created spirit, some being immeasurably more intelligent than any human person, but still finite. St. Thomas' fifth way, on the other hand, does lead to God."[25]

Some atheists have argued that unless we know how the laws of physics are conserved, we cannot comment on the designer's nature. Aside from the scientistic frame of mind that seems to be behind this allegation, there is something right and wrong about it. From Aquinas' perspective, we know that the Supreme Governor exists, but not his inner essence—let alone comprehend how he exists or sustains the universe in being. Yet we know this *is* the case. Thus the question of how the universe is preserved in being is impossible to answer.

The infinite causal action upon a spatial and limited universe must itself be a spaceless and timeless act. "If God is invoked as an explanation for the physical universe," says David Kelsey, "then this explanation cannot be in terms of familiar cause and effect."[26] Therefore, it is safe to say that "God's 'productive' and 'causal' relation with the world is strictly unique, and so we are bereft of analogies by which to suggest how God is 'creative.'"[27] If final causes are the result of the Governor's eternal decision to sustain the world, his creative act cannot be subject to the same kind of determinacy that creatures within the universe are subject to. The asymmetric character of the relationship between Creator and the *creatum* cannot be emphasized too much.

A third strength is that the Fifth Way demonstrates one designer, avoiding the curious atheist allegation that the design argument can lead one to accept many designers. Thomists have always had the philosophical capital to respond to the question of polytheism. If there were more than one Unlimited Governor, then there would have to be something that distinguishes the one from the other(s). But there is no way for one infinite

24. Dawkins himself does not hold that God's nonexistence can be proven, but only shown to be highly probable. See *The God Delusion*, 51.

25. Crean, *God is No Delusion*, 43.

26. Kelsey, "The Doctrine of Creation from Nothing," in McMullin, ed., *Evolution and Creation*, 177.

27. Davies, *The Mind of God*, 58. Cf. 68.

being to differ from another infinite unless there is some potential for differentiation inherent in them. But an Undesigned Designer has no limitations whatsoever. Since it has no potential for differentiation, there can only be one of them. The very nature of the Unlimited Governor entails that there can only be one of them.

Fourth, the issue of who designed the designer, while relevant to the fine-tuning argument, is not successful against Aquinas. Since the cosmic design argument is not a metaphysical argument, the proponent of the design argument cannot demonstrate that there is only one designer. Faced with the Thomist argument, the challenge of "who caused God?" is misguided. As atheist philosopher Peter Angeles rightly said: "If God is eternal, then He is uncaused. It would be silly then to ask 'What caused God?'"[28] The point to be underscored is that this objection can be refuted because of Aquinas' underlying metaphysics.

Closely linked to the "who designed the designer?" issue is how God can be simple (noncomposite), given that we live in a complex universe. Though we may speak of the different aspects of a complex universe, the idea of the universe in the mind of the Eternal Governor is not complex. Can we speak of the different facets of his idea in the same way that we can speak of the spatial location and temporal duration of things within the universe? Of course not. The universe is made up of different materials, but the idea of the universe is not made up of different parts. One can have an idea of a hill, but no one can have a hilly idea. One can have the idea of a square, but no one can have a square-shaped idea. As Thomas Crean puts it:

> Professor Dawkins would have been correct if he had stated, not that the designer of a complex product must himself be complex, but rather that a designer must be at least as *perfect*, at least as "rich in his reality" as the thing that he designs. Because he produces it, he must first possess it within himself in a certain way. He must "have" it in an intellectual way, in order to cause it to exist in the material world. In this sense, a designer must have it in an intellectual way, in order to cause it to exist in the material world. In this sense, a designer must have the same "richness" as what he makes. But he need not have the same *complexity*. The idea of a cathedral is as rich as the cathedral, in the sense that it contains, in an intellectual way, all that the cathedral is. But it is much simpler than the cathedral.[29]

28. Angeles, *The Problem of God*, 27.
29. Crean, *God is No Delusion*, 16.

The objection that a simpler being must be less perfect rests upon a simple mistake. Simpler beings are less perfect to the degree that they are material beings. As Crean states: "But when we pass from the material world into the world of knowledge, there is no longer a correlation between complexity and perfection. In fact, the opposite is true; there is a correlation between simplicity and perfection."[30] To be sure, intellectual knowledge is much simpler than sense knowledge. In order to see a million birds, one would need an extraordinary apparatus of vision. But the thought of a millions birds can be conceived (and not imagined) all at once. In the realm of intellectual knowledge, simplicity is a sign of greater perfection, not less.

A fifth advantage is that chance is at least a viable option over against the design argument, but in Aquinas this option is eliminated. The atheist exploitation of chance is a problem only for proponents of the modern design argument. Aquinas admits the reality of chance, but for him it is no substitute for the general tendency of agents to act toward certain ends. Notice that Aquinas does not maintain that everything acts for an end, but only that *agents* act for an end. Aquinas would be fine to allow that certain objects do not have any purpose—in the sense that they are accidental by-products of processes that generally converge toward certain ends.

One can responsibly argue that the fine-tuning argument is not diametrically opposed to Aquinas' proof, but it undoubtedly remains short-sighted without Thomas' metaphysics in the background. God may have directly "designed" the fundamental laws of nature with the built in potential for forming greater compounds of physical elements that would be necessary for biological evolution. These more complex formations of material reality allow for a wide spectrum of further possible outcomes. From the inception of the creation, therefore, a master plan is given by the Creator that eventually ascends through a continuous hierarchy of being.

Conclusion

Thomas Aquinas once said that "a small error in the beginning is a great one in the end." Consequently, this maxim applies in the current theism-atheism debate on the moral argument and the design argument (which is usually engaged by the theistic descendants of Paley on the one side, and Darwin and Hume on the other). Both sides continue to fuel each other's fire because of mutually shared starting points.

One way to help resolve the impasse is to re-introduce the soundness of Aquinas' metaphysics and arguments for God. Although the modern

30. Ibid., 30.

design argument has been reignited in many philosophical circles in recent years, it unwittingly accepts the mechanistic conception of nature that was devised at the dawn of modernity. Notwithstanding the commendable features of these design arguments, it is heavily plagued by problems. Aquinas' Fifth Way can overcome these difficulties and deal satisfactorily with the atheist critiques.

PART THREE

God Reveals Himself in Jesus

— 7 —

For Us and Our Salvation

GIVEN THE ASSUMPTION THAT an infinite, personal God exists, our minds inevitably want to ask: does the nature of God and the human race provide us with defensible reasons to think that God will reveal himself to humans in a special way? If God is likely to reveal himself, what form will this disclosure take? When and where will this special disclosure take place? How will God ensure that his message is accurately understood and preserved? From St. Thomas Aquinas to Richard Swinburne, theists across the ages have attempted to answer similar kinds of questions.[1] Philosophical reflection is able to provide some thought provoking ideas in response to these questions. The Catholic Church's teaching on special revelation corresponds with the expectations that one might anticipate from an infinite, personal God.

Various considerations indicate that the revelatory claims of Christianity and the Catholic Church are consistent with the expectations of a personal God. Though I do not spend much time with the historical evidence in support of the incarnation or the ecclesial attributes of the Church, my argument in this chapter merely posits these doctrines as revelatory truths and shows how they resonate with a certain type of revelation that may be expected from an infinite God. These answers are plausible in their own right and ought to be seriously considered by Jews and Muslims in dialogue with Catholics. It does not seem that other religions' claims on revelation can convincingly match up with the framework of the likelihood of God's message to humanity.

1. See Swinburne, *Revelation*.

119

Types of Revelations

Many religions endorse the existence of an infinite God. All three major monotheistic religions of the world teach that God's existence can be known through the natural light of human reason (Ps 19:1; Rom 1:18–20; Sura 17:44). Whether this bland understanding of God is accessible to persons by an intuition or by philosophical reasoning is insignificant to the Scriptural writers in the different monotheistic religions. They appeal to reasoning (at least of a common-sense kind) that is accessible to all persons. Statistics indicate that the majority of the world's population, whether they are religious or not, believe in some sort of God. Atheism has never been a majority world and life view. Although many of the world's religions tend toward some version of monotheism, their understanding of God is formulated in different ways.

The deistic conception of the natural knowledge of God remains unstable. Typically, deists hold that God exists, but that he remains aloof from the world, unable or unwilling to disclose himself to humanity in any special way. Theists, on the other hand, maintain not only that a transcendent God exists, but also that he is active, purposive, and caring for the human race. In this view, God seeks communion with human beings.

It is easy to see why deists typically deny the possibility of supernatural disclosures from God. Since they emphasize that a perfect God will necessarily create a perfect universe, there would be no subsequent need for this kind of God to "interfere" or "tune it up" again by performing a miracle on behalf of his creatures. A perfectly created universe ought to run on its own steam without any form of divine-human communication. The idea that an infinite, personal God would want to communicate with humanity seems not only possible, but also makes sense with the following concern in mind: what personal being would not want to respond to other persons who are in need of personal attention?

For some deists to argue that God would not want to communicate with the human race because creation must have been perfect seems to diminish the perfect nature of the deity—not enhance it. If a perfect, personal God had enough reason and love to create humanity in the first place, then it seems that he would address and help persons with their most vexing problems about human life. "If God were so cold and detached," says Avery Dulles, "it is impossible to conceive why He would have made the world in the first place."[2] God would try to help those persons that he is responsible for creating in the first place. The Dionysian principle still rings true: a good

---

2. Dulles, *Apologetics and the Biblical Christ*, 71.

person does not remain enclosed within himself, but diffuses his goodness outward for the betterment of others.

Some of the deepest questions that most, if not all, persons ask during their lives include the following: where have we come from?; why do we suffer?; what makes life worth living?; what is good and evil?; who are we?; and what awaits us at death?[3] These common questions stem from our natural inclinations. So, it makes sense that a perfectly good and loving God would want persons to have insight into the answers to these questions. God may intervene in human history to not only identify with human beings but to show them that they have intrinsic dignity and that he cares about them. God may concern himself with giving personal creatures some answers and practical solutions to the kinds of questions that they ask. Although the common person has natural knowledge of God, it makes sense to think that God will bring this vague knowledge of his existence to an even greater fulfillment by revealing himself to persons.

The existence of so many theologies and ways of speaking about God in the world's great religions strongly attests to the fact that humans are not content with merely knowing that God exists, but that they have a longing to know more about God and precisely how life is meant to be lived. Humans ceaselessly search for answers to their problems in the light of the divine. Certainly, it seems to be cruel that God would refrain from providing some sort of human fulfillment that goes beyond the bare knowledge of his existence. Consider for a moment that in this world, real needs can probably be satisfied. If there is a real need for food, then food probably exists. If there is a real need for camaraderie, then friendship can probably be attained. The same principle holds true about human needs with respect to ultimate concerns.

The nature of God and the needs of the human race provide us with good reasons to hope for some kind of divine disclosure. Human action requires some sort of architectonic principle that has the capability of specifically organizing human life around it. As theologian Charles Morerod explains: "As it is impossible to build a house if all workers just keep moving without any global purpose, it is impossible to live a somehow efficient life without a main organizing principle."[4]

God created us with the desire to understand our own identity and other moral truths. Morerod says: "To know the final end matters supremely for all human actions. As long as we do not know it, we can make different kinds of mistakes, that is, substitute the final end with partial ends (a kind

---

3. Vatican II, *Nostra Aetate*, 1.

4. Morerod, *The Church and the Human Quest For Truth*, 5.

of idolatry), or choose the wrong means to reach the final end, or simply refuse God to be our final end."[5] A divine revelation will be able to help persons to focus on their final end in order to help them live in the way they were meant to live. Although it is not necessary for God to reveal himself to humanity, there are nevertheless good reasons to think he would do such a thing in light of the divine nature and the intrinsic needs of humanity.

How many revelations should we expect? What form will this/these revelation(s) take? What time and place will it/they occur? These are some other questions that are worth reflecting upon, and these may be answered before one analyzes the arguments for the different revelatory claims pronounced by the adherents of the world's other monotheistic religions.

If God chooses to communicate with human beings in a special way, we would expect him to meet us on our grounds so that we can understand and respond to him. The message(s) will not take the form of a language or some other communicative means that humans are incapable of understanding. Considering that human persons are constituted with a body and soul, we would expect this revelation to meet us in material and spiritual forms. Conversely, if this special revelatory disclosure from God does not reach us both body and soul, then we would have good reason to question whether it was a revelation. How are we supposed to understand an intelligible message from God unless it reaches us through some physical channel?

It also makes sense to think that this public message to human beings will be supported by miraculous occurrences. "A miracle," says René Latourelle, "is a religious wonder that expresses the cosmic order (human beings and the universe), a special and utterly free intervention of the God of power and love, who thereby gives human beings a sign of the uninterrupted presence of his word of salvation in the world."[6] Miracles can be defined as naturally impossible events. Miracles, then, confirm that the message(s) is not coming from a false teacher, but is from God.[7] Such "naturally impossible events" would greatly assist persons to know that the message(s) is/are coming from God, and not from a religious pretender or a false prophet.[8]

In the case of private revelations, God speaks to each individual to let them know what to do in their circumstances—to steer them toward their final end. Private revelations will not contradict any public revelations. God cannot contradict himself, for he is the source of all truth.

---

5. Ibid., 7.

6. Latourelle, *The Miracles of Jesus and the Theology of Miracles*, 276.

7. For the credibility of miracles, including miracles outside the context of Christianity, see Keener, *Miracles*.

8. See Latourelle, *The Miracles of Jesus and the Theology of Miracles*, 281–98.

But what about the time and place of God's public revelation(s)? Here we can say a few things. It is adequate to maintain that the revelation will have to occur when human persons are able to understand and absorb its contents. God's revelation will not occur at an exceedingly early stage in evolutionary history when human brains are undeveloped. On the other hand, it is likely that a revelation will have to occur at a time and place that will enable the original witnesses or recipients of the revelation(s) to successfully bring the message outward to others. God could also communicate with each nation as it rises and falls, through prophets assigned to those particular people-groups.

Perhaps there will have to be an adequate communication system in the surrounding region where the revelation occurred in order to allow the original recipients to keep the message and its following going. The message is necessary for others to hear, understand, and live out themselves. The revelatory message will be given at a time and place where humans can successfully spread the message to many other individuals. A perfect God will want as many people as possible to hear his answers to their questions and concerns.

Perhaps there will be a reliable oral and written tradition process in the culture where the revelation will occur. The transmission of this revelation in either written or oral forms will be able to satisfy every subsequent generation's questions about it. Furthermore, the original recording of the event ought to be able to withstand critical scrutiny in the modern world. If the revelation occurred thousands of years ago in a very obscure part of the world, then modern individuals should expect to have a convincing amount of evidence for the event to satisfy them to believe in it.

Let us draw some conclusions about the probability of different types of divine revelation(s). First, it makes sense that God will disclose something of himself to humanity. Secondly, it will occur in a form that is conducive to human understanding. So it will arrive through a physical and spiritual channel. Lastly, a revelation will occur at a time and place that is culturally and technologically conducive for humans to propagate the message successfully. In this context, "successfully" means that subsequent generations who are exposed to the message will be intellectually satisfied by the meaning and evidence for that revelation.

How about the amount of revelations? Here one of the reasons why God would reveal something about himself is directly linked to helping persons to become the individuals they were meant to be. Hence it makes sense that we should expect the number of revelations to satisfy every human person's need in reaching his or her final end. Although we could never know how many revelations to expect from God (and this would have to include the number of public revelations), we can safely surmise that there will be a direct correlation between the number of divine revelations and human needs. In a later chapter of this book I discuss and answer the challenges surrounding the number and kinds of revelations by subsuming the problem of invincible ignorance of the Church as a subset of the problem of evil (chapter 14).

Monotheistic Religions and Divine Revelations

Without actually appealing to the historical evidence for the divinity and resurrection of Jesus (the central claims of Christianity), the writing of the Qur'an (Islam), or the whole exodus event (Judaism), one might advance some compelling a priori reasons for accepting the ways in which Christianity in general and Catholicism in particular teaches God's revelation over and against the revelatory claims defended by the world's other monotheistic religions.

All three monotheistic faiths teach that God's public revelatory disclosures have been circumscribed to just a few historical occurrences. However, in Catholicism, divine revelation culminated in the person of Jesus, and is preserved indefectibly through many persons in the Church. A providential God knows in advance how quickly persons can forget, break, or substantially modify his revealed message to humanity. According to Catholic teaching, however, God reveals himself decisively in the person of Christ, and he also provides some means for the transmission of that revelation in the power of the Holy Spirit. Avery Dulles observes: "It is logical to suppose that if God deems it important to give a revelation, he will make provision to assure its conservation."[9] Thus the means for the transmission of God's revelation is found in the Catholic Church itself. Vatican II confirmed this longstanding teaching of the Church: 'In his gracious goodness, God has seen to it that what He had revealed for the salvation of all nations would abide perpetually in its full integrity and be handed on to all generations."[10]

It is difficult to see how the Catholic answer could be more satisfactory in response to the amount of revelations that should be expected from God. More revelations would seem to trivialize Christ's sinless life. Thus the "amount of revelations criteria," is therefore satisfied by Catholic Christianity—one unique revelatory event that is indefectibly preserved and defended

9. Dulles, *Magisterium*, 4.
10. Vatican II, *Dei Verbum*, 7.

by many persons. Judaism is hardly a missionary religion, claiming only thirteen million members. While Muslims were primarily concerned to evangelize Arabia (when Mohammed was still alive), Islam has never been as inclusive and peaceful as Christianity has been in the missionary mandate. In many cases, the condition of Islamic mission work has been to offer peace on the condition of conversion. While Christians have been violent, it is difficult to square forced conversions with the teachings of Jesus.

As far as the time and place of divine revelation goes, Christianity originated in a time and place where the first established road system had been developed. "All roads lead to Rome!" encaptures one slogan of the day. Never before had long distances been easier to travel than in the Roman empire. The newly formed travel system around the Mediterranean basin was able to preserve communication for long distances within a reasonable amount of time. The first Christians began to proclaim the gospel in the city of Jerusalem—a city that was, in the words of Larry Hurtado, "the key initial venue for the proclamation of the christological claims" about Jesus.[11] Hurtado argues that the rapid spread and success of Christianity is due, in part, to beginning in Jerusalem. Like Rome, it had enough safe roads going to and from the city to get the message out at an astoundingly rapid rate.

It is difficult to imagine a religious movement that grew at a faster rate (in the peaceful way) than earliest Christianity did.[12] This point also has apologetic potential for Christianity. As the Jesuit theologian Gerald O'Collins observes:

> A number of "this-worldly" factors, which help explain the propagation of Buddhism, Confucianism, and Islam by the Gautama, Confucius, and Muhammed, respectively, do not apply to Christianity. . . . In these three instances we can point to publicly verifiable causes which furthered the spread, respectively, of Buddhism, Confucianism, and Islam: the long careers of the founders, financial resources, and success in battle. In the case of Christianity, the founder enjoyed none of these advantages: his public career was extremely short, he lacked military and financial support, and his life ended in a humiliating failure and a disgraceful death on a cross. After all this, the subsequent propagation of the message of universal salvation in his name remains an enigmatic puzzle unless we admit a cause (the resurrection) adequate to account for the effect.[13]

11. Hurtado, *Lord Jesus Christ*, 195.

12. Hart, *Atheist Delusions*.

13. O'Collins, *Easter Faith*, 40.

Therefore Catholic teaching on God's revelation in Jesus seems to satisfy the second criteria about the "time and place of revelation." As a religious institution, the Catholic Church has had a huge and beneficial impact on civilization. Both Christians and non-Christians have recently argued that history reveals that Christian beliefs have improved society in the physical, scientific, artistic, social, and political lives of countless individuals. This is a point that will be argued later on in this book (chapters 11 and 12). These studies indicate that Christianity has had much more of an impact on the Western world than either Judaism and/or Islam. Reason alone can legitimately apprehend the change that the Church has had on civilization. We would expect to see these changes, given God's purposes of bringing people together and giving them the answers to their deepest questions when understanding God's special revelatory message(s) to them.

The Catholic Church claims that God will ensure that the teachings of its founder will be faithfully and indefectibly preserved by a reliable body of interpreters. Although Swinburne is not a Catholic, he arrives at a similar conclusion: "if the revelation is to be available to future generations and cultures, God must ensure that in the end, . . . the correct interpretation of the original revelation emerges. The Church must have divine guidance."[14] Without the doctrine of unfailing divine guidance, nobody could ever know (or even say responsibly) in the midst of human error and confusion who is accurately relaying the lessons of revelation or who is supposed to speak on behalf of the Church.

Neither Judaism nor Islam can make this kind of claim, for the divisions within their communities are usually compensated by either political or secular unities of action.[15] Although there are official interpreters in these traditions, neither one of them claims to have ongoing, unfailing interpreters. The doctrine of authoritative interpretation, which is found in the Catholic Church, complements the emphasis that was placed on the building up of community. As people become united to one another, they also agree with one another (and vice versa). Likewise, authoritative and unfailing interpretation is a sign of the unity of the Church. So strong is the love of God for humanity that the message of salvation is offered indefectibly through human means!

With respect to the mode of revelation, I have emphasized that if God were to reveal himself that he would do it in a way that corresponds with human nature. It will appeal to both body and soul. Christianity avoids the extremes: it is not so otherworldly that it forgets the material, and it is not so

---

14. Swinburne, *Was Jesus God?* 75.

15. Blau, *Modern Varieties of Judaism*; Jansen, *Militant Islam*.

physical that it forgets the spiritual. Nowhere is this emphasized better than in the Son of God and then in the transmitter of this revelation, the Catholic Church. "For this reason," says Morerod, "Jesus gathers a community, a structured community, that goes on until the end of time. God acts fully for our salvation, but he associates with his work active human 'instruments': the Church. As human beings are visible (by their body) and have an invisible soul, and since God respects human nature in his dealings with us, the Church then is inseparably visible and invisible. Any saving act of God at least starts building the body of his Church."[16]

In Catholicism, God speaks to persons in human words through the incarnation, and consequently in the life of the Church, with authoritative interpreters of revelation. The Church is thought to have a spiritual and physical aspect. The Church is in the world, but is not of the world.[17] Anyone who notices the details of Catholic worship will almost immediately recognize the emphasis on developing the entire person, body and soul. Catholic worship attempts to unite the bodily aspect of human nature with its spiritual, mystical other-worldly aspect, but still revering both.

Given that an infinite, personal God is the type of God who would want to identify with human beings, it is all the more remarkable that in Christianity one of the divine persons of the Godhead is said to have revealed himself by becoming a human. Whether it is Orthodox, Catholic, or Protestant Christianity, all Christians agree that it was not possible for God to identify with the human race in a more intimate way than when he became man in the person of Jesus, the lowly carpenter from Nazareth. The incarnation serves as a remarkable example of how importantly God esteems and loves the human race. The God-man helps persons to understand the answers to their questions about human identity and morality.

While God could have merely spoken through one or more prophets and remained distant from human beings and creation, Catholic theologians argue that God not only used prophets but that he reached us immediately on our grounds—by becoming one of us. This assuredly reveals the extent to which God cares about humanity and the condition in which we struggle to live. The physical world is not to be shunned, but to be affirmed. The incarnation helps us to recognize the great lengths that God went to get our attention. While God could have used a person to deliver his message to humanity, in the Catholic view God became a person to give us his message and answers to our deepest questions about identity and morality.

16. Morerod, *The Church and the Human Quest For Truth*, 140.
17. Vatican II, *Lumen Gentium*, 8, 13.

According to classical Christian theology, God is a triunity of divine persons.[18] At the heart of the doctrine of the Trinity is a theology which insists that in order for human persons to understand themselves, they must become relational with one another. Trinitarian doctrine, which is found in Christianity alone, provides the means by which Christian apologists can make sense of the legitimacy of other religions and still propose Christianity as the one distinctively true religion. S. Mark Heim asserts:

> the question is whether one faith's sense of the ultimate is such as to allow it to recognize that real (if limited or less than full) relation to that ultimate exists in another tradition, *in terms largely consistent with the distinctive testimony from that tradition itself.* The faith that proves able to do this for the widest possible range of compelling elements from other traditions will not only be enriched itself, but will offer strong warrants for its own truth.[19]

Mono-personal understandings of deity seem incapable of explaining other religions as bearers of divine truth—while remaining true to their unique and distinctive religious claims. While Muslims and Jews have been adamant about God's oneness—a naturally knowable truth—Christianity alone claims to be united on revelatory truths: incarnation, resurrection, and Trinity. These revelatory truths help to make sense of Christian truth (unity) in the face of different religions and life-views (plurality).

Above it was argued that a theistic God is the type of God who may respond to our deepest questions about morality. Although all normally functioning persons are aware of basic moral truths, Catholics and all other Christians affirm with conviction that God's revelation brings human moral awareness to greater fulfillment through the person of Jesus Christ. The sinless and all-holy Christ serves as the model by which all persons are to live out their everyday lives. Moral norms are made much clearer because of Christ's perfectly lived life.

Undoubtedly Judaism and Islam teach that morality and spirituality plays a significant role in the spiritual life. Yet neither religion has stressed the importance of forgiveness and love of neighbor as Jesus did for his followers. Moreover, neither Judaism nor Islam have developed a mystical tradition that easily complements their orthodox beliefs and practices.[20] The mystical traditions of Islam and Judaism stand in an uncomfortable and sometimes a hostile relationship with their orthodoxy.

---

18. O'Collins, *The Tripersonal God*.

19. Heim, *The Depth of the Riches*, 128.

20. Scholem, *Major Trends in Jewish Mysticism*; Weisel, *Souls on Fire*.

Not only has Jesus given the human race clear moral guidance, but the incarnation also reveals that God cared enough about humanity to share our condition and suffer not only with us, but on our behalf. As Swinburne eloquently puts it:

> If we ordinary humans subject our children to serious suffering for the sake of a greater good to others, there comes a point at which it is not merely good but obligatory to identify with the sufferer. Given the amount of pain and suffering which humans endure involuntarily, it seems to me highly plausible to suppose that, even if not obligatory, it would be a unique best act for God to share that sort of life, including the paradigm crisis which humans have to face: the crisis of death. And the sharing needs to be not entirely incognito. The parent needs not merely to share the child's suffering, but to show him that he is doing so. This reason is connected with a number of reasons which Christian theologians have given as to why, even if there was no need for atonement, God might have become incarnate; but it is not quite the same as them . . . by becoming incarnate, God shows us how much he loves us. He manifests his love by getting as close to us in our condition as possible. Under this heading it is appropriate to mention Kierkegaard's parable of the king and the maiden. The king seeks to win the love of the humble maiden, but if he appeared to her as a king he might elicit her love for the wrong reason. So he comes as a servant—not in disguise, for that would be deception, but really becomes a servant.[21]

In correspondence with the questions related to meaning and suffering mentioned above, the Christian view claims that God became a man and suffered for us. Moreover, he suffered one of the most heinous methods of execution in the history of human civilization—Roman crucifixion. This type of God's intervention in human affairs is striking: no matter how much humans suffer, we are never alone: "Never will I leave you; never will I forsake you." No matter what kind of suffering humans might experience, the good news teaches that God cares about our sufferings. While the other monotheistic religions insist on the otherness of the Creator, Christianity holds that God has entered this vale of tears and has suffered on behalf of all in the person of Jesus.

Prescinding from the questions related to identity, morality, meaning, and suffering are questions related to human destiny. The story of Jesus' life and death by execution does not have a tragic ending. Jesus' resurrection anticipates our own resurrections from the dead. When confronted with the

---

21. Swinburne, *The Resurrection of God Incarnate*, 44–45.

ultimate questions about destiny, Catholicism gives historical credence to what will happen when human beings die. If we take the big questions about human destiny seriously, we will inevitably search for clues in history that will enable us to understand some answers about what lies beyond the grave.

Judaism and Islam also teach that all persons will be raised from the dead, but neither religion offers evidence in support of the afterlife. Swinburne confidently reports: "No other of the major (or medium sized) religions is founded on a purported miracle for which there is even a moderate amount of historical evidence."[22] Writing after he had become a theist, Antony Flew said that the evidence for Christian revelation is stronger than what can be found in any other religion: "As I have said more than once, no other religion enjoys anything like the combination of a charismatic figure like Jesus and a first class intellectual like St. Paul. If you're wanting omnipotence to set up a religion, it seems to me that this is the one to beat! . . . Today, I would say the claim concerning the resurrection is more impressive than any by the religious competition."[23]

Conclusion

A God who is in control of human events would certainly not expect persons living in a scientific age to blindly believe in a revelatory disclosure that is supported by weak evidence. Rather, God's message should be able to meet us (persons living in the twenty-first century) on our grounds. Christianity and, specifically, Catholicism, offer historical evidence in support of the answers provided by Christ about human destiny. The next chapters are dedicated to the evidence for Jesus and his resurrection. Islam and Judaism merely posit the bodily resurrection with little or no evidence. The doctrine has been practically abandoned by most contemporary followers of Judaism.[24] Islam merely asserts that the resurrection will happen on the basis of Qu'ranic teaching. By way of summary, Christianity is the only monotheistic religion that can provide modern individuals with some evidence to believe in such a supernatural event.

Catholic Christianity provides excellent answers to humankind's deepest questions about ultimate origins. Apart from the fact that the incarnation can show that God has created humanity with a special place in the cosmos (in comparison with God's impersonal creatures), God's sovereignty is brought to light when the full ramifications of Jesus' resurrection

22. Ibid., 62.
23. Flew, *There is a God*, 157, 187.
24. Levenson, *Resurrection and the Restoration of Israel.*

are spelled out. The human creature is not absurd, but has been dignified in light of the Christ-event. The doctrine of creation out of nothing involves God intending to create the world. If God intended to create, then human beings are not monstrous accidents, but are capable of loving, thinking and being responsible for others in this journey toward the eschaton.

— 8 —

Access to the Historical Jesus

MANY OTHER RELIGIONS COULD survive without their founder, but historic Christianity is based on an individual whom the Church regards as divine. The Nicene Creed brings home the significance of God's historical revelation in Jesus of Nazareth:

> For us men and our salvation he came down from heaven, and by the Holy Spirit was incarnate of the Virgin Mary, and became man. For our sake he was crucified under Pontius Pilate, he suffered death and was buried, and rose again on the third day in accordance with the Scriptures.

Notice the awkward inclusion of Pontius Pilate in the ancient Creed. By mentioning Pilate, the Creed emphasizes that Christianity is based upon events that occurred in human history.

God's personal entry into the world implies that many Christological claims of the Church are, in principle, open to historical investigation. So long as the Catholic faith makes claims about individuals and past events, historians are within their intellectual rights to ask relevant questions about the subject matter to decide whether these events occurred or not.

In the apostolic testimonies of the Church, there is an inseparable union of historicity (horizontal dimension) and theological import (vertical dimension). As the apostle Paul says: "Christ died (the event) for our sins" (the theological meaning). The theological discipline known as Christology involves a knowledge of who Jesus was. At the heart of any apologetic must therefore stand the figure of Jesus. Who did Jesus claim to be? A revolutionary? A cynic sage? A religious prophet? What did Jesus teach concerning himself?[1]

---

1. For some recent scholarship on Jesus' self-understanding, see McKnight and Modica, eds., *Who Do My Opponents Say I Am?*; Grindheim, *God's Equal.*

From Jesus to the Gospels

Most biblical scholars, classicists, theologians, and scholars of antiquity take it for granted that Jesus existed, and do not spend much time on whether Jesus existed.[2] We can set aside the debate on Jesus' existence, and turn to some of the more fruitful discussions that should be addressed. How did Jesus understand himself? Much of the answer to this question will be determined by the way in which one approaches the Gospels.

If one sees a radical break between the event of Jesus and the earliest Church's belief in the risen Christ, then the question concerning Jesus' self-understanding will be difficult to answer. By proposing a divide between the "Jesus of history" and the "Christ of dogma" (Kahler, Bultmann), historians are necessarily prevented from knowing anything substantive about Jesus' life, ministry, and deeds.[3]

In recent years, however, many more scholars have argued convincingly for the reliability of major portions of the Gospels by situating Jesus within the world of first-century Palestine.[4] Distancing themselves from previous generations of scholarship, the majority of scholars today hold that the Gospels are fundamentally trustworthy.[5] The most impressive studies on the historical Jesus in the twentieth and twenty-first centuries reflect significant continuity between Jesus and the Gospels.[6] This conviction is consistent with Catholic theology. For, in Catholic thinking, there is no opposition between the earthly Jesus and the Christ of the Gospels, but substantial unity and continuity. Historical reason and faith can complement and strengthen one another.

Scarcely any contemporary scholars think that the terms "myth" or "legend" are important interpretive categories for understanding the Gospels. E. P. Sanders expresses well the general consensus when he writes: "The dominant view today seems to be that we can know pretty well what Jesus was out to accomplish, that we can know a lot about what he said, and that

2. Even the skeptical scholars, Bart Ehrman and Maurice Casey, have provided a strong case for the historicity of Jesus. See Ehrman, *Did Jesus Exist?*; Casey, *Jesus*.

3. This older trend is discussed by Latourelle, *Finding Jesus through the Gospels*, 19–31.

4. For a defense of the trustworthiness of the Gospels, see Bauckham, *Jesus and the Eyewitnesses*; Boyd and Eddy, *The Jesus Legend*; Keener, *The Historical Jesus of the Gospels*; Dunn, *Jesus, Paul, and the Gospels*.

5. For a discussion on the positive developments in twentieth century scholarship on the reliability of the Gospels, see Latourelle, *Finding Jesus through the Gospels*, 33–45.

6. See, e.g., the multivolume works of James D. G. Dunn, John Meier, and N. T. Wright.

those two things make sense within the world of first-century Palestine."[7] Raymond Brown adds "that extreme positions on either end of the spectrum (no difference, no continuity) have fewer and fewer advocates."[8] When Brown speaks of "no difference" and "no continuity," he is speaking of the degree of change from the "historical Jesus" to "the Christ of dogma."

A variety of factors have encouraged many critical scholars to accept the Gospels as reliable sources of knowledge about Jesus. This confidence was regained as a result of different avenues of research carried out on various levels. According to René Latourelle:

> there is the literary level, with the methods of the School of Forms, . . . and of Redaction Criticism; the theological level, by representatives of the "New Hermeneutic" (Robinson, Fuchs, Ebeling); . . . the formal historical level, by authors concerned with establishing valuable criteria for finding Jesus of Nazareth. . . . All these works came to the same conclusion: finding Jesus through the Gospels, long thought impossible by historical positivism and by the holders of the theology of the kerygma, now may be acknowledged as a necessary and possible enterprise. . . . And so, after two centuries of history, criticism has *made a full turn* We find ourselves, at the end of the venture, before the same initial affirmation: through the Gospels we truly know Jesus of Nazareth (message, action, project and destiny). What a difference, though, between the acritical confidence of the past and the critically proven and laboriously acquired confidence of the present. . . . No matter how complex it may be, the knowledge of this history, far from frightening us, reassures and confirms us.[9]

Latourelle spends a considerable amount of time garnering the arguments in the relevant studies to defend the reliability of the Gospels.

Another major reason for the scholarly turnaround was the critics' identification of the genre of the Gospels and their purpose. Today the Gospels are widely categorized as "ancient biographies."[10] That the Gospel writers describe what they at least think happened to Jesus cannot be denied. The Gospels intend to show that Jesus is the Messiah and the risen Christ. In the positive sense of the term, their intentions are historical.

---

7. Sanders, *Jesus and Judaism*, 2.

8. Brown, *An Introduction to New Testament Christology*, 15.

9. Latourelle, *Finding Jesus through the Gospels*, 17–18, 77–78. Cf. 243–58.

10. Burridge, *What are the Gospels?*

Now the Gospels are not biographical in the modern sense of the term. Unlike modern biographies, they are only concerned with matters in the last two to three years of Jesus' life. The core message of the Evangelists is similar, but each of them identified, understood, and presented the message differently. Perhaps a better way to characterize the genre of the Gospels is to call them "theological biographies." Far from garnering some neutral facts about Jesus, the Evangelists present a kerygmatized history, with its underlying tradition history. They are in the line of ancient Greco-Roman biographies, or Greek and Jewish "historiography."

While some might be troubled by the lapse of time before the Gospels were written down, this "problem" is not as daunting as some skeptics might wish to think.[11] Part of the reason for the delay in writing was due to the gradual emergence of the Church itself. Believers needed to communicate the story and message of Jesus and identify who he was. Jesus was already well known in ancient Palestine. But by the time the Church expanded beyond Israel's borders, there was a new need that had to be addressed:

> The inhabitants of Judea, of Galilee, knew the characteristics, the works, the tragic destiny of Jesus. He had too strongly upset the religious life of the nation to be so soon forgotten. . . . But it was not the same for the pagans, strangers in Palestine and to the faith of Israel. . . . For all of them [read: the Greco-Roman world], to announce the survival of an unknown would have been to lead them to think there was involved some new esoteric doctrine. Typical in this regard is the reaction of the Athenians to the preaching of Paul (Ac. 17:18). Salvation, is too, linked with the historical person of Jesus: it was necessary to present Him. Clement of Alexandria states that Mark wrote his Gospel in response to the express desire of his audience in Rome. The Canon of Muratori states that John wrote his Gospel at the request of the bishops in Asia. . . . One thing is certain, in contact with the pagans, and on being diffused, the Gospel, necessarily, and each day more so, must be related to the person of Jesus. This is why the teaching to the Gentiles has less scriptural arguments and more and more insists on details . . . which enables the placing of Jesus of Nazareth. . . . The Gospels were written to oppose excessive spiritualizing tendencies, which manifested themselves in Corinth, or against the gnosis, that is, against the currents which abandon the earthly and historical figure of Jesus in order to reduce Christianity to a formless doctrine, or one

11. For scholarly treatments on the reliability of oral tradition, see Byrskog, *Story as History—History as Story*; Dunn, *The Oral Gospel Tradition*.

which confines Christian revelation to individual or collective spiritual experiences.[12]

The Gospels were written to promote and defend the identity, teachings, and actions of Jesus against the dangerous drifts of gnosis, myth, and ideology. Hence, one might conclude that the Gospels submit *themselves* to the criteria of historical research.

Another reason why the Gospels were probably not written down earlier is that most people could not read or write at this time. Christianity was a religion concerned with spreading the word of God, and was not about writing. Moreover, oral cultures are not so prone to write as modern day cultures. Consequently, the transmission of sacred oral tradition was highly developed in ancient Palestine.[13] The Evangelists had abundant sources that were passed down to them from the eyewitnesses (cf. Luke 1:1–4).[14]

Apropos the complaint that there is not adequate amount of evidence to construct a full and reliable portrait of Jesus, it should be noted that Christianity began as a humble religion with disciples who were not well educated. Christianity began in a remote location on eastern frontiers of the Roman Empire. Secondly, we know that there were more Christian writings, but they have been lost. Nonetheless, the best posture to take in the light of the amount of sources we have is to interact with them. In terms of practicing ancient history, we are fortunate to have as much documentation as we do about Jesus.

An Implicit Christology

Although most scholars accept the reliability of the Gospels, they are divided on whether the Christology of Jesus was explicit or implicit. The former involves designations or titles that Jesus would have used to identify himself as divine. An implicit Christology would attribute the divine titles of Jesus to early Church usage; yet Jesus' attitudes, teachings, and actions strongly implied an exalted status that was made explicit by his followers.

When people ask "did Jesus call himself God?" they do not realize that the question is awkwardly phrased. Such a question cannot be answered and should not be posed. For, in first-century Palestine, the word "God" was synonymous with YHWH, the Father who dwelt in heaven. Thus the claim that Jesus did not think of himself as God is correct. However, many New

---

12. Latourelle, *Finding Jesus through the Gospels*, 103–5.

13. Ibid., 169–83.

14. Keener, *The Historical Jesus of the Gospels*, 126–62.

Testament critics have argued for an implicit Christology drawn from the pre-Easter ministry of Jesus.[15] The Christological titles ascribed to Jesus in the Gospels serve to express explicitly what Jesus claimed about himself implicitly.

During the time of Jesus, Israel had hoped to be delivered by YHWH (see Isa 52:7–10; Ezek 34:7–16, 22–24). This restoration narrative forms the backdrop for understanding Jesus' identity. For, Jesus was conscious that in himself YHWH was returning to restore Zion (Jerusalem) and renew the covenant. Moreover, it is indisputable that Jesus preached the Kingdom of God, a rare theme in first-century Judaism.[16] The "Kingdom of God" can be defined as God's intervention in the world to liberate Israel from suffering by giving them salvation. Although the Kingdom would eventually make itself known in the future (the restoration), Jesus believed that it had come in himself, and this conviction was expressed by his message, exorcisms, healings, and actions. There is no Jewish precedent for understanding the Kingdom in this way.

Jesus so identified himself with the Kingdom that if anyone wanted to accept the Kingdom, they had to accept him. Here it might be useful for us to outline afresh some of Jesus' teachings, actions and deeds that illustrate his divine status. In Jesus, YHWH was returning to liberate Israel. For instance, his attitude toward the Mosaic Law indirectly reveals his identity. Although Jesus obeyed the law by attending major Jewish feasts, paying the Temple tax (Matt 17:24–27), and wearing the prescribed tassel on his robe (Num 15:38–41; Matt 9:20), he was at odds with some of the religious authorities of his day about correct interpretations of the Mosaic Law. His disagreement with the law reveals his authority over the Mosaic Law.

Jesus clashed with the Pharisees over the issue of the observance of the Sabbath (Mark 2:23–28, 3:1–6; and Luke 13:10–17).[17] The law says that Jews cannot harvest on the Sabbath (Exod 16:25–26; 34:21). Yet Jesus maintained that (Mark 2:27) "The sabbath was made for man, not man for the sabbath." It is also reported that Jesus challenged major portions of Jewish ritual laws. With regard to the law's insistence on purity and hand washing, for instance, Jesus affirmed (Mark 7:15): "Nothing that enters one from outside can defile that person; but the things that come out from within are what defile." Jesus also challenged the Pharisees' common understanding of divorce (Mark 10:2–12; Matt 19:3–12).

Similarly, in a remarkable series of passages in the Gospel of Matthew (Matt 5:17–48), Jesus contrasts what God said to the nation of Israel in the

---

15. O'Collins, *Christology*, 66–67.

16. Meier, *A Marginal Jew*, 2.289–506.

17. Keener, *The Historical Jesus of the Gospels*, 223–37.

wilderness with what he himself commands: "You have heard that it was said to your ancestors . . . . But I say to you." Thus, he deepens and radically internalizes the law by concentrating on the heart rather than the mere outward observance. Commenting on these passages, John Meier affirms:

> Jesus revokes the letter of the Law and replaces it with his own diametrically opposed command. Despite the permissions and commands of the law, there is to be no divorce, no oaths or vows, no legal retaliation. Given the highly Jewish coloration of this material, the claim Jesus makes for the authority of his own word is astounding. . . . As regards the Law and authority over it, Jesus stands where God stands. In a Jewish or Jewish-Christian context, a higher status could not be imagined.[18]

Jesus regarded himself as authoritative over the law by issuing a new understanding of it in such a way that made him not only superior to Moses, but literally equal to the God of Israel.[19]

Another area where scholars have reached something of a consensus pertains to Jesus' authority to forgive sins (Mark 2:5, 10; Luke 7:48) independent of the location of the Temple. Such declarations must have been perceived by first-century Jews as blasphemous. By showing authority in the forgiveness of sins, Jesus stands and speaks in the very place of God.[20] Since the exile was seen as a result of Israel's sin, Jesus' pronouncement of the forgiveness of sins indicates that Israel was being reconstituted in and through his presence and works. In this way, Jesus saw himself as the new Temple, bringing salvation to Israel. Jesus did not require formal repentance, sorrow for sins, or any other sacrificial act (cf. Mark 2:1–12). He forgives sins on the basis of his own authority, and sought out table-fellowship with tax collectors and sinners.

Another way that Jesus helped to inaugurate the Kingdom was through his miracles and exorcisms.[21] A series of convergent clues in the New Testament has led many scholars to accept the historicity of what the earliest disciples interpreted as miracles. Jesus' miracles take up so much room in the Gospels that it becomes difficult to accept his teachings without also accepting his miracles. In Mark's Gospel, 209 out of the 666 verses speak

---

18. Meier, *The Vision of Matthew*, 64.

19. Neusner, *A Rabbi Talks with Jesus*, 30–32.

20. Kasper, *Jesus the Christ*, 102.

21. The notion that miracles can occur will naturally assume that a personal God exists. For the credibility of miracles, see Latourelle, *The Miracles of Jesus and the Theology of Miracles*; Keener, *Miracles*.

about Jesus' miracles. If the miracles were excised from the Gospel of John, the overall message would vanish.[22]

The reported miracles of Jesus are multiply attested. They appear in the Gospel of Mark. These miracles also appear in the other canonical Gospels, as well as other miracles that do not appear in Mark (Matt 8:5–13; Luke 7:1–10). Within the Gospels, the miracles appear in different literary genres: disputes (Mark 2:1–12; John 9:1–41), summaries (Mark 6:12–13), and discourses (John 6:11). The miracles appear in the primitive kerygma as retained in the book of Acts[23] (2:22; cf. 10:37–39): "You who are Israelites, hear these words. Jesus the Nazarean was a man commended to you by God with mighty deeds, wonders, and signs, which God worked through him in your midst, as you yourselves know."

Other sources for establishing the miracles of Jesus would be the Letter to the Hebrews (2:3–4), the apocryphal gospel of Thomas, and the writings of Josephus.[24] A passage in the Babylonian Talmud also refers to Jesus' thaumaturgic activity: "On the eve of the Passover, Yeshua was hanged. For forty days before the execution took place, a herald went forth and cried: 'He is going forth to be stoned because he practiced sorcery and enticed Israel to apostasy.'"[25] Notice that the passage says that Jesus was "hanged" because of his "sorcery." This is an obvious reference to Jesus' miracles and healings.

Further, it becomes difficult to explain how Jesus could have generated a faithful following—and generated controversy—unless the miracles occurred. For, Jesus' preaching and actions were intimately related to one another: "He went around all of Galilee, teaching in their synagogues, proclaiming the gospel of the kingdom, and curing every disease and illness among the people" (Matt 4:23). Jesus publicly displayed his wonders and exorcisms; those who did not believe in him could have challenged the veridicality of the miracles. But, as a matter of fact, no one seems to have denied Jesus' miracles. "What they challenged was not his activity as wonder-worker but the authority he claimed for himself on the basis of it [cf. Mt 12:22–32]."[26]

---

22. The first twelve chapters of John's Gospel are often referred to as the "book of signs."

23. It is a relatively uncontroversial that the creedal statements embedded in the book of Acts can be traced back to within a few years after Jesus' death; see, for example, O'Collins, *Interpreting Jesus*, 109.

24. For an account, see Latourelle, *The Miracles of Jesus and the Theology of Miracles*, 56–58.

25. Found in Sanhedrin 43a. Cited in Latourelle, *The Miracles of Jesus and the Theology of Miracles*, 55.

26. Ibid.

In sum, one of the most widely accepted fact about Jesus is that he performed what his contemporaries perceived as miracles: "Even the most critical historian," Luke Johnson states, "can confidently assert that that a Jew named Jesus worked as a teacher and wonder-worker in Palestine during the reign of Tiberius."[27] John Meier concurs: "The statement that Jesus acted as and was viewed as an exorcist and healer during his public ministry has as much historical corroboration as almost any other statement we can make about the Jesus of history. Indeed . . . it has much better attestation than many other assertions made about Jesus, assertions that people often take for granted."[28]

Jesus' self-designations also attest his divine nature. References to the "son" (Mark 12:1–12, 13:12; Matt 11:27) seem to imply Jesus' claim to a unique relationship with the Father.[29] Although Mark's presentation of the parable of the vineyard seems to have undergone some allegorical developments before being written down, the general thrust of the teaching probably goes back to Jesus. In the parable, "the son" is not vindicated after his death. So, it is strange that Mark would not include a vindication of the son, especially given the post-resurrection milieu in which the early Church emerged. The story does not make sense without the inclusion of the son. Hence the title probably did not emerge as an accretion to the original story, but probably goes back to Jesus himself.[30]

Apropos of the saying in Mark 13:32, "But of that day or hour, no one knows, neither the angels in heaven, nor the Son, but only the Father," it is unlikely that Mark would have included Jesus' ignorance in the saying unless the statement goes back to Jesus. The criterion of embarrassment attests to the authenticity of the saying. Brown concludes that these Synoptic passages, including Matthew 11:27, provide valuable evidence, making it "*likely that Jesus spoke and thought of himself as 'the Son,' implying a very special relationship to God that is part of his identity and status.*"[31]

Likewise, one expression that reinforces the essence of Jesus' claim to have a unique relationship with God is the word *abba* (Mark 14:36; Rom 8:15; Gal 4:6). Very few scholars would dispute the authenticity of Jesus' use of *abba*. This Aramaic word is preserved in the New Testament (which were written in Greek) to emphasize how endearingly Jesus addressed God

27. Johnson, *The Real Jesus*, 123.

28. Meier, *A Marginal* Jew, 2.970.

29. The reference to the "son" in the Mark 12:1–12 is also mentioned in the apocryphal gospel of Thomas.

30. Keener, *The Historical Jesus of the Gospels*, 283–87.

31. Brown, *An Introduction to New Testament Christology*, 89.

in prayer. Jesus spoke with God in the same way that a child would speak with his or her dad.

Many scholars have debated the significance of the title, "Son of Man," for understanding Jesus' identity. Raymond Brown says that the title appears in all four Gospels (eighty times), and is expressed in fifty-one sayings (some of these sayings appear in a collection of Jesus' sayings called Q).[32] Undoubtedly, the "Son of Man" is Jesus' favorite self-designation. In the Old Testament, the term refers to humanity in general (cf. Num 23:19; Job 25:6; Ps 144:3), or it can be used to identify a prophet (Ezek 2:3–6, 3:1, 4:16, 5:1, 6:2).

In Daniel 7, the phrase is used either as a symbol for Israel or for a person who will represent the people of Israel. By the time of Jesus, many Jews were interpreting Daniel's "Son of Man" as involving a human being who would be enthroned, glorified, and judge Israel and her enemies (cf. 1 Enoch 37–71; 4 Ezra 13). Given this newer interpretation, some even saw the Son of Man as being equal to the God of Israel. Critical scholars have argued that Jesus drew from this apocalyptic tradition, and deepened its meaning by applying the term to himself.

In Mark 14:61–62, Jesus is on trial and asked a question by the high priest: "Are you the Messiah, the Son of the Blessed One?" Jesus' answer highlights the apocalyptic terms that are involved with the Son of Man. "I am; and you will see the Son of man seated at the right hand of the Power and coming with the clouds of heaven." Considering that this "prophecy" went unfulfilled (the high priest never saw Jesus sitting at the right hand of God), it was probably not something that the earliest Church fabricated out of nothing. As indicated by Brown: "If Christians produced such a statement post-factum, presumably they would have clarified it."[33]

It is increasingly acknowledged that another early Christological title for Jesus is the "Messiah." Israel's hope for the Anointed One (the *mashiach*) had revived in the centuries before Jesus.[34] By the time of the earliest Christians, the title *Christos* (the Greek word for Messiah) is so closely connected with the name "Jesus" that Paul practically uses it as a surname: "Jesus Christ" (or, in less frequent cases, "Christ Jesus").[35] The opening lines of Mark's Gospel read: "The beginning of the gospel of Jesus Christ [the Son

32. Ibid., 90.

33. Ibid., 99n157.

34. There were a variety of expectations as to how the Messiah would intervene on Israel's behalf. See Brown, *An Introduction to New Testament Christology*, 155–61.

35. In Romans 1:1–4, Paul cites an ancient creedal formula that mentions "Jesus Christ." Some critical scholars believe that this creed can be traced back to the 40s. Also relevant is Paul's recitation of another creed: 1 Corinthians 15:3–5. See Brown, *An Introduction to New Testament Christology*, 79n109.

of God]." John's Gospel also closes with an explanation for its composition (20:31): "But these are written that you may [come to] believe that Jesus is the Messiah, the Son of God, and that through this belief you may life in his name." The primary question is whether the early Christians (those who follow the "Christ;" cf. Acts 11:26, 26:28; 1 Pet 4:16) fabricated this title or whether it goes back to the earthly lifetime of Jesus.

It is difficult to see why the earliest Christian communities would have taken it upon themselves to assign the title "Messiah" to Jesus.[36] A plausible alternative is that Jesus had a messianic sense of his own identity. The Gospels unambiguously teach that Jesus was aware of his Messiahship (see Mark 8:27–29; Matt 16:15–23; Luke 9:18–20; John 1:19–27). Mark reports that Jesus asked the disciples: "Who do people say that I am?" They said in reply, "John the Baptist, others Elijah, still others one of the prophets." And he asked them, "But who do you say that I am?" Peter said to him in reply, "You are the Messiah. Then he warned them not to tell anyone about him." Jesus' strange warning is used by Mark to inculcate in them a deeper meaning of the Messiah than what was current: the Son of Man must suffer and be raised from the dead (Mark 8:31; Matt 16:20–21; Luke 9:20–24).

Moreover, all four Gospels closely link Jesus' Messiahship with a title that was mockingly put on the cross: the "King of the Jews" (Mark 15:32; Matt 27: 11, 17, 22; Luke 23:2; John 19:3, 19–21). This title is probably authentic; there is no indication that Christians called Jesus the "King of the Jews" during his lifetime. Thus the criterion of dissimilarity seems to increase the likelihood of its historicity. In this very way, Jesus provided the grounds for his own death sentence from both Jewish authorities (blasphemy) and the Romans (treason and sedition). Walter Kasper explains the significance of this title: "There can be little doubt of the authenticity of the inscription on the cross, and this allows conclusions about the course of the trial. . . . It can be concluded with fair probability, therefore, that before the Council Jesus was forced to declare himself the Messiah."[37]

Jesus never understood himself as the Messiah in the way that Second Temple Jews probably understood that term. He had no intentions of establishing an earthly kingdom and serving as its ruler, or conquering the Romans. "Parodoxically," says Brown, "this attitude points to a higher christology than if he regarded himself as fitting all that was generally expected of the Messiah."[38]

---

36. An acceptance of the post-resurrection experiences does not automatically render Jesus as the Messiah. For a Jewish scholar's defense of Jesus' resurrection, see Lapide, *The Resurrection of Jesus*.

37. Kasper, *Jesus the Christ*, 106.

38. Brown, *An Introduction to New Testament Christology*, 80.

For these obvious reasons, practically no scholar denies that Jesus was executed as a messianic pretender. This fundamental event is not only widely reported in the New Testament (1 Cor 15:3; Gal 3:1) and non-canonical sources (Ignatius of Antioch and gnostic writings), but is also mentioned by Josephus, Tacitus, Lucian, and Mara ben Serapion.[39] Affirming that Messiah Jesus was crucified on a cross did not make things any easier for the earliest Christians in the attempt to convert the Jews and Gentiles. And, it is clear that they preached "Christ crucified" (1 Col 2:2). On the basis of these two factors (the crucifixion is independently attested by early sources, and it is embarrassing), the crucifixion may be considered historically certain. Johnson concludes: "The support for the mode of his death . . . is overwhelming: Jesus faced a trial before his death, [and] was condemned and executed by crucifixion."[40] Gerd Lüdemann adds that: "Jesus' death as a consequence of crucifixion is indisputable."[41]

Early Devotion to Jesus

Those who deny that Jesus made any special claims about himself (or that he did not engage in any acts that implied his divinity), must explain how the earliest Church came to suddenly and sincerely *worship* Jesus and God together.[42] The earliest Christians infused belief in one God with a definitive, new meaning at an exceptionally early date (Rom 3:28–30; 1 Cor 8:1–6). As Richard Bauckham affirmed: "With the inclusion of Jesus in the unique identity of YHWH the faith of the Shema is affirmed and maintained, but everything the Shema requires of God's people is now focused on Jesus. Exclusive devotion is now given to Jesus, but Jesus does not thereby replace or compete with God the Father, since he himself belongs to the unique divine identity."[43]

The earliest Christology was accompanied by a particular pattern of liturgical worship. This pattern of worship strongly implies the divinity of Jesus. In a powerfully argued study on early devotion to Jesus, Larry Hurtado lists and defends six cultic actions in the earliest worship practices that

39. One of the best scholarly treatments on ancient non-Christian sources for understanding Jesus is Van Voorst, *Jesus Outside the New Testament.*

40. Johnson, *The Real Jesus,* 125.

41. Lüdemann, *The Resurrection of Christ,* 50.

42. For more on the antiquity of devotion to Jesus, see Bauckham, *Jesus and the God of Israel;* Dunn, *Did the First Christians Worship Jesus?;* Hurtado, *One God, One Lord;* Hurtado, *How on Earth Did Jesus Become a God?;* Hurtado, *Lord Jesus Christ.*

43. Bauckham, *Jesus and the God of Israel,* 106.

should be distinguished from Jewish worship practices. Although there is some precedent and analogy between the two, the earliest Christians took worship one step further by giving Jesus cultic devotion—the best indication that Jesus was seen as divine.

Hurtado outlines and discusses the following cultic practices which can be found in Paul's letters: (1) Prayer was offered to God *through* Jesus Christ (Rom 1:8); (2) in the Church's rituals, Jesus was invoked and confessed (this implies that Jesus was given a divine status); (3) Jesus' name was invoked in the ritual of baptism; (4) The association of Jesus with the Lord's Supper connotes that he was a living divine power who owns the meal and presides over it. These were novel practices, especially considering that it was celebrated in contradistinction to the cult meals of the pagan gods in Roman religion; (5) In the early Church's hymns, the Christians literally sang to Jesus by using Old Testament Psalms, interpreted Christologically; (6) The use of prophetic speech in the context of Christian worship was seen and experienced as the voice of the risen Jesus.[44] Such devotion to Jesus, says Hurtado "erupted suddenly and quickly, not gradually and late, among first century circles of followers."[45]

Noting that there was nothing in Judaism to compel the first Christians to fabricate such cultic actions, early devotion was characteristically expressed in terms of Jesus' special relationship to God, and in conjunction with God's action in the world. This is attested by Paul's belief in Jesus' pre-existence, which denotes that Jesus' very being lies exclusively in God, and that his appearance in history corresponds to his role in the redemption of the human race (Col 1:16).[46]

On the one hand, Second Temple Jews viewed YHWH as the only sovereign being. On the other hand, Christians saw Jesus as sovereign. While YHWH has a unique divine name in the Old Testament, so Christians also give Jesus the same unique name. Bauckham concludes:

> if we attend carefully and accurately, on the one hand, to the ways in which Second Temple Judaism characterized the unique identity of the one and only God and, on the other hand, to what New Testament writers say about Jesus, it becomes abundantly clear that New Testament writers include Jesus in the unique identity of the one God. They do so carefully, deliberately, consistently and comprehensively, by including Jesus in precisely

44. Hurtado, *One God, One Lord*, 100–114.

45. Hurtado, *Lord Jesus Christ*, 2.

46. For more on the early Church's belief in the pre-existence of Jesus (which implies Jesus' divinity), see Gathercole, *The Preexistent Son*.

those divine characteristics which for Second Temple Judaism distinguished the one God as unique. All New Testament Christology is, in this sense, very high Christology, stated in the highest terms available in first-century Jewish theology.[47]

Lastly, Jews held that God was to receive exclusive worship, not worship alongside other pagan deities. But the first Christians exclusively worshipped Jesus (alongside God the Father, and the Holy Spirit[48]). No other gods in the Greco-Roman world, according to early Christianity, deserved honorable worship.

The single biggest distinction in earliest Christianity was its insistence on worshipping a human being. This in itself was a huge mutation and also has no parallel, let alone linguistic parallel, in Judaism: "in what became the dominant view, Jesus' real human and historical reality remained as crucial as the heavenly glory that he was believed to share."[49] Moreover, there is hardly any indication that there was "any controversy or serious variance about this exalted place of Jesus among the various other Christian circles with which he was acquainted."[50]

Second Temple Judaism forbade the apotheosis or divinization of human persons. This makes the phenomenon of early devotion to Jesus all the more remarkable. As Bauckham writes:

> When New Testament Christology is read with this Jewish theological context in mind [a strictly monotheistic context], it becomes clear that, from the earliest post-Easter beginnings of Christology onwards, early Christians included Jesus, precisely and unambiguously, within the unique identity of the one true God of Israel. They did so by including Jesus in the unique, defining characteristics by which Jewish monotheism identified God as unique.[51]

The worship of Jesus was not in competition for the devotion given to God, but both were included by believers. Earliest devotion to Jesus was not possible by "applying to Jesus a Jewish category of semi-divine intermediary status, but by identifying Jesus directly with the one God of Israel, including

---

47. Bauckham, *Jesus and the God of Israel*, 32.

48. Dunn's major contribution demonstrates that early worship was always directed to Jesus, the Father, and the Holy Spirit. See Dunn, *Did the First Christians Worship Jesus?*

49. Hurtado, *How on Earth Did Jesus Become a God?* 55.

50. Hurtado, *Lord Jesus Christ*, 135.

51. Bauckham, *Jesus and the God of Israel*, ix.

Jesus in the unique identity of this one God."[52] What made earliest Christianity unique is that, unlike the Jews, they introduced a binitarian pattern of worship directed to God and Christ. Such a pattern of worship was seen as heretical, because it contravened the prayers, hymns, and devotion reserved for the God of Jewish biblical tradition.

With all of this historical evidence in mind, who did Jesus think he was? What kind of person would say and do the things that he did? As we have seen, Jesus proclaimed that he was the divine embodiment of the Kingdom. He had an intimate relationship with God (*abba*), and claimed to have the authority to change the Mosaic Law. He imparted forgiveness to sinners, and initiated table fellowship with some of the outcasts of his day. Jesus is God's unique son (Mark 12:1–12), and he has unique knowledge of the Father (Mark 13:32). His wonder-working and exorcisms characterized his ministry, and as a result he was able to gather a group of disciples around himself. Calling himself the "Son of Man," Jesus shared in God's glory and sovereign rule over the nations. In early Christianity, Jesus was being worshipped as the risen Christ. Thus Sigurd Grindheim concludes:

> The Jesus who emerges then is a Jesus who said and did what only God could say and do. His claims are unmatched by Jewish expectations of the Messiah, by Jewish ideas regarding the glorious characters of Israel's past, the most exalted of the angels, and even the heavenly Son of Man. According to the contemporary Jewish sources, these divine agents do not engage Satan directly, and they do not inaugurate the new creation. They do not forgive sins, and they do not autonomously pass the ultimate, eschatological judgment. They do not pit their own authority against the authority of the word of God. Nor do they demand a loyalty that takes precedence over the commandments of God.[53]

Hellenization and the Historic Christ

While many critical scholars firmly maintain that the New Testament offers a reasonably accurate portrait of Jesus, every so often there are critics who challenge the origin of belief in the divinity of Jesus. Bart Ehrman, for instance, tries to undercut the case for Jesus' unique identity by laying out some evidence to suggest that in pre-Christian Judaism there was

---

52. Ibid., 3.
53. Grindheim, *God's Equal*, 220.

no absolute divide between God and created realities.[54] Instead there was a continuum of deities, graded by a pyramid of power and grandeur.[55] As a result, he affirms that belief in Jesus' divinity came about as a gradual evolutionary development after his death. This development was fostered by theological reflection in the earliest Christian communities, not by the teachings of Jesus.

At most, Ehrman says, Jesus may have been understood as divine in the same way that other human beings were deified in the ancient world (Emperor Augustus was said to be deified after his death, and Moses was declared to be a god by the philosopher Philo), but he was definitely not equal to God.

Now, anyone who lived around the Mediterranean world would have known about the worship of other deities. Paul himself shows an awareness of these deities (1 Cor 8:5–6). It follows that the primary issue is how one should relate belief in these gods to the relevant New Testament passages. Part of the problem with Ehrman's hellenization thesis is that belief in Jesus should be understood within the context of Second Temple Judaism. Although Hellenic ideas affected the language, political structure, arts, architecture, entertainment, and intellectual life of Jewish society, it rarely affected the latter's underlying religious and philosophical culture.[56]

The antiquity and rapid speed with which early devotion arose in Christianity devastates Ehrman's reconstruction of earliest Christianity. Hurtado notes: "The named disciples who made up Jesus' own entourage (men and women) were all Jews from Roman Judea (mainly Galilee, it appears)", and even when the evidence comes from Paul's letters, "the named figures . . . are mainly fellow Jewish Christians."[57] He concludes: "It is simply not very credible, therefore, to allege influence of the pagan religious environment as the crucial factor generating devotion to Jesus as divine."[58]

Critical scholars have long recognized that some parallel elements between different sources does not automatically mean that there is a causal relationship between them. One should recognize that there are similarities and differences between parallel sources, and not merely highlight the similarities between them.[59] As a case in point, the worship of a crucified and risen Messiah was utterly unique at the time, and was scandalous to both

54. Ehrman, *How Jesus Became God*.

55. Ibid., 43.

56. Boyd and Eddy, *The Jesus Legend*, 91–132.

57. Hurtado, *How Earth Did Jesus Become a God?* 38–39.

58. Ibid., 41.

59. Boyd and Eddy, *The Jesus Legend*, 133–64.

Greeks and Jews alike. So, if Christian ideas about Jesus were so compatible with the religions of the day, then why did the Jews flog the apostle Paul (2 Cor 11:24)? Luke reports that the Greek philosophers laughed Paul out of the Areopagus (Acts 17:32). It seems unlikely that, if the Christians tried a syncretistic experiment with other religions, they would have experienced as much persecution as they did.

A much more likely scenario is that early Christianity reconfigured Jewish monotheism. This is why some scholars have used the phrase, "christological monotheism," to describe the innovative Christian inclusion of Jesus with God. These scholars have demonstrated that Jews were strict about their belief in one God.[60]

How, then, should one understand the status of intermediary figures in pre-Christian Judaism? Jewish thought allowed for honorific titles that should be given to angels (see Metatron) and exalted humans (Enoch). These figures, per Judaism, were not depicted as divine beings, but were seen as aspects of God's reality (Word, Wisdom, and Logos). Still other figures were merely seen as creatures exalted by God (angels, patriarchs).[61] They still retained their status as creatures. None of these nuanced views of the intermediary figures blurred the very sharp line that Jews made between the worship that was reserved for God alone and all other creatures.

Conclusion

When the historical quest for Jesus was re-launched in the middle of the twentieth century, many critical scholars renewed their commitment to approaching the Gospels from an historical standpoint. Critical scholars began to produce major studies on the historical Jesus. These studies are important for apologetics because they help to improve the credibility of Christian faith. At the center of these works stands the unique character, teachings, and person of Jesus.

---

60. Hurtado, *One God, One Lord*, 17–39; Hurtado, *Lord Jesus Christ*, 29–52; Bauckham, *Jesus and the God of Israel*, 1–59.

61. Bauckham, *Jesus and the God of Israel*, 3, 13–17.

— 9 —

Resurrecting Jesus and
Critical Historiography

How do Christian apologists verify the identity and teaching of Jesus? Traditionally apologists have furnished arguments for his divinity and well-founded faith in his resurrection from the dead. In the earliest Christian communities, Jesus' resurrection was seen as God's stamp of approval upon Jesus' teachings (Rom 1: 3–4). Viewed in this way, the case for the resurrection helps to vindicate Jesus' claims about himself. The resurrection intensifies the belief that Jesus had a unique relationship with God.

The main evidence for the resurrection is usually understood to consist of a series of post-mortem appearances, the empty tomb, and the origin of the earliest disciples' belief in and worship of the risen Christ. Gary R. Habermas has developed what is called the "minimal facts approach" to defending the resurrection. According to Habermas, there are twelve reported facts that have been accepted by the majority of critical scholars:

> (1) Jesus died due to the rigors of crucifixion and (2) was buried. (3) Jesus' death caused the disciples to despair and lose hope. (4) Although not as frequently recognized, many scholars hold that Jesus was buried in a tomb that was discovered to be empty just a few days later.
>
> Critical scholars even agree that (5) at this time the disciples had real experiences that they believed were literal appearances of the risen Jesus. Because of these experiences, (6) the disciples were transformed from doubters afraid to identify themselves with Jesus to bold proclaimers of his death and resurrection, even being willing to die for this belief. (7) This message was central in the early church preaching and (8) was especially proclaimed in Jerusalem, where Jesus had died shortly before.

As a result of this message, (9) the church was born and grew, (10) with Sunday as the primary day of worship. (11) James, the brother of Jesus and a skeptic, was converted to the faith when he also believed he saw the resurrected Jesus. (12) A few years later Paul, the persecutor of Christians, was also converted by an experience that he, similarly, believed to be an appearance of the risen Jesus.[1]

Habermas wants scholars to begin with the conclusions set by the scholarly consensus: "one of my interests is to ascertain if we can detect some widespread directions in the contemporary discussions—where are most recent scholars heading on these issues? Of course, the best way to do this is to comb through the literature and attempt to provide an accurate assessment."[2]

The "consensus" is known from the conclusions set by most scholars who study the subject, including conservative and liberal scholars. In his ambitious article: "Resurrection Research from 1975 to the Present: What are Critical Scholars Saying?" Habermas explains how he is able to determine what counts as the consensus. In Habermas' words: "Since 1975, more than 1400 scholarly publications on the death, burial, and resurrection of Jesus have appeared. Over the last five years, I have tracked these texts, which were written in German, French, and English. Well over 100 subtopics are addressed in the literature, almost all of which I have examined in detail."[3] By cataloguing the major trends in the field, Habermas wants everyone in the debate to begin with the same basic evidence. This chapter will not only posit the best attested evidence, but also defend the reasons why the majority of scholars have come to accept it.

Jesus' Resurrection and Critical Historiography

Professional historians recognize that historiography is not concerned with pronouncing mathematically certain conclusions about the past. Rather, it aims to establish probable conclusions about the past. Some events are much more likely than others. Various considerations show that the argument of this chapter constitutes a probabilistic case for the resurrection. First, in any attempt to establish and describe a past event, historians must (1) choose which sources should be used, (2) interpret them within the context in

---

1. Habermas and Flew, *Did Jesus Rise from the Dead?* 19–20.

2. Habermas, "Resurrection Research from 1975 to the Present," 135–53.

3. Ibid., 135.

which they were composed, and (3) then explain how they came about in the form in which they did.

The fact that unknown evidence could alter the historical argument for the resurrection, or that we do not have absolute certainty when it comes to understanding each piece of evidence, or that there is a supernatural component to the resurrection itself, does not mean that historians and other critics should refrain from using the evidence that is currently at their disposal. We will garner the relevant evidence from the New Testament and then attempt to account for it. The resurrection claim proceeds on the assumption that other hypotheses are rational, but that they are not as rationally warranted as the Christian hypothesis.

As far as (1), the choice of sources, goes, there may be as yet unknown evidence that could, in theory, radically alter either the overall balance of the evidence or one's understanding of the evidence. Consequently, historians should not make hard apologetic claims in the light of this possibility. But the fact that unknown evidence might alter the argument for the resurrection does not mean that historians should refrain from using the evidence that is currently available to them. They should use the evidence that they have instead of constructing hypotheses on the basis of sheer possibility or of silence. Since ancient historians rarely find new sources to supplement the present evidence, apologists are justified in drawing on the New Testament to develop their arguments. Unless critics can provide positive evidence to establish that the early Christian movement remained deliberately silent about some unknown evidence, historians remain completely within their rights to use the New Testament to make arguments about the origins of Christianity. These documents provide, in point of fact, the only direct sources that we have to assess the resurrection and its competition.[4]

When it comes to (2), understanding and interpreting the sources, historians should recognize the personal bias that affects their understanding of history. Undoubtedly, the best insights of postmodernism have enabled historians to realize that they should be cautious in making assertions about the past, for historical arguments and conclusions are always tentative and capable of revision. Nevertheless, a proper historical "relativism" does not mean that critical historians should give up the attempt to retrieve the shape of the past in the best way that they can. These considerations should also dissuade contemporary apologists from making hard apologetic claims.

Although historians may discuss how much evidence is needed to draw conclusions about the undeniability of some past event, it is still

---

4. Understanding first century Jewish beliefs about the afterlife might help one to determine whether Jesus' resurrection occurred.

accurate to say that history discloses truth. The historical kind of truth, however, does not have the same status as mathematical or logical truth. As Gerald O'Collins explains, "one can very well argue that, although they cannot be demonstrated by mathematical calculations, repeated scientific experiments, or philosophical logic, historical truths can certainly be established beyond any reasonable doubt. . . . There are very many historically certain truths from which we can argue and draw conclusions."[5] Even more to the point, he says that "there are very many historically certain truths from which we can argue and draw conclusions, including those which affect faith."[6]

Skeptics are completely within their epistemological rights to insist that all the evidence for the resurrection comes from believers. However, they are mistaken if they conclude that the biblical authors' beliefs prevent us from having reliable information about the origins of Christianity. In fact, the New Testament witnesses' beliefs might be an even *greater* indication of historical accuracy. To be sure, reliable documents can contain some inaccurate information, and unreliable documents can contain accurate information. Even so, the responsible thing for historians to do is utilize the sources they have to establish what they think should count as reliable evidence.

When it comes to (3) determining the cause(s) of the evidence, historians normally appeal to law-like regularities, not miraculous ones. But, in a sense, all events are unique and without parallel. So if a naturalist explanation does not seem to account for the facts because the evidence is pulling in a direction which strongly suggests that a miracle has happened, and if the context in which the event is thought to have occurred is religiously oriented, then it would be feasible for the historian who already believes in a God who is likely to reveal himself in human history to conclude that a supernatural miracle has in happened.

Troeltsch's "principle of analogy"[7] is not a hard and fast rule. It can be qualified and subsequently recast in a way that is hospitable to the likelihood of miracles. Historicism is no longer a prevailing view in the academy in a postmodern age. As Avery Dulles wrote:

> According to a positivist view that was widely accepted fifty or
> a hundred years ago, history is a science analogous to physics

5. O'Collins, *Christology*, 8–9.

6. O'Collins, *Easter Faith*, 34.

7. The "principle of analogy" is a general rule in historiography which says historians should draw inferences about the past that bear some similarty with observable events in the present. The principle does not propose rigid uniformity.

or chemistry. It proceeds on the assumption that the world is a closed system in which causes and effects are connected by strict necessity. History, in that view, leaves no place for the unique, the exceptional, and especially not for events brought about by God's direct activity.[8]

But such a view of history has been widely abandoned.

All of the above requirements (namely, choosing the sources to use, understanding them accurately, and explaining what accounts for them) should not prevent historians from offering what they believe is the best explanation for the historical evidence. Should historians stop reaching conclusions because there are other possibilities that may account for the evidence? Of course not. What is more interesting for critical historians is not positing a range of historical possibilities but the chance of developing arguments that can outstrip rival hypotheses and possibly convince those who might think otherwise.

For instance, a few writers used to propose the swoon theory (according to which Jesus merely appeared to die on the cross, was taken down alive and recovered). While such a theory is a historical possibility, other hypotheses are currently seen as much more plausible and defensible. For this reason, no serious critic upholds the swoon theory or the fraud theory anymore.[9] In particular, many contemporary apologists have argued that the hypothesis that "God raised Jesus bodily from the dead" is the most epistemologically respectable hypothesis and ought to be accepted over rival theories.

William Craig, for instance, describes his position in "soft apologetics" terms in the way that we have defined. In his public debate with John Dominic Crossan, Craig stated:

> I do not assert that belief in the resurrection of Jesus "is the only reasonable option, and thus it would be irrational not to believe in it." Rather, I argue that four established facts . . . "provide adequate inductive grounds for inferring Jesus' resurrection," and that "it's very difficult to deny that the resurrection of Jesus is the best explanation" of these four facts. . . . These statements are carefully chosen and indicate that I am employing inductive

8. Dulles, "Historians and the Reality of Christ," 21.

9. Swoon theorists insist that Jesus merely fainted on the cross and did not die. After he was buried alive, Jesus came out of the tomb and convinced the disciples that he was risen from the dead. For obvious reasons, this theory is not seriously considered by contemporary scholars. Fraud theorists insist that the disciples conspired together to fabricate a new religion. Such a theory is almost unanimously rejected by New Testament scholars as well.

reasoning understood according to the model of inference to the best explanation. This model holds that there may be a number of reasonable explanations for a body of evidence, and that one is to choose from this pool of live options that explanation which is the best, that is, which most successfully meets such criteria as having explanatory power, explanatory scope, and not being ad hoc. . . . Again, I did not say that it is irrational to fail to believe in the resurrection.[10]

Such theories in competition with the hypothesis that "God raised Jesus" are sometimes not irrational, but need to account plausibly for the data. Apologists might play a significant role in helping doubters and unbelievers overcome intellectual obstacles blocking the path of the Christian faith. Let us now turn to the most salient evidence which has been accepted by the majority of critics who study the resurrection as an event of history.[11]

The Honorable Burial and Empty Tomb

The majority of scholars who investigate the resurrection accept that Jesus was properly buried. Closely linked to the burial is the discovery of the empty tomb by a group of Jesus' women followers.[12] Usually cumulative-case arguments are employed in support of the burial and the empty tomb. While each piece of evidence may be individually suggestive, when combined together the case becomes all the more plausible. Here I will briefly comb through the relevant literature to present the most common arguments used in support of the reported facts.

The first argument in support of the empty tomb lies in establishing the burial account. If Jesus was properly buried, then the place of his tomb would have been known. By recognizing the burial of Jesus, those who want to deny the empty tomb must explain how the disciples preached

10. Craig, "Resurrection and the Real Jesus," in Copan, ed., *Will the Real Jesus Please Stand Up?* 160.

11. According to Catholic teaching, the resurrection of Jesus is both a transhistorical and historical event. While the resurrection occurs *in* history, it is not *of* the historical process.

12. These conclusions are consistent with the judgment of many critical scholars. See Allison, *Resurrecting Jesus*, 332, 334; Brown, *An Introduction to New Testament Christology*, 170; Crossan, "The Resurrection," in Stewart, ed., *The Resurrection of Jesus*, 33; also see Crossan's "Bodily-Resurrection Faith," 176; Dunn, *Jesus Remembered*, 828–41; O'Collins, *Believing in the Resurrection*, 80–99; cf. Perkins, "The Resurrection of Jesus of Nazareth," in Chilton and Evans, eds., *Studying the Historical Jesus*, 435–37, 442; Vermes, *The Resurrection of Jesus*, 140–41; Wright, *The Resurrection of the Son of God*, 321, 686, 696, 709–10.

the resurrection in the city of Jerusalem. For the enemies of Jesus and his followers could have easily gone to the tomb and paraded the body across the streets to subvert the new religious movement. The case for the burial and empty tomb deals with verifiable public data, and so resembles a very sober case. Nothing is miraculous about Jesus' burial or the discovery of his empty tomb.

The burial is mentioned in the primitive confession cited in 1 Corinthians 15:3–5, which can be traced back to within a few years after the crucifixion. In 1 Corinthians 15:4, we read: "For I delivered to you as of first importance what I also received, that Christ died for our sins according to the scriptures, and that he was buried . . . ." The Greek verb in verse 4 means to "bury" and would not be used of the unceremonious dumping of a criminal in an unidentifiable place.

Second, when Mark wrote his Gospel, he probably had an earlier source which mentioned Jesus' burial (in the pre-Markan Passion story). Throughout Mark there are independent stories of Jesus' teaching and other anecdotal events. But by the time we get to the final week of Jesus' life, there is a continuous narrative that begins with the Jewish plot during the feast of unleavened bread, the passion, death, burial, and discovery of the empty tomb. This abrupt change to the continuous narrative strongly suggests an earlier source which predates the Gospel itself. James Dunn notes: "The most obvious explanation of this feature is that the framework was early on fixed within the tradition process and remained so throughout the transition to written Gospels. This suggests in turn a tradition rooted in the memory of the participants and put into that framework by them."[13] Many scholars have argued that the pre-Markan passion narrative can be traced back many years before Mark and the other Gospels were composed.[14]

Notably, the Gospel of Mark also says that Joseph of Arimathea was responsible for burying Jesus (Mark 15:43). Joseph was one of the members of the court responsible for crucifying Jesus (Mark 15:1). The embarrassing admission only seems to increase the likelihood of the burial. In his magisterial commentary on the Passion narratives, Raymond Brown wrote:

> I have been outlining a detectable pre-Gospel account of the burial of Jesus by Joseph. . . . How much of that is history? That Jesus is buried is historically certain. That Jewish sensitivity would have wanted this done before the oncoming Sabbath . . .

13. Dunn, *Jesus Remembered*, 765–66.

14. Bauckham, for instance, says that the pre-Markan Passion narrative was formed no later than the 40s. *Jesus and the Eyewitnesses*, 243. Also see Johnson, *The Real Jesus*, 110–11.

is also certain, and our records give us no reason to think that this sensitivity was not honored. That the burial was done by Joseph of Arimathea is very probable, since a Christian fictional creation from nothing of a Jewish Sanhedrist who does what is right is almost inexplicable, granted the hostility in early Christian writings toward the Jewish authorities responsible for the death of Jesus. . . . While high probability is not certitude, there is nothing in the basic pre-Gospel account of Jesus' burial by Joseph that could not plausibly be deemed historical.[15]

Next, the burial stories do not show many signs of legendary traces and are written in a straightforward way (Mark 15:42–47; John 19:38–42). It is well known that Mark is not very creative from a literary point of view. Each Gospel contains additional traditions, which presuppose that Jesus was not thrown onto a pile for criminals but was rather interred (Matt 27:62–66; 28:11–15; Mark 14:8; 16:1–8; Luke 24:13–35; John 20:1–10, 11–18).

More importantly, the burial seems to pass through the criteria of multiple attestation. When early, independent sources all mention the same incident, then this increases the likelihood of historicity. For instance, we have already mentioned that Paul refers to the burial in 1 Corinthians 15:4. Mark also refers to an independent tradition that mentions Jesus' burial.

But this is not all we have. Many scholars maintain that the Gospel of John is literarily independent from Mark. Thus the two Gospels probably used independent sources for their compositions. Further, although Matthew and Luke probably used Mark, both of them probably utilized other traditions that were independent of Mark's chosen sources. As E. L. Bode concluded: "It would seem rather difficult to explain all the additions of the later evangelists to the Markan narrative (for example, Matthew's guard or Luke's visit by Peter) as all stemming from the tradition presented by Mark. Thus there would appear some justification for speaking of independent traditions within the framework of the empty tomb tradition."[16]

Another piece of evidence concerns the women who saw where Jesus was laid to rest in the tomb (Mark 15:47). The crucial point here is that the Gospels claim that the location of Jesus' tomb was known to the women (Mark 15:47; Matt 27:61; Luke 23:55; John 20:1). The women wanted to anoint the dead Jesus shortly after his burial (Mark 16:1; Luke 24:1), as Jewish custom demanded. This suggests that none of the disciples, and certainly

---

15. Brown, *The Death of the Messiah*, 2.1240–41.

16. Bode, *The First Easter Morning*, 18. For a more comprehensive discussion, see 5–24.

not the women, expected his resurrection. Therefore, it is implausible that Jesus was not buried or that the place of his tomb was unknown.

Closely linked to the burial account are further arguments given in support of the empty tomb. For instance, the earliest Jewish polemic against the Christians' belief in Jesus' resurrection maintained that the tomb was empty because the body had been shifted elsewhere (Matt 28:11–15; see John 20:2, 13, 15). We have no early evidence that anyone, either Christian or non-Christian, alleged that Jesus' grave still contained his remains. Thus the earliest Jewish argument against the resurrection did not dispute the emptiness of the tomb, but who or what emptied it.

Moreover, the relevant Gospel texts mentioning the empty tomb are not creative in scope; instead they seem intent on providing historical information about what happened (cf. Mark 16:1–8; John 20:1–2, 11–18). To appreciate how sober Mark's account is, one ought to read the account of the resurrection in the apocryphal gospel of Peter. This Gospel describes Jesus' egress from the tomb with angels accompanying the risen body of Jesus into the heavens. A talking cross and a voice from heaven are heard in a magnificent scene. The event is witnessed by the Roman guard, the Jews, and a multitude of other people. Unlike the canonical Gospels, this kind of description is characteristic of a legendary account.[17]

Moreover, the Gospels report that it was women who discovered the open tomb of Jesus (Mark 16:4–6). In a purely fictional narrative one would have avoided making women the first witnesses of the resurrection, since they were considered in rabbinic Judaism incapable of giving valid testimony (cf Luke 24:11). Legend-makers do not invent positively unhelpful information.

The wording, Jesus was "buried and then raised," in 1 Corinthians 15:3–5 also implies an empty tomb. Even though the empty tomb is not explicitly mentioned, this would not mean that Paul did not know about it, or that we cannot infer that the tomb was empty. As N. T. Wright remarked,

> Early Christianity did not consist of a new spirituality or ethic. It consisted of the announcement of things that had *happened,* whose significance lay precisely in their happenedness: specifically, the messiah's death, burial, and resurrection. . . . The empty tomb, though not mentioned here, is presupposed. It is we, not the early Christians, who have made the empty tomb a major

17. For more on Mark's account of the empty tomb, see Waterman, *The Empty Tomb Tradition of Mark.* Like Habermas, Waterman indicates that the majority of critics who study the final ending of Mark accept the historicity of the burial and the empty tomb.

focal point of discussion. For Paul the Pharisee, saying "he was raised, leaving an empty tomb" would have been tautologous.[18]

It is not difficult to understand why the empty tomb was not articulated until the Gospels were written. The early preachers were not giving continuous accounts of all that had happened but were proclaiming the risen Jesus.

Still other reasons might be given to explain why Paul did not mention the empty tomb. Perhaps he was disinclined to mention it because he has been at pains to persuade his readers that he is just as much as an apostle as James and the others (cf. 1 Cor 9:1–5). Maybe Paul knew that the Corinthians already knew about the discovery of the empty tomb and did not feel the need to mention it. Maybe it was not as important as the appearances and/or salvation (cf. 1 Cor 1:23). It must be remembered that in the Jewish mindset the empty tomb would have been self-evident given what was meant by resurrection. Resurrection in Jewish thought involved one's physical body.

In addition, since the gravesite was not venerated by the early Christians, this connotes that it was empty; for there were no remains to be venerated (cf. Matt 22:29). As Dunn puts matters: "This is indeed striking, because within contemporary Judaism, as in other religions, the desire to honour the memory of the revered dead by constructing appropriate tombs and (by implication) by veneration of the site is well attested."[19] N. T. Wright explains why the disciples would have venerated the gravesite: "The practice is usually thought to reflect a belief in resurrection, in that the bones of the individual person continued to matter."[20]

Each of the Gospels, with indirect references in Acts and in 1 Corinthians 15, provide an empty tomb scene (Matt 28:1–8; Mark 16:1–8; Luke 24:1–12; John 20:1–8; Acts 2:27–29; 1 Cor 15:3–5). In each of the Gospels the tomb is vacated and confirmed by an angel who says Jesus is *not there* (cf. Matt 28:6; Mark 16:6; Luke 24:6; John 20:12).

Like the case for the burial account, the empty tomb is part of the pre-Markan Passion story. In this part of Mark we do not see any kerygmatic coloring, prophecy citations from the Old Testament, and/or use of christological titles. This has led some critics into thinking that we are working with material that must have preceded the first written Gospel.

Lastly, since the disciples originally preached the resurrection in Jerusalem, it is difficult to believe that the tomb still contained the cadaver of Jesus. Enemies of Easter faith could have easily gone to the tomb to prove

18. Wright and Borg, *The Meaning of Jesus*, 119.

19. Dunn, *Jesus Remembered*, 837.

20. Wright, *The Resurrection of the Son of God*, 579.

that Jesus was not raised. Instead, we see no resistance from the Jews or Romans. Hence, we can infer responsibly that the apostles' proclamation of the resurrection was successful precisely because nobody was able to produce the corpse.

In conclusion, the historicity of the burial and empty tomb are consistent with a cumulative case argument. As Hans Freiherr von Campenhausen concluded: "If one examines what there is to examine, one cannot avoid accepting as fact the news of the empty tomb itself and of its early discovery. There is a great deal that is convincing and definite to be said for it and little to be said against it; it is, therefore, in all probability, historical."[21] N. T. Wright says that the strength of the evidence for the empty tomb is "in the same sort of category, of historical probability so high as to be virtually certain, as the death of Augustus in AD 14 or the fall of Jerusalem in AD 70."[22]

The Post-Mortem Appearances

The historical case for the resurrection of Jesus also depends on establishing the earliest disciples' experience of what they at least thought were appearances of the risen Lord.[23] These experiences occurred over a period of time to individuals, groups, and enemies of Jesus and his closest followers. The appearances occurred under radically different circumstances.

There are many lines of evidence in support of the historicity of the appearances. First, the earliest and most reliable testimony is found in the ancient creed cited by in 1 Corinthians 15:3–8. Exegetically speaking, the wording for "received" and "passed on" in verses 3–5 were technical standard terms for the handing down of sacred tradition in rabbinic Judaism.[24] Paul is therefore trying to convince his readers in the most solemn way

21. Quotation from von Campenhausen, *Der Ablauf der Osterereignisse und das leere Grab*, 42; cited in Kasper, *Jesus the Christ*, 128.

22. Wright, *The Resurrection of the Son of God*, 710, cf. 707. He affirms that "the evidence is as watertight as one is likely to find."

23. The historicity of the post-resurrection appearances are almost universally acknowledged by critical scholars who study the subject. See Allison, *Resurrecting Jesus*, 269; Brown, *The Virginal Conception and Bodily Resurrection of Jesus*, 89–92; Brown, *An Introduction to New Testament Christology*, 169; Crossan, "The Resurrection," 33; Crossan, "Bodily-Resurrection Faith," 176; Dunn, *Jesus Remembered*, 841–57, 864; O'Collins, *Believing in the Resurrection*, 61–79; cf. Perkins, *Resurrection*, 88–89, 102–3; Vermes, *The Resurrection of Jesus*, 17, 92, 102, 108, 120, 140, 148, 150; Wright, *The Resurrection of the Son of God*, 686–96.

24. Cf. Brown, *The Virginal Conception and Bodily Resurrection of Jesus*, 81.

possible that Jesus appeared to Peter, the Twelve, the more than 500, James, all the Apostles, and Paul himself.

Paul's list of percipients, coupled with the "more than five hundred brethren" in verse 6, was deliberately chosen to convince his readers of the truth of the appearances. The appearance to the more than five hundred cannot be a secondary construction explained by development in the history of oral tradition. Paul calls attention precisely here to the possibility of checking his assertion by saying that most of the five hundred are still alive. There is hardly any reason for Paul to mention the "more than 500" unless he wanted his readers to question them as living eyewitnesses.

Paul's letters are not constructed by second-hand evidence as in the Gospels; they are firsthand reports of eyewitness testimony. For instance, Paul also knew other disciples who experienced appearances of Jesus (Gal 1:11–19). The creed of 1 Corinthians 15 can be traced back well before Paul wrote his letter to the Corinthians (55–56 A.D.). He probably received the creed from the other apostles when he visited Jerusalem in 36 A.D. (Gal 1:18). It is also possible that he received it earlier in Damascus. Not to be overlooked, the sources used by the author(s) of the creed must stretch back even further to the original events themselves. N. T. Wright, for instance, states that it "was probably formulated within the first two or three years after Easter itself" and is "the earliest Christian tradition."[25] Walter Kasper concurs; it goes back to "30 AD."[26] James Dunn dates it to "within months of Jesus' death."[27] The atheist critic, Gerd Lüdemann, says it can be traced back to within "30 and 33 A.D."[28] Here it might be recalled that the ancient creed of 1 Corinthian 15:3–5 mentions the historicity of the burial account. As mentioned before, the burial serves as indirect evidence for the empty tomb.

An analysis of the creedal list seems to indicate the percipients' belief in the extramental and bodily nature of the appearances. Any neutral or hostile observer, who did not yet have faith in Jesus, *could* have seen an appearance (for example, the apostle Paul, James, the more than 500). The suggestion that only the eyes of faith could "see" the risen Jesus comes much later on in theological reflection, and is quite foreign to New Testament tradition. 1 Corinthians 15:3–8 indicates that enemies and perhaps those who were indifferent to Jesus saw these appearances, and in doing so came to enjoy "eyes of faith."

25. Wright, *The Resurrection of the Son of God*, 319.

26. Kasper, *Jesus the Christ*, 125.

27. Dunn, *Jesus Remembered*, 855.

28. Lüdemann, *The Resurrection of Jesus*, 38.

Before we turn to Paul's understanding of the nature of the appearances, it may be worthwhile to explain why reports of Paul's experience on the Damascus Road in the book of Acts does not rule out corporeal appearances. Some scholars like to refer to Acts as a basis for affirming that the appearances mentioned in 1 Corinthians 15 must have been incorporeal.

First, it must be remembered that Acts 9, 22, and 26 report a post-ascension vision to Paul. The same Luke who wrote Acts is the Luke who presents a truly bodily resurrection (Luke 24; Acts 1). Thus those who begin with Acts in order to understand the resurrection faith of Paul unseemingly presuppose a shift from Luke to Acts: from the corporeal to the non-corporeal.

If one wants to begin with Acts in order to understand Paul, then one must admit that Luke is explicit on the bodily nature of the appearances. Luke clearly depicts the risen Jesus as physical in the first of his two volumes. The differences between what Paul reports of his encounter with the risen Christ (1 Cor 9:1; 15:8; Gal 1: 12, 15–16) and the appearances in the Gospels do not rule out corporeal appearances in Acts. Luke is forced to construe Paul's encounters with Jesus (in Acts) as heavenly visions, since Jesus has already ascended bodily.

Second, anyone who wants to begin with Acts to understand Paul's experience should be asked: why would Luke want to change his interpretation of the experiences of the risen Christ from a corporeal to a non-corporeal one? Would potential converts have found it more palatable to believe in a non-corporeal body? Jewish expectations of a resurrection of the body created great difficulties for the earliest Christians. Paul's proclamation of the resurrection (Acts 17:32) shows how precarious the thesis was in the early days of the Christian mission to the Gentiles.

Third, it is also disputable whether Acts teaches a non-corporeal risen body. Jesus' body "did not see decay" but was raised up (Acts 2:30–32; 13:35–37). As Christopher Bryan puts it:

> This element of physicality in Acts' narrative of Paul's conversion is entirely consistent with Acts' general descriptions of the resurrection preaching. This preaching has, as Wright points out, a "robust and bodily" character, emphasizing the Psalms which speak of God's holy one 'not seeing corruption,' and making a contrast between Jesus and David, who died and was buried whose tomb "can be checked." At the same time, it stands in marked contrast to other divine revelations, including visions of the risen Christ, that are clearly understood to

be entirely inward and personal (e.g., Acts 8:26; 9:10–16; 10:3, 10–16; 16:6–10; 22:17–21; 27:23–24).[29]

Let us now turn to the New Testament evidence for the appearances that can be derived from Paul's letters.

1 Corinthians 15:3–8 does not enter into details and say, for instance, whether or not the appearances were corporeal. However, Paul maintains that Jesus' resurrection was/is the model for understanding the eschatological resurrection (1 Thess 4:14; 1 Cor 6:14, 15:20; 2 Cor 4:14; Rom 8:11). If Paul says something about the nature of the eschatological body (Rom 8:11; 1 Cor 15:42–54, 2 Cor 4:16–5:8; Phil 3:21; cf. Col 2:9), we may gain some additional insight into the appearances. For example, in Romans 8:11 he says that our mortal bodies will be raised just as Jesus' body was raised. The Spirit who raises the believer's body is the same Spirit who raised Jesus' body. Also relevant is Philippians 3:21: "He will change our lowly body to conform with his glorified body." Note that Paul says our bodies will be transformed to be like Jesus' glorified body.

Perhaps the most important set of passages is found in 1 Corinthians 15:42–54. Here Paul teaches that there is a one-to-one identity between the body that dies and the body that rises (42–44): "So also is the resurrection of the dead. *It* is sown corruptible; *it* is raised incorruptible. *It* is sown dishonorable; *it* is raised glorious. *It* is sown weak; *it* is raised powerful. *It* is sown a natural body; *it* is raised a spiritual body. If there is a natural body, there is also a spiritual one" (italics mine). The body that goes down in burial is the same body that comes up in resurrection. This conclusion is in accordance with the earliest Christian belief about Jesus: namely, that Jesus had been bodily raised from the dead.

What then of Paul's teaching about the "spiritual" body? When the body is earthly, it is material, but when it is raised it is spiritual (1 Cor 15:42–44). The Greek word for "spiritual" (*pneumatikos*) is used to mean spiritually mature (see 1 Cor 2:14, 15; 3:1; 14:37; cf. Gal 6:1), not immaterial or ethereal. It may also refer to something that has its origins in the Holy Spirit (1 Cor 2:14–15; 9:11; 10:3–4; 12:1; 14:1). When Paul speaks of the "spiritual body" he does not refer to an ethereal body, but to a person who is dominated by the Spirit. The "spiritual person" is not immaterial, but is someone who is under guidance of the Spirit (1 Cor 2:14–15).

Some critics have cited 1 Corinthians 15:50 to argue against the resurrected body: "flesh and blood cannot inherit the kingdom of God, nor does corruption inherit incorruption." These commentators maintain that

---

29. Bryan, *The Resurrection of the Messiah*, 218.

"flesh and blood" is a synonym for "merely physical."[30] However, many more would agree that the term is a figure of speech. Anthony Thiselton reports: "flesh and blood" denotes "humankind in its weakness and vulnerability" and that 15:50a refers to "holiness in place of sin" and 15:50b refers to "the reversal of weakness, degeneration, and decay."[31] The phrase "flesh and blood" refers to mortality, not to mere physicality.

Paul is not saying the risen body will be immaterial. Rather, he is contrasting a holy body that is dominated by the spiritual with a body that is vulnerable to decay. Immediately after 15:50, Paul says that our current bodies will be "changed" (1 Cor 15:51–53). In fact, "we will all be changed" (15:51–52; cf. 1 Thess 4:16–17). Paul maintains that the body which dies is the same body that rises; the risen body is more than physical, but is definitely not less than physical. To conclude: Paul recognizes that the appearances were bodily manifestations of Jesus from the "other side."

Since the evidence decisively points in the direction of bodily resurrection appearances, it follows that Jesus' tomb must have been empty. The skeptical scholar Maurice Casey sees the implications: "Some Jews [of the Second Temple period] believed . . . that resurrection involved the resuscitation of the earthly body. Those who converted to Christianity would naturally assume that if Jesus rose from the dead and appeared to his disciples, there must have been an empty tomb."[32] He continues: "If this view of bodily resurrection were applied to the resurrection of Jesus, it would follow that his tomb was left empty."[33] Conversely, if there was no empty tomb, then there was no bodily resurrection.

Usually in ancient history one or two sources renders the reported fact unimpeachable Ancient historians do not usually have all that much material to work with. But in the case of the resurrection appearances, we have many sources, including Paul's letters, the Gospels, and Acts. Let us now turn to the testimonies of the Evangelists.

While some argue that the Gospels were written too long after the central events reported in them, others urge that there was still an insufficient amount of time for legends to develop because of the apostles' influence during the emergence of the early Church. Many more generations would have been needed for the Evangelists to completely refashion their depictions of Jesus. Certainly, it is well known that a later dating of the Gospels

30. Borg and Wright, *The Meaning of Jesus*, 133. Also see Borg, *Jesus*, 289.

31. Thiselton, *The First Epistle to the Corinthians*, 1291.

32. Casey, "Response to Michael F. Bird," in Bird and Crossley, *How Did Christianity Begin?* 193.

33. Casey, *Jesus of Nazareth*, 476. Cf. 467. For those Jews who held to the eschatological resurrection, it would have been axiomatic that the risen body was corporeal.

does not necessarily render them unreliable. Though many scholars do not believe that we have eyewitness accounts, a strong case can be made for the eyewitness traditions behind them.[34]

The prominence of women, for instance, lends credibility to the appearances (Matt 28; John 20). James Dunn claims: "Paul's omission of any women witnesses in his 1 Cor. 15 list may reflect something of the same bias. In what has the appearance of being a fairly formal list of witnesses, the inclusion of appearances to women would be regarded as a weakening of the claim not a strengthening. Contrariwise, the inclusion of such testimony elsewhere, *despite* the bias against women as witnesses, is all the more impressive."[35] Women were regarded as inferior to men at the time. They were, for all intents and purposes, unable to be counted as legal witnesses. If the narratives were purely legendary, then the evangelists would have probably made men the original percipients, not women.

Second, the diverse reporting of the appearances does not give the impression that they were contrived or wholly fabricated. Dunn continues: "Particularly in Matthew, Luke, and John 21, there has been no real attempt to provide a sequence or structured listing. Overall, the impression is given of a number of reported sightings which occurred on what might otherwise be called a random basis." The writers (esp. Matthew) make hardly any attempt to pacify the doubts of the original percipients. Therefore, the appearances were most likely "part of the original eyewitness testimony."[36] Nowhere are the appearances described as a miracle, or as an event of salvation, a fact which tends to support the plausibility of the reports. The Evangelists composed their narratives to primarily relay theological lessons, but signs of historicity can be traced in them.

A final line of evidence stems from the multiple sources from which the appearance traditions originate. All four Gospels give witness to them, including the ones found in the Pauline corpus. The appearance to Peter is independently attested to by Paul and Luke (1 Cor 15:5; Luke 24:34); the appearance to the Twelve is mentioned by Paul, Luke, and John (1 Cor 15:5; Luke 24:36–43; John 20:19–20); and the appearances in Galilee are mentioned by Mark, Matthew, and John (Mark 16:7; Matt 28:16–17; John 21).

Moreover, both 1 Corinthians 15:3–5 and Mark 15:37–16:7 (and Acts 13:28–31) share *sequential similarities*: the first episode is the crucifixion; second is the burial; third is the resurrection; fourth is the appearances. The fact that these independent sources agree on the sequence is noteworthy

---

34. Bauckham, *Jesus and the Eyewitnesses*.

35. Dunn, *The Evidence for Jesus*, 70.

36. Ibid.

for historical purposes. Many different individuals experienced what they at least thought was the risen Jesus at different times and places under radically different circumstances and expectations.

These conclusions about the historical reality of the appearances are nearly universally acknowledged by New Testament scholars who study the resurrection. In the words of E. P. Sanders: "That Jesus' followers (and later Paul) had resurrection experiences is, in my judgment, a fact. What the reality was that gave rise to the experiences I do not know." Says Sanders: "Finally we know that after his death his followers experienced what they described as the 'resurrection:' the appearance of a living but transformed person who actually died."[37] Gerd Lüdemann asserts that "It may be taken as historically certain that Peter and the disciples had experiences after Jesus' death in which Jesus appeared to them as the risen Christ."[38]

The nature of the appearances is somewhat nuanced by the earliest percipients' beliefs about Christ's risen body. Thus the appearances were seen as unique historical occurrences:

> It is, therefore, impossible to categorize the Easter appearances in any available this-worldly language, even in that of religious mysticism. It is not really satisfactory to call them "objective visions," for that introduces a nominal form which the New Testament, apart from the otherwise explicable exception in Acts 26:19, is careful to avoid. The ultimate reason for this difficulty is that there are no categories available for the unprecedented disclosure of the eschatological within history.[39]

The appearances were interpreted as unique divine acts in history, commissioning the disciples as apostles and leaders in the earliest church (cf. Matt 28:18–20; 1 Cor 9:1; 15:3–11).

The exegetical details in the Gospels and Paul's letters are not as significant as the emphasis placed on the uniqueness of the appearances. Indeed, the resurrection appearances ceased (John 20:29; 1 Pet 1:8) and should be distinguished from later Christic visions in the earliest Christian communities. Gerald O'Collins, for instance, carefully delineated the appearances from other early Christian experiences of Jesus.[40] Paul also says that he was the last one to see a resurrection appearance (1 Cor 15:8).

---

37. Sanders, *The Historical Figure of Jesus*, 280. Cf. 11, 13.

38. Lüdemann, *What Really Happened to Jesus?* 80.

39. Fuller, *The Formation of the Resurrection Narratives*, 33.

40. For a discussion, see O'Collins, *Jesus Risen*, 116–18.

Believing in the Risen Jesus

But the appearances and empty tomb are not all we have to argue for the resurrection. Most historians have no difficulty speaking about the earliest disciples' *belief in Jesus' resurrection*, since this is a matter of public record. It is historically certain that some of Jesus' followers came to believe that he had been raised. So strong was the earliest Church's belief in the risen Jesus that they proclaimed him as the "Jewish Messiah." Unlike pre-Christian Judaism, believing in the resurrection was at the front and center of the newly formed faith.

Whatever critics may think about the empty tomb and the appearances, the first Christians for whom we have evidence at least believed that Jesus had been raised (and not ascended, assumed, or immortalized to heaven). This belief was at the very heart of earliest Christianity. N. T. Wright recognized that "the historical study of early Christian practice and hope leaves us no choice but to conclude that this unfortunate belief was what all early Christians held. Indeed, they professed that it was the very centre of their life."[41] Not only is this belief "unanimous" and "unambiguous," but the sources we have are "sober," "critical," and "reserved," without a shred of "extravagant enthusiasm" which we would expect to hear in legendary accounts.[42]

Phrases referring to this belief are probably the oldest and most distinctive in early Christianity. Indicated by the Greek words *egeirein*, a transitive verb that means "to awaken" or "to raise up," and *anistēmi*, which means "to arise," reference to Easter faith is firmly embedded in the Scriptures (Acts 3:15, 4:10, 5:30, 10:40, 13:30, 37; Rom 4:24–25, 6:4, 7:4, 8:11; 1 Cor 6:14, 15:4, 12, 20; 2 Cor 4:14, Gal 1:1, Col 2:12, 1 Thess 1:10; Eph 1:20; 2 Tim 2:8; Heb 13:20; 1 Pet 1:21). O'Collins rightly observes: "The primary claim was not that Jesus' cause continued or that the disciples had been 'raised' to a new consciousness and the life of faith . . . , but that the crucified Jesus had been personally brought from the state of death to that of a new and lasting life."[43]

In order to appreciate the remarkable modification of earliest *belief* in Jesus' bodily resurrection, Wright argued that one should understand the prevailing views of the afterlife in Second Temple Judaism.[44] Wright indi-

---

41. Wright, *The Resurrection of the Son of God*, 705.

42. Kasper, *Jesus the Christ*, 125.

43. O'Collins, "The Resurrection of Jesus," in Fisichella and Latourelle, eds., *Dictionary of Fundamental Theology*, 769.

44. The definitive work on Second Temple Jewish views of the afterlife at the time of Jesus is Wright, *The Resurrection of the Son of God*.

cates that Jews held that (1) all people, or at least a large group of the Jewish nation, would be raised from the dead together (not one individual apart from the rest); (2) the resurrection would occur at the eschaton, never in the middle of history (as the earliest Christians said about Jesus); (3) none of the risen would play a role in the divine judgment; (4) the Messiah would not die, much less rise from the dead. Nor did they think that (5) God, or YHWH, would be raised from the dead in human form (cf. 2 Clem 1:1).

Conversely, says Wright, the first followers of Jesus proclaimed specific things about the resurrection of Jesus: (1) the Christians believed in a resurrected and crucified rabbi, which was seen as a curse from God (cf. Deut 21:23); (2) they claimed that the general resurrection had somehow already begun, in Jesus (1 Cor 15:20–23); (3) they unanimously placed the resurrection at the center of their message, excluding all other views of the afterlife (unlike the Jews, whose resurrection doctrine was peripheral and even debatable among other eschatological beliefs); (4) the Christians argued that the resurrected body was "incorruptible" and "imperishable" (unlike the Jews, who never commented on the nature of the risen body); (5) they spoke of God's Kingdom as having come—and still having to come—a very nuanced position to be in; (6) and they propagated the good news to all people, regardless of race, gender, or social status—something the Jews did not feel the need to do, either before and during the rise of Christianity. All of these drastic changes have prompted historians to ask: what could have caused such modifications?

Conclusion

The historical status of the event of Jesus' rising from the dead has been queried, every now and then, even by those who accept the resurrection. Was the resurrection of Jesus then a historical event, just as much as the assassination of Julius Caesar in 44 BC or the destruction of Jerusalem in AD 70? While we know through faith that the resurrection occurred, can historical investigation provide rational support for this belief and show the resurrection to be an event of history?

Catholic apologists have compelling evidence for defending the resurrection. Currently, many scholars indicate that there are some generally established facts that all critics must take into consideration when assessing whether "God raised Jesus from the dead." So strong is the evidence that even John Dominic Crossan, has come to accept it in recent years: "I do not for here and now debate the historicity of either Jesus' burial or the empty tomb's discovery. Instead, for here and now (*dato non concesso*, to be sure) *I take the Gospel stories of the empty tomb's discovery and of all those risen apparitions as historically factual in their entirety.*[45] Although Crossan believes that the appearances should be categorized as apparitions, his point should be well-taken.

45. Crossan, "Bodily-Resurrection Faith," 176; also see Crossan's "The Resurrection," 33.

— 10 —

Assessing the Evidence
for Jesus' Resurrection

TODAY MANY BIBLICAL SCHOLARS argue that the resurrection of Jesus is the best explanation of the tentatively established evidence that was discussed in the last chapter. Such a contention seeks to demonstrate the rationality of the resurrection hypothesis. It does not attempt to demonstrate the irrationality of the alternatives. Both belief and unbelief can be rational. By wording their arguments with greater precision, Catholic apologists can be more persuasive to contemporary, postmodern audiences. In this chapter I argue that the resurrection of Jesus outstrips other rational hypotheses. I will also attend to the most salient criticisms against the resurrection.

With the assumption that an infinite, personal God exists, apologists usually lay out two steps in defense of Jesus' resurrection. In the first step they establish what should count as evidence. That evidence has already been discussed in the last chapter. After the evidence has been agreed upon, the next step assumes the conclusions established in the first step and is dedicated to pinpointing the causal theories that can responsibly account for the data. If Jesus was indeed raised by God, this miracle would add crucial support for his identity and teachings.

Objections to Easter Faith

(1) The first argument against the historicity of the resurrection is that *there are numerous contradictions in the resurrection narratives for them to be considered reliable.* By contrast, this complaint shows a hesitancy to take the evidence seriously. Since we have already admitted certain facts as evidence, this objection acts as a smokescreen in taking the explanation of that evidence seriously. Historians are not trying to demonstrate the resurrection of

Jesus, and so they admit that other possible explanations might account for the data. The more interesting question, however, is whether the resurrection hypothesis is the best explanation of the evidence.

Further, this complaint is no more significant than an event reported by a number of individuals with different perspectives. The different theological emphases in the Gospels might correspond to different figures and/or past events. Although it may be the case that no details in these narratives can be harmonized, this does not mean, *tout court*, that they are contradictory. As Kasper states: "these irreconcilable divergences . . . agree on one thing: Jesus appeared to certain disciples after his death; he proved himself living and was proclaimed to have been risen from the dead. That is the centre, the core, where all the traditions meet."[1]

Notwithstanding the theological emphases in the four Gospels, this does not preclude the possibility of historicity. The similarities outweigh the differences in the Gospels. Of the differences which do appear, many simply reflect varying theological interpretations of the same historical events without calling into question the fundamental historicity of the events themselves.

Considering that the appearances were in history, but still had a mysterious quality about them, we should not be surprised to see at least some "contradictions" in the texts. So, it would be a mistake to consider the narratives purely legendary because they are not "word for word" translations of what the risen Jesus said or did. Nor is it a problem that the narratives do not agree about the chronology of reported events. As the Pontifical Biblical Commission explained:

> The truth of the Gospel account is not compromised because the Evangelists report the Lord's words and deeds in different order. Nor is it hurt because they report His words, not literally but in a variety of ways, while retaining the same meaning. . . . Since these books were to be so authoritative, He undoubtedly guided and directed the sacred writers as they thought about the things which they were going to write down; but He probably allowed each writer to arrange his narrative as he saw fit.[2]

The Commission goes on to say:

> Of the many elements at hand they reported some, summarized others, and developed still others in accordance with the needs of the various churches. They used every possible means to

1. Kasper, *Jesus the Christ*, 129. Cf. Wright, *The Resurrection of the Son of God*, 614.

2. Pontifical Biblical Commission, *The Historicity of the Gospels*, 7–8.

ensure that their readers would come to know the validity of the things they had been taught. From the material available to them the Evangelists selected those items most suited to their specific purpose and to the condition of a particular audience. And they narrated these events in the manner most suited to satisfy their purpose and their audience's condition. Since the meaning of a statement depends, among other things, upon the context in which it is found, the Evangelists reported Christ's deeds and words in varying contexts, choosing whichever one would be of greatest help to the reader in trying to understand a particular utterance. Hence the exegete must try to ascertain what the Evangelist intended by reporting a certain saying or event in a particular manner or a particular context.[3]

We must also keep in mind that we are dealing with texts that have been analyzed and pulled apart, if you will, more than any other work of literature in the past 300 years. Clearly we should expect to see a few "contradictions" in them. Be that as it may, no reputable historian who finds a few contradictions in his or her sources would automatically conclude that the narratives are purely legendary. Some contradictions may provide greater weight to the reliability of the central events reported in them. These kinds of "contradictions" would give the careful reader the strong impression that the stories were not harmonized in order to promote an unnecessary agenda.

Lastly, even if the Gospels were completely unreliable, this would not leave us with nothing: we still have to reckon with Paul's account in 1 Corinthians 15:3–8, the early speeches in Acts, and the early creeds that precede his writings (for example, Rom. 1:1–4; Phil 2:5–11).

(2) The second argument given by some critics is that *the oral traditions undergirding the Gospels are unreliable.* However, this objection confuses the two steps in our argument for the resurrection (step one is about gathering the relevant evidence, and step two is about explaining the evidence). No matter what uncertainties are surrounding the agreed upon evidence, the reader should concede the historicity of the empty tomb, the post-mortem appearances, and the origin of the disciples' faith.

Nonetheless, let us try and address this objection from another standpoint. The critic may be confusing the deposit of oral teaching and the way it was expressed (or applied) in different circumstances. If Jesus meant so much to his followers, then it is overwhelmingly improbable that they would have remembered so little about him, or that they so completely refashioned the content of their memories and the sources they used that there would be nothing reliable in the final texts.

3. Ibid., 7.

Moreover, the fact that we have multiple sources within such a short generation after Jesus's ministry makes us fortunate as critical scholars. Bart Ehrman states: "Therefore, if there is a tradition about Jesus that is preserved in more than one of these documents, no one of them could have made it up, since the others knew of it as well, independently. If a tradition is found in several of these sources, then the likelihood of its going back to the very beginning of the tradition from which they all ultimately derive, back to the historical Jesus himself, is significantly improved."[4]

Usually ancient historians have much less material to work with than scholars who study the modern period. In ancient history one or two sources render the reported fact unimpeachable. But in the case of Jesus' resurrection, we have multiple, early, and independent sources. Thus there was an insufficient amount of time for legends to develop substantially because the apostles served as living restraints on the tradition. More than one or two generations would have been needed for the Evangelists (and Paul) to completely refashion their depictions of Jesus.

A final consideration brings us back to the creed of 1 Corinthians 15:3–5.[5] Because this creed can be traced back well before the writing of 1 Corinthians (to within the 30s), it seems to nullify one's uncertainty about the oral traditions which preceded the final, written accounts.

(3) *The Gospels were not written by eyewitnesses. They were written too far after the Christ event to be considered reliable.*[6] Once more this objector confuses the notion of evidence and the best way to explain the evidence. Even if the Gospels were not written by eyewitnesses, this does nothing to undercut the evidence that has already been produced.

Nonetheless, let us still try and respond to this criticism. Most (many?) New Testament scholars are well aware that later compositions would not make the texts unreliable. Surely later sources can be just as reliable as earlier sources; firsthand reports are not necessarily preferable. Sometimes later interpreters understand the original events better than the eyewitnesses. So instead of always valuing firsthand accounts over subsequent reports, historians recognize that in times of upheaval people may not immediately write things down, and that later compilers may be in a better position to grasp the nature of the events. Avery Dulles illustrates this point:

> Anglicans and Orthodox, as well as Roman Catholics, have generally rejected the Protestant position, in so far as this is purely Biblicist, and have insisted that the Bible cannot be the rule of

4. Ehrman, *The New Testament*, 217.

5. See chapter 9 for details for the tradition history behind 1 Corinthians 15:3–8.

6. Allison, "Rational Apologetics and the Resurrection of Jesus," 325–26.

faith except when conjoined with a continuous Church tradition. In this perspective, which is fundamentally Catholic, the very sections of the New Testament which the liberals tend to discount as too far removed from the events can be seen as providing privileged interpretations, for, as [John Henry] Newman pointed out, events of great importance require a considerable span of time in order to be rightly comprehended.[7]

Later compilers may have more well-rounded evidence from various perspectives at their disposal to determine what should be included in the most up to date reporting. Historians do not need earlier sources to ensure that their case is more historically accurate.

What is more, the concern about having eyewitness accounts does not apply in the case of Paul. Paul himself wrote that he saw an appearance (1 Cor 9:1). He was originally an enemy of the earliest Christians. He did not expect Jesus to appear to him. He became a believer several years after the Christian movement began in Jerusalem. The ancient creed found in 1 Corinthians 15:3–5, moreover, was formulated within years (or even months) after the crucifixion. In short, skeptics should engage the evidence and account for it, rather than dismiss it for being limited, one-sided or occurring too far after the alleged original event.

(4) The next skeptical challenge states that *the evidence is biased*. For these skeptics the evidence is furnished by individuals who already believed in the resurrection and so cannot be trusted by critical historians. Here the principle of disinterestedness seems to be upheld. Again, this challenge has nothing to do with the evidence already established in the first step.

Few, if any, historians would want to stop at this point, throw up their hands and quit simply because the sources may have been shaped by passionate believers. Testimonies and other artifacts of history, whether oral or written, are sometimes transmitted because the original compiler(s) firmly believed in their truth. Historical validity is not diminished by the use of such sources. If the resurrection occurred, then we would expect Jesus' followers to transmit zealously and faithfully his message to subsequent generations. An absence of personal commitment on the part of the original witnesses would render their testimony less than credible.

It should also be said that "bias explains everything and so explains nothing." Notwithstanding the issue of bias, the resurrection is said to be the *best* explanation of the known evidence, not the *only* explanation. Other explanations are certainly possible, but Ehrman and the other critics have not provided one thus far. Alternative explanations can be given, but unless

7. Dulles, *The Catholicity of the Church*, 97.

skeptics can provide positive evidence to establish that the early Christian movement remained deliberately silent about some alleged, hitherto unknown source(s), historians remain completely within their rights to use the New Testament documents to make arguments about the origins of resurrection faith. Critics should use the evidence that is currently available instead of constructing a causal theory on the basis of sheer possibility or of silence.

What is more, no historical account is written from a neutral, objective standpoint. But this does not mean that the Evangelists could not (or did not) report anything accurate about Jesus. Given the genre of the Gospels (see chapter 8), the Evangelists were somewhat concerned about presenting accurate depictions of Jesus in the face of different situations facing the earliest Christian communities.

Lastly, the issue of bias seems to be drastically undercut in the case of Paul and James (and possibly to the "more than 500"). Paul was not always a believer, and presumably some of the 500 did not know or believe in Jesus either. To be sure, Paul challenges the Corinthians to ask any of the "more than 500" who were alive at the time of his writing to convince the former of the reality of the appearances (1 Cor 15:6).

(5) The next argument is that *other figures of history were said to perform miracles and be resurrected.* Ehrman lists figures such as Apollonius of Tyana, Honi the Circle Drawer, Hanina ben Dosa, and the Roman Emperor Vespasian.[8] If we already accept Jesus' resurrection, Ehrman says, then why couldn't we say these figures were raised too? Let me say from the outset that apologists should not affirm that Jesus was the only figure ever to be raised. This closed-minded attitude is detrimental to the virtue of open-mindedness about the miraculous. But notice that the admission of special divine acts in other religious contexts does not undercut the credibility of Jesus' resurrection either.[9]

Second, even if there is evidence for these divine acts, this would not mean that the evidence is equally compelling in all cases. Poorly evidenced miracles scarcely rule out the validity of well attested evidence in other scenarios, especially in the historical case for the risen Jesus. By contrast, in these other scenarios there is minimal evidence appearing literally hundreds of years after the event.[10] They are usually uncorroborated by multiple,

---

8. Ehrman, *Jesus, Interrupted,* 172.

9. The Protestant Reformers held that the only true miracles were recorded accurately in the Bible. By contrast, Catholic teaching does not limit where miracles can or will occur.

10. Habermas, "Resurrection Claims in Non-Christian Religions," 177.

independent sources. Consequently, the evidence for these special divine acts allows for many plausible explanations.

Third, Ehrman asserts that many Christians naively reject miracle claims in other religious contexts because they are not found in Scripture or church teaching. But this is a textbook example of committing the genetic fallacy: how one comes to believe in X does not have anything to do with the truth of X. Christians might believe in the resurrection of Jesus because of the circumstances they found themselves in (for example, upbringing, and living in a Christian culture), but this does not mean that it is a false belief or that Jesus' resurrection is not the best explanation of the evidence. Many Christians (and atheists, agnostics, and other religionists) may have poor reason for holding to specific beliefs and rejecting other ones.

Both faith and reason can lead individuals to certain conclusions. But in the case of critical historians, they do not claim to establish, demonstrate or prove the resurrection. Instead the resurrection hypothesis is cast as a piece of inductive reasoning on the basis of agreed upon evidence.

(6) The next argument is that *historical understanding seeks multiple causes, not exclusively one.* It is true that the early Church could have had more than one cause for its existence, but this would not prevent historians from positing Jesus' resurrection as the ultimate cause that set off a chain reaction of additional causal conditions that brought the Christian movement into full bloom. Various causes have different values and contribute variously to forming historical phenomena. True, historians rarely affirm that entire movements can be accounted for by a single cause. Many conditions surrounding the primary event under consideration, the resurrection of Jesus, likely contributed to its ongoing influence.

Larry Hurtado, for instance, has recently outlined and explained some of the many reasons why the earliest Christian movement spread at the astounding rate it did. First, it began in Jerusalem—a city that allowed for many persons to hear the good news in order for the first disciples to take the message out to a wider world.[11] Outsiders found the strict nature of Christian worship attractive[12] including its exclusive stance with respect to Christianity's relationship to all other religions.[13] Christianity, moreover, was unlike any other religion at the time. It did not discriminate on the basis of gender or social class. It called on everyone to repent and believe in the gospel.[14] Christian worship was more intense than the conventional

---

11. Hurtado, *Lord Jesus Christ*, 195–96.

12. Hurtado, *At the Origins of Christian Worship*, 4.

13. Ibid., 18; cf. 39.

14. Ibid., 46.

liturgies of Judaism.[15] The earliest Christian worship featured the belief that God was active in the midst of ritual action.[16] Lastly, says Hurtado, the Christian attitude in worship was not passive, but one in which the believer could expect to be changed by the Spirit. The early Church's intense charismatic experience of the risen Jesus in the context of worship was attractive to outsiders.[17]

(7) Seventh, *bereavement experiences can account for the appearances.* Offering this explanation as a sheer possibility, some critics have said that the appearances can be explained by the experience that widows and widowers sometimes have of their deceased spouses. Undoubtedly, bereavement experiences have some similar characteristics to what the evidence has produced for the appearances of the risen Christ.

For one thing, both groups find themselves immersed in grief after the recent death of a loved one. Second, both groups came into contact with the beloved. Third, these meetings were not initiated by the living, but came from "the other side." As a result of these experiences, the living felt enlightened and empowered.

Notwithstanding these similarities, there are many more differences that preclude this explanation from being taken seriously. First, they usually affect spouses that were married to one another for decades, not disciples of dead religious leaders. O'Collins writes: "before the 'bereavement,' the disciples of Jesus had enjoyed a different kind of relationship with a remarkably different kind of person who made quite extraordinary claims about his identity and mission. This dissimilarity affects the 'point of departure' for the proposed analogy."[18]

Moreover, one might argue that Paul had no acquaintance with Jesus during his earthly ministry. Thus the experience of grief would not apply in his case. "From the outset," says O'Collins, "any analogy between his meeting and with the risen Jesus on the road to Damascus and the experience of widows and widowers seems to be ruled out."[19]

Next, there are no indications that those who appeared to their living spouse died in the same way as Jesus. Indeed, they passed away from natural causes or accidents. There are no reported cases of suicides or homicides, let alone horribly cruel public executions.

15. Ibid., 53, 55.
16. Ibid., 56–57.
17. Hurtado, *Lord Jesus Christ*, 134–53, 619–24, 649–53.
18. O'Collins, "The Resurrection and Bereavement Experiences," 229.
19. Ibid.

Another reason for differentiating the two experiences is that bereavement experiences do not happen to groups. But in the New Testament there are simultaneous group experiences of the risen Jesus (Matt 28:9–10; Luke 24:13–35; John 21:1–14; 1 Cor 15:6). Another factor to consider is that these bereavement experiences can continue for many years after their spouses die. Aside from Paul, the resurrection appearances ceased shortly after Jesus was executed and buried.

Another difference is that the vast majority of the bereaved do not tell anyone about these episodes. The disciples of Jesus, however, told others about Jesus and inaugurated a new worldwide mission. Lastly, in the case of these bereavement episodes there is no life-long change. But the disciples set the world ablaze with their new convictions about Jesus' rising from the dead. Faced with the bereavement hypothesis, apologists should appeal to a simpler hypothesis which has greater explanatory power and a much broader scope: Jesus was supernaturally raised and appeared to individuals and groups of people. Some of these percipients included enemies and/or skeptics who did not expect Jesus to be raised.

What is more, belief in the bodily resurrection makes mere bereavement experiences untenable, especially in light of the Jewish matrix from which it came. As Wright suggested: "Meetings with Jesus, likewise, could by themselves have been interpreted in a variety of ways. Most people in the ancient world (though not so many, it seems, in the modern world) knew that visions and appearances of recently dead people occurred."[20] So it might be asked: why didn't these experiences lead the apostles to say Jesus was in Abraham's bosom? Or that he was in apocalyptic glory as some martyr-prophet? These inferences would have made more sense to make in the context of first-century Palestine. As Kasper asserted: "In neo-Judaism exaltation (or ecstasy) was available to express the fact that a human being on earth would still play a part in the eschatological events. Exaltation was therefore a current category, which was used in an attempt to express a person's eschatological importance."[21]

The earliest believers could certainly discriminate between physical, post-mortem encounters with Jesus and other visionary experiences. Pannenberg says: "one must at the same time take into consideration that primitive Christianity itself apparently knew how to distinguish between ecstatic visionary experiences and the fundamental encounters with the resurrected Lord."[22] Such explanations of these so-called meetings would

---

20. Wright, *The Resurrection of the Son of God*, 689.

21. Kasper, *Jesus the Christ*, 149.

22. Pannenberg, *Jesus—God and Man*, 94.

have confirmed for the percipients that Jesus was truly dead, not gloriously risen from the dead, never to die again. Lastly, that Jesus' tomb was found empty would also serve as evidence for the physicality of the appearances and distinguished them from mere visionary experiences.

(8) An eighth argument comes from Ehrman. *He claims that it is not within the province of historians to discuss the probability of miracles.* He writes: "I'm willing to grant that miracles—that is, events that we cannot explain within our concepts of how 'nature' normally works—can and do happen. There still remains, however, a huge, I'd even say, insurmountable problem when discussing Jesus' miracles. Even if miracles are *possible*, there is no way for the historian who sticks strictly to the canons of historical evidence to show that they have ever happened."[23] Lest historians commit the "god-of-the-gaps fallacy," methodological restraints prevent the historian from responsibly inferring that Jesus was raised. The "god of the gaps" fallacy is committed when historians prematurely invoke the supernatural to explain uncertainties about the past. For miracles are a matter of faith, not historical argument.

Now, when it comes to determining the cause(s) of the evidence, historians normally appeal to law-like regularities, not miraculous ones. Notice the indispensability of the arguments for the existence of God in responding to this argument. If an all-powerful and good God exists, then miracles will most likely occur on those occasions where God is going to communicate with humans. Miracles serve as confirmation of the divine message that will be given to humanity. As John Meier writes: "Whether we call it a bias, a *Tendenz*, a worldview, or a faith stance, everyone who writes on the historical Jesus writes from some ideological standpoint; no critic is exempt."[24]

Even if the historian is precluded from inferring a miracle because of methodological restraints, this would not mean that intellectually curious individuals cannot take the reins from professional historians at this step in the argument and draw the conclusion that Jesus was supernaturally raised. Indeed, it would be a tragedy if scholars were prevented from correctly describing the past because of methodological restraints. Background theories are inevitable and have an impact on the kind of conclusions that are made. No one can do history from a strictly neutral standpoint.

(9) When discussing the resurrection, Dale Allison is primarily concerned to rule out two extremes: hard apologetic claims—that is, demonstrative claims—and complete skepticism. "I tend to focus on the extremes"

23. Ehrman, *The New Testament*, 225–26. Cf. 228–29.
24. Meier, *A Marginal Jew*, 1.5, 6.

he says, "the convinced believer and the strident unbeliever."[25] While many apologists are convinced believers, this does not necessarily affect the soft form that historical apologetics takes. Explanations competing with the resurrection hypothesis are not seen as irrational. The more interesting question is whether naturalist explanations ought to be preferred over the resurrection hypothesis, given the evidence that many apologists and Allison already agree with. While most of Allison's book can be commended by defenders of Christian faith, he has unwittingly taken his concerns about "the convinced believer" and projected them onto historical apologists (such as Craig, O'Collins, and Wright) who have never attempted to cast the historical argument for Jesus' resurrection as an undeniable logical conclusion.[26]

Allison misunderstands Wright for holding, along with Craig, that the resurrection hypothesis is the "best historical explanation."[27] Allison thinks that Wright is trying to prove Jesus' resurrection; he places Wright in the same camp as William Hetherington, a rationalistic apologist from the late nineteenth century. But both Craig and Wright argue that the resurrection hypothesis is the best historical explanation, not in the sense that non-Christian explanations are irrational, but in the sense that it is the best explanation of the available evidence.

The Jewish scholar Alan Segal adopts a similar approach to Allison: "the vast majority of modern historians looking at the very same story would say that *no evidence at all would ever demonstrate that a unique resurrection took place*."[28] Segal's presupposition steers him in a direction that prevents him from seriously examining the credibility of Jesus' resurrection. Instead, he says, the issue is a matter of faith: "For me, this is the mark of faith; it does not depend on reason. If it did, it would be reason, not faith."[29] Like Allison, Segal overreacts to the perennial enterprise of historical apologetics, because Jesus' resurrection cannot be strictly demonstrated.

Most apologists concede that the resurrection cannot be absolutely proven. But this should not become an excuse to quit making any historical arguments. Most historical conclusions are tentative and, in theory, capable of revision. Saying that Jesus' resurrection is the best explanation of the

---

25. Allison, "Rational Apologetics and the Resurrection of Jesus," 327–28.

26. Allison, *Resurrecting Jesus*, 345. While Allison conclusively demonstrates the errors of hard apologetics, he mistakenly projects these concerns onto the arguments provided by apologists who merely want to say that the resurrection, cast as an historical hypothesis, is the best explanation of the known evidence.

27. Ibid., 345–46.

28. Alan Segal, "The Resurrection," in Stewart, ed., *The Resurrection of Jesus*, 135.

29. Ibid., 137.

known evidence is not a hard apologetic claim, but is a piece of inductive reasoning that historians can and should accept.

Allison moves on to critique Stephen Davis: "one can still land upon a new book or article with the assertion that 'alternative theories that have been proposed are not only weaker but far weaker at explaining the available historical evidence than the claim that God raised Jesus from the dead.'"[30] But here too Allison misses Davis' point. Davis is not saying that the resurrection is the best explanation, without qualification, but that the resurrection is the best inference to make in the light of the agreed-upon evidence. The inference is not presented as logically airtight. But are scholars supposed to refrain from making any arguments and reaching any conclusions on the basis of the available evidence? None of these scholars—Wright, Davis, and Craig—are pretending to do apologetics in the hard sense of the term.

(10) Allison argues that we do not have enough evidence to make a convincing case for Jesus' resurrection.[31] Here he is in agreement with many skeptics. Unquestionably, miracles are difficult to establish on historical grounds when the evidence is slight. Be that as it may, what one historian thinks is an insignificant amount of evidence will be significant to another. More important for our purposes is that Allison does not seem to notice that his complaint about the limits in evidence does not mitigate the force of the apologetic argument presented here.

Let us grant that the evidence is meager. Such an admission does not mean that historians should not try to explain that evidence to the best of their abilities. How much evidence is needed before one will proceed to test all the various hypotheses? Nowhere does Allison assess the amount of evidence available. Moreover, he does not seem to realize that in historical matters "a lot of evidence" can sometimes make it even more difficult to reach defensible historical conclusions—even when some alleged event is recent, has numerous witnesses, and is relatively simple. A significant amount of evidence does not necessarily make things easier for the "critical historian."

(12) Allison limits himself to possibilities instead of taking the initiative and presenting a defensible position that can account for the four reported facts mentioned above. The following point is not exactly interesting: "one can draw any number of curves through a finite set of points to create a thousand different pictures."[32] But the issue is not whether historians can construct viable hypotheses that can compete with the resurrection hypothesis, but whether other hypotheses can outstrip the latter through their use

---

30. Allison, *Resurrecting Jesus*, 345.

31. Allison, "Rational Apologetics and the Resurrection of Jesus," 325–26.

32. Allison, *Resurrecting Jesus*, 339.

of defensible arguments. Allison retorts: even if the resurrection happened, this does not mean that we can show that it happened; and if the resurrection did not happen, this would not mean that we can show that it did not happen.[33]

However, we must insist that the more appropriate alternative is to develop a defensible argument that might persuade others when they look at the available evidence. Allison reflects on what might count as legitimate evidence for the resurrection of Jesus, and concludes that some facts are relevant. Why then does he refuse to propose an hypothesis that can account for the reported facts?

(13) In a final argument, Allison maintains that apologists are already biased in favor of orthodox conclusions about the resurrection.[34] He endorses an allegedly "impartial" ideal: "we should try to establish the historical truth whether or not it upholds our theology." This leads him to defend his skeptical procedure and results: "I question the notion that I found what I was looking for, or that my theological uncertainty unduly infected my historical thinking."[35] Yet no scholars are simply "impartial." It is with their own philosophical presuppositions that they approach issues and interpret reality, and these presuppositions can be modified and changed through argument and experience.

While apologists, like anyone else, must work with a certain set of presuppositions, this does not exclude the possibility of Jesus' resurrection being the best explanation of the given evidence, when it is assessed. Believers can retain their presuppositions when comparing and contrasting their views with competing claims. The issue is: whose worldview or particular position makes the most sense out of the agreed-upon evidence? Simply put, for Allison and everyone else, there is no such thing as a "purely historical" approach to Jesus' life or resurrection.

Yet Allison maintains: "pure historical reasoning is not going to show us that God raised Jesus from the dead."[36] But is "pure historical reasoning" either desirable or even possible? Critical historians inevitably develop their arguments on the basis of some philosophical presuppositions, including some that pertain to religion. Allison himself plans to be as skeptical as possible: "the subject matter demands this."[37] In effect Allison privileges his presupposition, skepticism, as embodying the "purely historical" ideal. While

33. Ibid., 338.
34. Ibid., 342.
35. Allison, "Rational Apologetics and the Resurrection of Jesus," 320.
36. Allison, *Resurrecting Jesus*, 342.
37. Allison, "Rational Apologetics and the Resurrection of Jesus," 321.

Allison is quick to fault the orthodox for finding what they were looking for, should the same be said about him?

Yet Allison does not completely rule out the contribution of philosophy to historical enquiry: "In like fashion, I understand why Richard Swinburne, in his recent defense of the resurrection, commences by first seeking to establish the existence of a certain sort of God and the likelihood of this God communicating with and redeeming the human race."[38] What shape does Swinburne's natural theology take and how does it bear on his evidential approach to the resurrection?[39]

Swinburne's first step in his overall argument for the resurrection consists of showing how God might want to become a human being and do certain things in human history. These are his "a priori reasons" which, in his words, arise "from the very nature of God and from the general condition of the human race" and which suggest "why we should expect them to be true."[40] While it is not necessary for God to become human, there are still good reasons to think that he would do such a thing. It would be appropriate for God to identify himself with human beings; such an act would provide reasons for thinking that people have intrinsic dignity and reveals the extent to which God loves the human race. The incarnate God would live an exemplary human life in terms of teaching the truth about God and being supremely moral. A divine stamp of approval would rest on his life, vindicating his central message. The nature of God and the human race provide us with reason to think that God is likely to reveal himself at least once in human history. More importantly, according to Swinburne we can discern a general form in which this revelation might take place.

After the a priori reasons, Swinburne turns to what he dubs the "a posteriori evidence" for resurrection faith (the empty tomb, the appearances, and so forth). Swinburne then concludes that the a posteriori evidence for Jesus' resurrection resonates with the a priori reasons better than any other hypothesis that excludes the resurrection. He concludes: "Alternative hypotheses have always seemed to me to give far less satisfactory accounts of the historical evidence than does the traditional account."[41]

Yet Allison, after showing some initial openness, refuses to consider Swinburne's natural theology as a framework for a historical examination of the resurrection and is agnostic about this natural theology. At times he

---

38. Allison, *Resurrecting Jesus*, 341.

39. Swinburne, *The Resurrection of God-Incarnate*, 33–68.

40. Swinburne, *Was Jesus God?* 5.

41. Swinburne, "Evidence for the Resurrection," in Davis, Kendall, and O'Collins, eds., *The Resurrection*, 201.

brushes aside philosophy when it comes to "doing history." But philosophy, including the arguments of natural theology, deserve to influence historical thinking and argument, especially in a postmodern age which stresses academic collaboration and interdisciplinarity. If historians follow philosophers in acknowledging good reasons to think that God might reveal himself to us in a particular way, then that could rightly predispose them to see God at work in the person of Jesus.

Let us now turn to a more sophisticated objection to the resurrection. In many ways it is relevant to the bereavement vision hypothesis which was already covered. Were the appearances ghostly apparitions? Before answering this question, we must understand something about apparitions.

Parapsychology and Apparitions

Most apparitional experiences are documented in anecdotal reports. Unlike experimental evidence, which can be controlled and repeated under laboratory conditions, anecdotal evidence can be provided only by eyewitnesses who merely pass on the information related to their experiences. Whether the experience can be explained by paranormal processes is hotly debated in parapsychology. Sometimes these experiences are explained by naturalist processes such as hallucinations. But in other cases paranormal explanations seem to makes sense of the data.

Apparitions should be distinguished from mirages, illusions and, more problematically, hallucinations (which usually stem from drug use and/or mental illness). One of the criteria used to delineate apparitions from hallucinations or illusions is that new information is sometimes gleaned from the apparitional experience (perhaps the percipient learns something from the encounter that could not have been ordinarily known). Another criteria is that apparitions are sometimes seen by many people at once, whereas hallucinations cannot be collectively shared.

Apparitional research has resulted in what might be called a taxonomy of apparitional experiences.[42] The first type is usually called an "experimental apparitional experience." In these cases the living can somehow make themselves seen to someone else in another location. Though very few examples are discussed, these occurrences almost always happen to experients who are asleep or in a trance-like state. Experimental apparitions have led

---

42. Sidgwick, et al., "Report on the Census of Hallucinations," 25–422; Tyrrell, *Apparitions*, 35–36; Green and McCreery, *Apparitions*; Haraldsson et al., "National Survey of Psychical Experiences and Attitudes Towards the Paranormal in Iceland;" John Palmer, "A Community Mail Survey of Psychic Experiences," 226–39.

some parapsychologists to maintain that at least some apparitions are not merely subjective.[43] However, almost two-thirds of all apparitions reported are of the dead, not the living.[44]

A second type is known as "crisis apparitions." These meetings occur when the person represented by the apparition is in some sort of crisis (such as an accident or is near death). As a general rule of thumb, parapsychologists hold that these experiences occur within twelve hours before or after the crisis begins. These apparitions are very short lived, meaning they do not reoccur over an extended period of time. In many cases the percipient does not expect or think about the person represented by the phantasm.

A third category is known as the "postmortem apparitional experience." Almost all of these represent someone who has been dead for at least twelve hours. Based on the famous Chaffin case (1927), the persons involved with these apparitions have been known to exchange unknown information to the experient(s). Irwin and Watt write: "Note also in this case the apparition had both a visual and an auditory component. As with the other types of apparition, the figure is lifelike and appears suddenly and unexpectedly."[45] Sometimes these experiences appear in a dream; but in other cases the apparition appears in ordinary circumstances. They are sometimes seen by a group of people, although all experients may not see the phantasm. Most apparitions are experienced visually, in about four-fifths of the reported cases.[46]

The fourth category is known as the common ghost experience (otherwise known as a "haunt"). In these cases a figure appears in the same locality over an extended period of time. Given this description of hauntings, usually many different people have the chance to see them. Ghosts do not show much awareness of the living. These characteristics seem to evade the common depiction of ghosts in folklore. "Additionally, ghosts seem more somnambulistic in their movements. Some ghosts reportedly perform the same actions in the same location on each occasion they are experienced."[47] They perform the same "behavior" whether they are seen or not.

With this fourfold classification of apparitional experiences in mind, we should focus on the "postmortem apparitional experience" if we are going to seek an analogy with the appearances. Like many of the reports that

43. Cf. Rogo, "Apparitions, Hauntings, and Poltergeists," in Mitchell and White, eds., *Psychic Exploration*, 376–77; Tyrrell, *Apparitions*, 142–48.

44. Palmer, "A Community Mail Survey of Psychic Experiences," 228.

45. Irwin and Watt, *An Introduction to Parapsychology*, 197.

46. Green and McCreery, *Apparitions*, 143.

47. Irwin and Watt, *An Introduction to Parapsychology*, 197.

describe the nature of apparitions, the appearances happened over a period of time, not merely within twelve hours after Jesus' death. Other types of apparitional experiences do not resonate with the reports given by the New Testament data. Andrew MacKenzie and Jane Henry observe: "The hardest apparitions to explain by normal means are crisis apparitions where information about the death of a person appears to have been transmitted correctly by the apparition, and collective cases where more than one person sees the same apparition."[48]

If a skeptic is going to focus on apparitions as a substitute for understanding and explaining the appearances, then the responsible thing to do is cite the relevant case studies from postmortem apparitions, not haphazardly cite studies from the other three types. Nor does it seem responsible for critics to patch together unrelated cases of apparitional experiences if we are going to link them to the nature of the appearances (simply because the other three types do not resemble what has been concluded by the New Testament witnesses). Because the current state of apparitions research within the field of parapsychology is highly indecisive and uncertain in this regard, it is exceedingly difficult to extrapolate individual cases of postmortem apparitional experiences as the exclusive and/or univocal basis for understanding the appearances.

To make matters more complicated, many apparitional experiences are not easily explained by paranormal processes. Many parapsychologists explain them away as naturalist occurrences. There is no general consensus in the community of parapsychologists heading in either direction about this problem.[49] MacKenzie and Henry comment: "Apparitions can be thought of as nothing more than hallucinations and the bulk of cases probably are just that."[50] For every apparitional case study that runs parallel to the appearances, another case study can be cited against it. Researchers do not usually know whether the apparitional experiences reported are indeed paranormal (instead of being naturalist), let alone that they could also be postmortem apparitional experiences that happen to individuals, groups and enemies of the deceased.

There is simply no end to this point-counterpoint contest. Consider the following case: "The apparition itself may appear solid and lifelike or semitransparent. It may be seen and heard by all present; or some people may not see it, even when their attention is drawn to the position where it is.

48. MacKenzie and Henry, "Apparitions and Encounters," in Henry, ed., *Parapsychology*, 182.

49. Houran and Lange, *Hauntings and Poltergeists*, 4. See also Irwin and Watt, *Introduction to Parapsychology*, 201.

50. See also MacKenzie and Henry, *Parapsychology*, 183.

It may appear and disappear in locked rooms."[51] Quite naturally, this single anecdotal report smoothly parallels the appearances in some specific ways. But notice that it says nothing about which of the four types of apparitional experiences that it might have been.

Further, we also have other reports in the literature where the phantasm ate food and was touched.[52] Perhaps, then, Jesus ate the fish! But, as Charles Green and Celia McCreery have emphasized, the referent person represented by the phantasm usually appears within three meters of the experient(s) and is not previously known by them.[53] Obviously this report paints a picture that runs contrary to the appearance to the disciples—and to those who knew of Jesus (such as the apostle Paul).

Other examples can easily be cited. Postmortem apparitional experiences almost always happen indoors. By contrast, the New Testament writers suggest that Jesus appeared both inside and outside. Or again, Alan Gauld says that apparitions (of the four types, we are *not* told) cannot be used as evidence for life after death.[54] Irwin and Watt agree: "The spirit hypothesis of apparitional experiences now is promoted by a minority of modern parapsychologists."[55] Still others maintain that apparitions provide evidence for the afterlife.[56] Of course, Catholic theologians have always held that Jesus' resurrection serves as the exemplar and forerunner of the eschatological resurrection.

Or again, one of the basic features of the appearances is that they were mission-inaugurating experiences (cf. Matt 28:18–20). But, in the majority of apparitional reports (again, which of the four types?), there seems to be no life-changing mission that accompanies the experience.[57] Brian Nisbet has mused: "The genuine apparition . . . is more likely to appear as a normally clothed figure, which is seen for a few brief moments and then vanishes or gradually fades away. Sometimes a reason for its appearance can be suggested; but more often there is none."[58]

Moreover, it should always be kept in mind that most anecdotal reports on apparitional experiences in the relevant literature do not resemble

---

51. Nisbet, "Apparitions," in Guinness, ed., *Psychical Research*, 92.

52. Green and McCreery, *Apparitions*, 102–13; Tyrrell, *Apparitions*, 63.

53. Green and McCreery, *Apparitions*, 123.

54. See Alan Gauld's chapter "Survival," in Henry, *Parapsychology*, 215–23.

55. Irwin and Watt, *An Introduction to Parapsychology*, 202.

56. One of the best current examples can be found in Haraldsson, *The Departed Among the Living*.

57. Ibid., 131–35.

58. Nisbet, "Apparitions," 91.

the appearances at all. Only certain cases will characterize certain (not all) features that run parallel to the appearances. Apparitions are not usually seen by groups (only 2–12 percent), let alone by "more than 500" at one time.[59] They are not usually seen by enemies (less than 1 percent of the deceased appear to one of their former enemies).[60] The vast majority of them are unable to be touched (only 2.7 percent can be touched). Less than 1 percent of the cases lead the experient(s) to believe that the referent person had been raised bodily from the dead. Yet all of these characteristics are featured at the origins of Easter faith.

So it would be an exceptionally rare case that an apparition would be characterized by all of these features in a series of different episodes over a period of weeks (or much later on, as in the case of Paul's experience of Jesus). Consequently, when each improbability is multiplied by the other improbabilities, we arrive at a staggering chance: 1:3,800,000.[61] In effect the chance that any one apparition would be described by all four features makes the possibility of a constructive comparison between apparitions and the appearances exceptionally implausible (and irresponsible). Even worse for the chances of constructive comparison, it is highly uncertain how any of these cases could be neatly categorized into any of the four types of apparitional experiences.

While most parapsychologists confidently hold to the reality of parapsychological experiences, they are highly divided as to whether paranormal factors can account for them. Added to this problem is the lack of understanding about the individual cases of apparitions and how the statistics pertaining to each of them might compare to the conclusions about the appearances. For every apparitional experience that is similar to the appearances, another case can be cited to highlight the dissimilarities between them.

It is not logically impossible to patch together unrelated apparitional experiences as a control belief to retranslate the original meanings assigned to the Easter appearances. But an agnostic position seem to be more justified about the nature of apparitional experiences. Although many parapsychologists are convinced that apparitions occur, there is not enough positive evidence for the nature and originating cause of apparitions to make a constructive comparison between them and the appearances. Those who disagree with my contentions are forced to demonstrate their case otherwise.

59. Green and McCreery, *Apparitions*, 41.

60. Allison, *Resurrecting Jesus*, 267, n283, 284.

61. 0.12 x 0.009 x 0.27 x 0.009 = 0.0000002644.

Resurrection Appearances
or Ghostly Apparitions?

For the skeptical scholar Dale Allison, the apologist's inference to the resurrection of Jesus would make sense only given the traditional meaning of the appearances. He disputes whether they were originally perceived by the disciples and Paul as resurrection appearances. Let us discuss Allison's position on ghostly apparitions and how they might affect the inference to the resurrection.

First, Allison grants that the disciples saw Jesus in a series of appearances in different times and places: "These appear to be the facts, and they raise the question of how we should explain them."[62] The emphasis is not exclusively placed on the disciples' experience. *Jesus also saw them.*[63] After experiencing the risen Lord (1 Cor 15:8), Paul believed in a one-to-one correspondence between the earthly body and the transformed, resurrected body that is to come: "there is no good evidence for belief in a non-physical resurrection in Paul, much less within the primitive Jerusalem community. . . . Even Paul, in 1 Cor. 15, when defending the notion of a 'spiritual body,' teaches—like 2 *Bar.* 51:10—the transformation of corpses, not their abandonment."[64] The earliest percipients were convinced that Jesus had been raised bodily, not just spiritually, or immaterially.[65] Thus the appearances are to be distinguished from later visual phenomena in the early Christian communities.[66]

Believing in the resurrection did not mean that the recently deceased was naturally present to the living, but it included one's physical body being transformed to new life (never to die again). Commenting on the possibility of understanding the resurrection as the continued presence of the recently deceased, Allison wrote: "I know of no evidence for this point of view."[67] He also speaks of the widespread belief of the earliest Christians in the bodily resurrection of Jesus.[68]

Anecdotal evidence for apparitions indicates cases where the referent person was seen and heard; seen by many individuals at a time; seen by some

---

62. Allison, *Resurrecting Jesus*, 269; cf. 346.

63. Allison, "The Resurrection of Jesus and Rational Apologetics," 315; Allison, *Resurrecting Jesus*, 346.

64. Allison, *Resurrecting Jesus*, 317.

65. Ibid., 314, 317, 325 n497.

66. Ibid., 260.

67. Ibid., 325n497.

68. Ibid., 230.

but not all; offered reassurance to the living; seen as real and/or solid; and seen less and less as time goes on.[69] Notwithstanding these parallels to the appearances, Allison himself recognizes that these cannot be used to retranslate the original meaning of the appearances: "I eschew explaining the appearances of Jesus in terms of typical appearances from the dead—an unfeasible task anyway given our limited knowledge and understanding of apparitions in general—but simply ask what light a wider human phenomenon might shed on some of the issues surrounding the resurrection stories."[70]

Allison goes on to say that apparitional experiences "cannot explain the specific content of the words attributed to the risen Jesus." Of the reported cases, he says, none of them led "to the founding of a new religion."[71] Because Jesus was a messianic figure, the appearances took on a different kind of significance for the original percipients, leading the first disciples to worship the Christ.[72] Context begets meaning. An empty tomb, to be sure, does not usually accompany an apparition either!

Allison does claim that apparitional experiences can be merely used as a heuristic tool for understanding what happened to Paul and the other percipients.[73] With apparitional reports in hand, Allison argues that a skeptic might wish to challenge apologists. According to Allison:

> A skeptic, however, would, with some justification readily respond that these defects of apparition reports apply equally to the New Testament accounts. For example, can anyone really come up with proof or even strong evidence that the stories in Luke and John in which the risen Jesus eats and invites himself to be touched (Luke 24: 36–43; John 20:24–29) comes ultimately from eyewitnesses? I freely grant that one cannot show that they do not; but this is scarcely the same as showing that they do. So are not these important gospel paragraphs, from an evidential point of view, "lacking" something? In other words, just like so many apparitional accounts, they are "questionable," because their origin cannot be established. Many scholars have no problem classifying Luke 24:36–43 and John 20:24–29 as later apologetic. Is this not a possibility?[74]

69. Ibid., 279–82.

70. Ibid., 285.

71. Ibid., 283. Cf. 284.

72. Bauckham, *Jesus and the God of Israel*, 232; Dunn, *Did the First Christians Worship Jesus?* 24; Hurtado, *Lord Jesus Christ*, 64–65; Hurtado, *How on Earth Did Jesus Become a God?* 151, 192–94, 199.

73. Allison, *Resurrecting Jesus*, 285.

74. Allison, "The Resurrection of Jesus and Rational Apologetics," 329.

Allison limits himself to possibilities instead of taking the initiative to present a defensible position. The issue is not whether historians *can* construct viable hypotheses that *can* compete with the resurrection, but whether other hypotheses can outstrip the latter through the use of arguments.

So, the more appropriate alternative is to develop a defensible argument that might persuade others when looking at the evidence. Allison reflects on what might count as evidence for the resurrection, and he concludes that some facts are relevant. Why then does he refuse to propose an hypothesis that can account for those facts? In other terms, Allison deduces what he thinks should count as evidence (by garnering the arguments to establish the burial, the post-mortem appearances, the empty tomb, and the origin of the disciples' faith in the resurrection), but he balks at the opportunity to explain those reported facts. Instead he flaunts the mere possibility that the appearances might have been apparitions to defuse the apologetic claim.

A paucity of evidence should indeed drive historians down the path of humility. But in some cases humility can be employed immoderately, strengthening an agnosticism that militates against the evidence which favors one position over the others. Such a problem is paramount in Allison's work. Even if we have "meager evidence" for a purported event, this would not mean that historians should not attempt to explain the evidence. Sometimes a lot of evidence can sometimes make it more difficult to explain what actually happened. Thus historians are not forced to disprove all competing hypotheses before they decide responsibly which explanation to defend. If a single hypothesis seems to stand out among the alternatives, then historians should accept that hypothesis.

Allison agrees with the biblical evidence in support of the frequency and nature of the resurrection appearances. Correspondingly, he should not always easily concede other possibilities. For every apparitional experience that is similar to the appearances, another case can be cited to highlight the dissimilarities between them. Thus agnosticism is the proper stance to take with respect to apparitions research (not an agnosticism with respect to whether apparitions occur, but an agnosticism that disallows speaking definitively on the origin, nature, and frequency of apparitions).

Positively speaking, apologists have something meaningful to say about the Easter appearances. They assess the New Testament writings not as the written Word of God but as a collection of reliable Greek documents coming down to us from the first century. Allison himself agrees with the conclusions tentatively established. Negatively speaking, there is not enough positive evidence to establish anything significant about the nature, cause and frequency of apparitions to make a constructive comparison between them and the appearances. Again, Allison agrees with the latter point.

Furthermore, Allison is well aware that the appearance narratives are not historical in every detail. He knows that this circumstantial problem should not preclude one from affirming the historicity of the appearances. Critical realism allows the historian to arrive at this conclusion. Parapsychologists are equally critical when analyzing the extraordinary experiences of many individuals, but have not arrived at an equally warranted positive conclusion. Rather, the established facts within the field of apparitions research are practically nonexistent.

So it is disanalogous for Allison to compare the "skepticism" of New Testament scholars and the "skepticism" concerning apparitional experiences. Practitioners within each of these fields arrive at two different conclusions with different degrees of certainty (or, uncertainty). Allison concedes the conclusions set by both camps.

By appealing to the pre-Easter predictions of Jesus, Allison's next argument is that a skeptic could responsibly hold that the resurrection appearances were in reality only apparitions but later retranslated into the language of the bodily resurrection. Jesus' predictions about himself are

> the sort of thing a skeptic would wholeheartedly welcome. Would not the evidence for the resurrection be stronger if we could believe that Jesus did not forecast his resurrection, so that the appearances were utterly surprising, totally unprepared for, and so out of the blue? . . . I am unsure of the apologetical payoff. Keeping in mind that religious movements tend to interpret events in terms of already established categories and expectations, . . . could one not argue that the disciples, upon having apparitional encounters with Jesus, interpreted them in terms of resurrection because resurrection was the category that Jesus had antecedently given them?[75]

Notice that Allison once again refers to the logical possibility of apparitions to explain the appearances. This historiographical problem has already been addressed. Further, Allison himself affirms the reality of the resurrection appearances. Moreover, he disputes the positive meaning that may be established (albeit tentatively) in the field of apparitions research. Thus Allison might wish to play the role of the apologist when facing the skeptical challenge that he mentions.

Even if Jesus predicted his resurrection, this would have added weight to the religiously charged context that is not only needed to advance the argument for Jesus' resurrection, but would have been useful for understanding the nature of the appearances. Nonetheless, Paul was unaware of these

75. Ibid., 331. Cf. Allison, *Resurrecting Jesus*, 347.

pre-Easter predictions. Presumably, at least some of the 500 (1 Cor 15:6) were unaware of them as well.

Allison responds that a skeptic's worldview might allow her to make the apparitions inference. Perhaps she has had a firsthand experience of an apparition and, consequently, strongly suspects that if the original percipients had the same experience(s), this would have driven them to affirm with unwavering constancy that Jesus had been raised bodily:

> While there is not a sliver of evidence for such a fantastic state of affairs, it cannot be dismissed as inconceivable, only wholly unlikely for utter lack of evidence. . . . The hypothetical scenario goes to show that proof of the Christian confession can never be achieved because possible alternatives can always be imagined. It also raises the question how Christians have come to the view that invoking space aliens beggars belief whereas crediting God with a resurrection is sensible. Science fiction . . . has certainly not hesitated to give aliens the power to raise human beings from the dead, so at least we find the notion intelligible.[76]

Allison repeatedly conflates the historians' use of the best explanation and the notion of proof. He needs to recognize that apologists usually cast their argument through the use of the former, not the latter. Second, Allison needs to assess the arguments of natural theology with the evidence for aliens in order for the analogy of the apparition hypothesis to work. Let us now turn to the role that background beliefs might have in constructing the case for the resurrection.

One of the deepest and most perennial questions that people ask pertains to life after death. These common questions stem from our natural inclinations. It makes sense that God will concern himself with personal creatures to give them some answers to help resolve the problem of death. If we take the questions about human destiny seriously, people must search for clues in history to get some answers about what lies beyond the grave. In the words of Walter Kasper:

> The question of man's purpose in life cannot be answered from within his own history but only eschatologically. Implicitly, therefore, in all the fundamental processes of his life, man is driven by the problem of life and its ultimate purpose. The answer will not be found until the end of history. For the moment all man can do is to listen to and look at history and try to find signs in which that end is portrayed or even anticipated. Those signs will always be ambiguous within history; they will only

76. Allison, *Resurrecting Jesus*, 340.

become clear in the light of faith's perceptions of that end of history, just as conversely that perception must constantly make sure of its own validity in the light of history. Only if the problem is seen in this comprehensive perspective can the testimonies of the early Church and of the later church tradition be understood meaningfully.[77]

In Christianity, life does not end at the grave, but continues on in a bodily life that is glorious, incorruptible, and eternal.

Allison is inclined to accept a bare deism. In a revealing admission, Allison says "I am reluctantly a cryptic Deist. My tendency is to live my life as though God made the world and then went away. It is hard for me to see the hand of providence either in history or in individual lives, including my own."[78] It follows that Allison's reference to aliens is disanalogous to support his case against the historical argument for the resurrection. Unless he can refute Aquinas' proofs for the existence of God and then provide convincing evidence for the existence of aliens—and then explain why those particular aliens would have a keen interest to raise Jesus, apologists seem to be justified in holding to the resurrection of Jesus over its competing causal theories. It is possible that a theistic God will make a personal entry into human history in order to provide human beings with answers to their deepest questions about their final destiny.

Conclusion

Most skeptics admit that there is some evidence for the resurrection. But these skeptics hesitate to take the evidence seriously because of ancillary reasons related to establishing what should count as evidence. Though some apologists might be passionate about the argument for Jesus' resurrection, this should not be confused with the attempt to demonstrate it. Rather, the most sophisticated critics generally speak in tentative terms about the evidence, affirming the resurrection as the best explanation of the known data, not the only or strictly exclusive explanation.

Ehrman and Allison, for instance, claim that the appearances can be reinterpreted as bereavement experiences, but this possibility is ruled out for a variety of reasons. Historians are not forced to disprove all competing views before they award historicity to the most defensible one. If a single conclusion seems to stand out among all other alternatives, then historians

---

77. Kasper, *Jesus the Christ*, 136.
78. Allison, *Resurrecting Jesus*, 215.

should accept that explanation. Ehrman's only significant argument against the case for the resurrection—let alone taking it as the best explanation of the evidence—has to do with his endorsement of methodological naturalism. But this restraint is outdated in an age where historians take philosophy and other disciplines seriously.

All historians are inevitably influenced by the social sciences, philosophy, and even religious commitments. There is no such thing as the historical method apart from the influence of presuppositions. In sum, the skeptics' case against the resurrection of Jesus is inadequate. The rationality of the resurrection should be upheld over its rival (rational) hypotheses.

PART FOUR

The Relevance of Christian Belief

— 11 —

Prospects for Developing
the *Via Empirica*

THROUGHOUT THE CHURCH'S HISTORY, many apologists have tried to demonstrate the truth of Catholic Christianity by showing how the Church epitomizes the four ecclesiastical attributes (oneness, holiness, catholicity, and apostolicity). As a result of the Second Vatican Council, many Catholic theologians have argued that the marks can be found in some measure— qualitatively speaking—in other churches and ecclesial communities. Gone is the preconciliar approach which insisted that the Catholic Church is the only Church that can achieve unity and holiness.[1]

Yet this decline in apologetics does not mean that arguments for Catholicism should be abandoned. For the ecumenical movement itself continues to grow out of the conviction that when Christians are truly one, holy, catholic, and apostolic, the gospel will increase in credibility. Thus apologetics needs to be modified in light of the Catholic Church's participation in the ecumenical movement, taking on a more holistic approach than before.

When Christians recite in the ancient creeds that the Church embodies the four marks, they are still affirming the fundamental features by which the true Church is recognized. Although the Council says that ecclesial elements, sanctification, and gifts of the Holy Spirit can be found outside Catholicism, this does not nullify her claim that she is the truest or fullest expression of the Church.[2] In no way does the Council endorse ecclesiastical relativism.

---

1. For an article length discussion of the preconciliar use of the marks for apologetics, see Fenton, "The True Church and the Notes of the Church," 282–97.

2. Vatican II, *Lumen Gentium*, 8; Vatican II, *Unitatis Redintegratio*, 8; Vatican II, *Dignitatis Humanae*, 1.

Prior to the Council, many Catholic theologians sought to establish the Church's distinctive doctrinal and moral claims over Protestant and Orthodox Christianities on the basis of the marks. Now, a postconciliar apologist would certainly be within his or her epistemic rights to show the superior expression of the marks within Catholicism,[3] but that is not the intention of this chapter. My aim is to reach outsiders and even hesitant believers with some reasons for perceiving the positive difference that Catholicism can make. Here the marks are utilized to lend credibility to the Divine Founder, not to provide support for Catholicism over other Christian groups.

The *via empirica* is a toned-down variation of the traditional argument from the four "notes" of the true Church mentioned in the Creed: one, holy, catholic, and apostolic, but is less triumphalistic and more modest in admitting both true holiness outside of Catholic Christianity and periodic limitations and corruptions within the latter. Nevertheless, one is justified in claiming that Catholicism has worked as a leaven to improve any society that embraces it in myriad ways.

The argument from the "transformative influence of the Christian faith upon the world" resonates well with the classical apologetics. If God raised Jesus from the dead, we would expect to see his life and teachings make a difference in the lives of those individuals who entrust themselves in faith as a member of the Church. Human beings have a real need to hear from God to answer their most perplexing questions about life.

Catholic Apologetics and the Ecclesial Attributes

In contrast to Pius XII's papal encyclical *Mystici Corporis*, which identified the Church of Christ directly with the Catholic Church, the Fathers of Vatican II inaugurated a remarkable shift by identifying more broadly the nature of the Church. In *Lumen Gentium*, for instance, the bishops declared that the church subsists in (and not simply is) the Catholic Church.[4] Given this more expansive view of the ecclesiastical landscape, the bishops envision the church as a complex reality, not a "perfect society" (as expressed in the older manuals of apologetics) or a single community holding to the four properties exclusively. Correspondingly, the Church is recognized as

---

3. Examples of the apologetic use of the marks (the *via notarum*) can be found in Rahner, *Foundations of Christian Faith*, 346–69; Latourelle, *Christ and the Church*, 133–63, 211–64; Ashley, *Choosing a World-View and Value-System*, 211–68.

4. Vatican II, *Lumen Gentium*, 8.

an invisible and visible reality, a mystical and hierarchical society, unable to be fully grasped.

According to Vatican II, the Church of Christ subsists in the Catholic Church. Hence Catholics can no longer hold to the older style of Catholic defense. Grace is not a quantitative thing, limited to Catholics alone. Rather, it is qualitative, dynamically and efficaciously working in the entire Church of Christ. As a result of the Council's teaching, many Catholic theologians think differently about the marks. Other churches and ecclesiastical communities can be one, holy, catholic, and apostolic.

One consequence of this remarkable shift is that other believers who take advantage of the gifts and callings they received can become more one, holy, catholic, and apostolic than Catholics: all churches can in fact attain an equal if not higher degree of sanctity than Catholics alone. As Avery Dulles concludes: "Unity, holiness, catholicity, and apostolicity are dynamic realities that depend on . . . the Holy Spirit. Evangelical communities that excel in love for Jesus Christ and in obedience to the Holy Spirit may be more unitive, holy, catholic and apostolic than highly sacramental and hierarchically organized churches in which faith and charity have become cold."[5]

Thus the Council makes it difficult for apologists to demonstrate that Catholic Christianity better embodies the ecclesial attributes than other Christian communities. The Church of Christ is a mystery. Grace, it should be stressed, is not quantitative. As a human institution, the Church fails to live up to her divine calling at times. However, all other things being equal, ecclesial vitality and institutional integrity can be found in greater measure in the Catholic Church than in other churches. In the words of Francis Sullivan: "What the Catholic apologist now has to justify is the claim of his church to have a certain fullness of what it means to be a church, and a fullness of the essential properties, such that it can rightly be said that the church of Christ subsists there in a way that is not found in other churches."[6]

Although the ambitious attempt of showing the superior quality of the marks within Catholicism is occasionally pursued by apologists in the postconciliar era, my goal in this chapter is to provide a defense of Christian faith in response to the secularist allegation that says Christian faith does more harm than good in the world. This argument was once known as the *via empirica*. My argument is more attentive to a more broadly ecumenical era. As Sullivan suggests: "there is reason to hope that in the future a Catholic apologist will be able to base the *via notarum* on an understanding

5. Dulles, "The Church as 'One, Holy, Catholic, and Apostolic," 27.

6. Sullivan, "Notes of the Church," in Fisichella and Latourelle, eds., *Dictionary of Fundamental Theology*, 174.

of these properties that would represent at least a convergence, if not a full convergence, that had been achieved through ecumenical study and dialogue."[7] Unlike the strict use of the *via notarum*, which was used to argue for Catholic Christianity, my argument will uphold and defend a contemporary version of the *via empirica*—itself a form of the *via notarum*.

By definition, grace manifests itself in persons and changes them for the better. That is why this argument should always remain valid, even in a postconciliar Church. As Joseph A. Komonchak observes,

> The church's very existence is supposed to make the world different. It would be a mistake, then, to imagine a tension, much less a dichotomy, between the texts of the council that, to use a not entirely happy distinction made at the time, speak of the *Ecclesia ad intra* and those that speak of the *Ecclesia ad extra*, to contrast a theological to a sociological or historical approach to the Church, or to divide the theological notions of the Church up between these two pretended oppositions. It is true, of course, that some notions direct attention more clearly than others to one or another of these dimensions, but it is a single dynamic historical agent that these dimensions constitute and these notions describe. . . . The mystery of the Church is realized in the history of the world.[8]

Each of the four marks logically implies the presence of the others. God's grace brings people together (unity), and it enables them to reach their potential as human beings (holiness). Part of what it means to be a human is to be inclusive towards others (catholicity). With this spiritual connection, there is historical continuity with other believers, reaching backward into the past (apostolicity).

The notion that the Church in its concrete existence can provide testimony to its Divine Founder has never been absent in Catholic thought. As the Canadian Catholic theologian René Latourelle once noted: "The argument is a traditional one in the church. From the first centuries, the Fathers, primarily Irenaeus, Tertullian, Origen, and Augustine, appealed to it to defend Christianity, its miraculous spread, the constancy of its martyrs, and the brilliance of its holiness."[9] In modern theology the argument was eventually taken up by Savonarola, Bossuet, Pascal, Lacordaire, Bautin, Dechamps, Kleutgen, and Franzelin.

7. Ibid.
8. Komonchak, "The Significance of Vatican Council II for Ecclesiology," in Phan, ed., *The Gift of the Church*, 90–91.
9. Latourelle, *Theology of Revelation*, 417–18.

Let us now turn to some philosophical arguments to understand how Catholic belief is thought to make a difference in the lives of those who entrust themselves in faith.

The Inner-Rationale of Catholicism and the Difference it Makes

Traditional Catholic theology holds that the strongest form of moral motivation can be discovered only by receiving God's grace, and pursuing a life that is lived in relationship with him. God's special infusion of grace is the necessary ingredient to live out the virtues in the way they are intended to be lived out. Healing the person, God's grace brings the acquired virtues to fulfillment by elevating believers to perform supernatural acts, securing them on the right path to their final end. These supernatural acts cannot be performed unless one receives God's grace.

Rather than merely stating that grace makes believers more virtuous than they would be without it, there are at least four reasons that can be philosophically adduced to provide an inner-rationale of the difference Christianity makes in the world. Only someone who has faith will recognize the effects of receiving grace. But, unbelievers can still apprehend the intrinsic connection between Christianity and the way in which believers develop stronger forms of moral motivation.

First, because human life does not end at the grave in a Christian universe, all persons are held accountable for their actions during their earthly lives. In the end the scales of justice will finally be balanced, and righteousness will prevail over evil. Every evil will be transformed for the greater good. In turn every decision that is made by Christians in this lifetime has eternal significance because there is something to hope for in the end. Christian believers can, therefore, make decisions that run strongly against temporal pressures and embrace acts of extreme self-sacrifice for the greater good.

Second, belief in the Christian God provides moral resolution in a world which is highly pluralist and uncertain with respect to moral matters. A radical moral pluralism can easily lead to skepticism about morality and despair, making it easy, if not inevitable, to doubt the moral efficacy of human beings altogether. One of the problems with atheism is that not only is objective morality undermined, but so is rational thought. A world of complete and total chance is not a world of reason, but of chaos. Rational beliefs may help us in our struggle for survival, but naturalism does not build up confidence in helping persons know that their beliefs are in fact true.

Sometimes moral skepticism makes it seemingly irrational to sacrifice oneself for another for the greater good, because there is no guarantee that this sacrifice is precisely what is needed to achieve that good. In this way, moral skepticism can lead to a deprivation of the motivating force in building virtue. Skepticism about morality does not take away the natural desire to be moral, but it does take away the motivating force because morality is intimately connected with commitments, expectations, and hopes. In order to transcend the impasse, something must provide moral guidance—something such as a divine revelation and providence.

Third, if people embrace the moral point of view, they need the satisfaction of knowing that they will have a reasonable chance of success at being moral. Atheists—whether they are of the critical or practical variety—do not have the benefit of knowing that they will have a good chance of success at being moral, because there are so many factors outside of their control that prevent them from reaching their full potential within the limited amount of time they have to live. To be fair, atheism is consistent with a deterministic view of human beings.

As one recognizes that it is very likely that the history of the universe will not be good on the whole, no matter what one does, it seems that this futility will induce a cynical sense of futility about the moral life, undermining one's moral resolve and one's interest in moral consequences. Belief in the living, revealed God, by contrast, enables one to overcome moral weakness and inefficacy when facing the difficulties of moral living. The grace that manifests itself in the infused virtues provides one with a greater chance of success in facing the challenge of living the moral life.

Fourth, Catholic belief in the communion of saints helps believers to live a more moral life by removing the feeling of cosmic loneliness, which can lead to despair. At the heart of this doctrine is the belief that there is a communication of spiritual gifts among the elect. This sharing includes those who have passed into the next life. With this conception of spiritual communication in mind, believers become more conscious of their obligation to contribute to the common good and also of the extent to which they are indebted to others for their own spiritual blessings. All believers, regardless of their situation—no matter how dismal life might appear—can contribute to the betterment of the entire world through their lived example, prayer, and other spiritual sacrifices (even if they are performed alone or in secret).

Now these arguments are suggestive and not individually probative. Each piece of evidence is presented to create a cumulative case argument. An accumulated amount of evidence, while unable to be persuasive if one takes one piece at a time, becomes more persuasive when combined together. By no means are these four points comprehensive accounts of the inner-rationale of Catholic or Christian beliefs; other doctrines could certainly be included. The point is that Christianity enables believers to embrace a distinctively moral life view that seems out of reach in worldviews antithetical to Christianity.

Given the inner rationale of Christianity, we should expect empirical traces of its influence in those societies it has deeply permeated. Karl Rahner once drew attention to this point: "God really *has* redeemed, he really *has* poured out his Spirit, he really *has* done mighty things for sinners, he *has* let his light shine in the darkness . . . she [the Church] must not declare this merely as a *possibility* provided by God . . . as if one could merely 'presume' that God has poured out his Spirit without giving any evidence at all of his mighty wind and his tongues of fire."[10]

The Church can count a large number of believers who have lived as heroic exemplars of sanctity in every historical age and circumstance. So confident is the Church's belief in the effects of Christianity that she has declared that the Church itself is a motive of credibility.[11] Exemplifying a type of sacrament, the Church "is not a force or entity which exists in its own right. On the contrary, it points away from itself, and beyond itself."[12] The transformation of so many people in different cultures across the ages requires an explanation.

Prospects for Developing
the *Via Empirica*

Observations from history strongly suggest that Christianity has led to an improvement in the physical, scientific, artistic, social, and political lives of countless individuals. The Church's beliefs and practices are distinctive in the sense that they form the worldviews of individuals to perceive reality in a certain way, inaugurating the Kingdom of God "on earth as it is in heaven."

Only someone who has faith will recognize the mystery of the four marks, but reason can apprehend the change that Christianity has had on a civilization. The *Catechism of the Catholic Church* remarks:

---

10. Rahner, *Theological Investigations*, 3.94.

11. For an apologetic discussion of the Church as sacrament, see Dulles, *A Church to Believe In*, 41–52; Dulles, "The Church," in Latourelle and O'Collins, eds., *Problems and Perspectives of Fundamental Theology*, 259–73.

12. Kasper, *Theology and Church*, 117.

Only faith can recognize that the Church possesses these properties [that is to say, the four marks] from her divine source. But their historical manifestations are signs that also speak clearly to human reason. As the First Vatican Council noted, the "Church herself, with her marvelous propagation, eminent holiness, and inexhaustible fruitfulness in everything good, her catholic unity and invincible stability, is a great and perpetual motive of credibility and an irrefutable witness of her divine mission."[13]

Some detractors might note that historical effects are usually accounted for by multiple causes, not just one. They might point out that Catholic beliefs cannot be exclusively responsible for any particular effect. Now, it is true that historical effects usually have more than one cause, but this does not mean that historians cannot point to specifically Christian beliefs that are widespread as a necessary cause for certain effects. Different causes have different values and contribute to forming various phenomena in history. Thus historians rarely affirm that entire movements and institutions can be accounted for by a single cause. Many necessary causes, however, might contribute to the ongoing influence of historical effects. Christianity is thought to be a major contributor to the positive differences made in different cultures.

The studies that will be mentioned below were not usually written with apologetic intentions, but they do happen to coincide with the apologists' use of the four marks. Beginning with the assumption that Christian beliefs can make a difference for the greater good, it is now time to briefly introduce the relevant evidence that seems to confirm the soundness of the philosophical arguments in the last section. We now turn to some *prospects* for developing the *via empirica*. Readers are encouraged to consult the notes for developing the argument in more specific ways.

From the beginning of the Christianity, a tradition developed in which believers encouraged the use of reason and celebrated the possibility of progress in light of their eschatological outlook. Unlike other religions focused on law, Christianity encouraged the use of reason and, in particular, when doing theology. Theological understanding is taken seriously in Christianity. Reason itself is seen as a gift from God. While many other religions are based on law, intuition, "esoteric knowledge," or even belief in capricious, humanlike deities, Christianity embraces reason and logic as God-given guides for understanding religious truth.

Christianity spread rapidly throughout Europe into the Middle Ages. Its emphasis on rational theology and eschatology continued to transform

---

13. *Catechism of the Catholic Church*, 812.

its adherents and entire societies. Though some antiquated works of history claim that after the Roman Empire collapsed Europe entered the so-called "Dark Ages," contemporary scholars have repeatedly called this contention into question. Rapid intellectual and material progress began as soon as the Church escaped from Roman rule and Greek idealism. Consequently, medieval Europe soon surpassed the rest of the world in science, culture and technology.[14]

Innovations in productive capability, including advanced military weaponry and improved transportation, were all significant features of medieval Europe. In the words of Rodney Stark: "So much progress took place during the so-called Dark Ages that by no later than the thirteenth century, Europe had forged far ahead of Rome and Greece, and ahead of the rest of the world as well. Why? Primarily because Christianity taught that progress was 'normal' and that 'new inventions would always be forthcoming.' This was the revolutionary idea."[15]

The novelty of earliest Christianity helps to explain why it was able to grow at such an astounding rate. Outsiders found the strict nature of Christian belief attractive, including its exclusive stance with respect to other religions. Christianity was unlike any other religion at the time. Unlike Judaism and many other religions, it did not discriminate on the basis of gender and social class. Christians called on everyone to repent and believe in the gospel.

Christian worship was highly intense, unlike the mundane liturgies of ancient Judaism. To be sure, earliest worship practices featured the belief that God was active in the midst of ritual action. The attitude in worship was not passive, but was one in which the believer could expect to be changed by the Spirit. The intense charismatic experience of the early Christians was highly attractive to outsiders. Thus the Christians' refusal to accommodate the substance of their worship to alternative pressures, and the rapid rise and success of worshipping a crucified Messiah in the face of secular opposition should all be explored.[16]

Closely linked to the Catholic concern for reason and innovative progress is the endorsement of natural law principles. No matter what is one's race, religion, or gender, every human being is created in the image of God. Different understandings of natural law can be found in Greco-Roman

14. Dawson, *Religion and the Rise of Western Culture*; White, *Medieval Religion and Technology*; Gimpel, *The Medieval Machine*; Gies and Gies, *Cathedral, Forge and Waterwheel*; Stark, *The Victory of Reason*; Harris and Grigsby, *Misconceptions about the Middle Ages*.

15. Stark, *The Victory of Reason*, 54–55.

16. Stark, *The Triumph of Christianity*.

cultures before the rise of Christianity, but it was Christian thinkers who held that *God* was the author of nature. This deeply held conviction set the stage for the defense of human integrity and universal rights in later centuries. Reference to human dignity is also used to defend labor and economic freedom. It has also played a significant role in liberation movements.

Although it may seem obvious today that everyone is created equal under God, the historical evidence points in the opposite direction. Without the influence of Catholic Christian faith, it is not at all evident that equality trumps inequality, given the various strengths, talents, and circumstances of so many different individuals. In Catholic faith, God creates and loves each person infinitely.

Christianity's revolutionary ideas about human beings eventually contributed to opposition to slavery.[17] When we look at the relationship between Christianity and slaveholding, it must be admitted that the Church originated and later developed in a world teeming with slavery. Because the institution of slavery was so widespread and uncontested in many parts of the world, it was rarely protested against. As someone once said, the history of *humanity* is a history of slavery. However, there has always been outrage at the practice of slavery in certain quarters in the Church (Justin the Martyr and St. Patrick of Ireland both abhorred the practice of slavery). The Church may have been one of the only organized groups that declared the diminution, if not the final elimination, of slavery to be meritorious. Even though it may have taken centuries to abolish slavery, many Christians contributed to overthrowing it.

Similar circumstances apply in the development of women's rights. While the earliest Christian movement did not immediately protest against patriarchy, it elevated the status of women in the face of Greco-Roman pressures to the contrary.[18] So different were the ways that Christians treated women in the ancient world that the Romans scorned the new religious sect as effeminate and soft, lacking strong "male virtues" such as justice. Likewise, courtly love can also be traced back to the Catholic Middle Ages.

Another fascinating area of research should center on the impact of theology upon the elevation of sexual norms.[19] The new standard set by the early Christians has had a monumental impact on civilization. Detractors of Christian morality have argued that Christians merely borrowed their ideas about sex from Greek philosophies and religions. But this contention is not sustainable in the face of contemporary scholarship. As Kathy L. Gaca

17. Stark, *For the Glory of God*, 291–376.
18. Stark, *The Rise of Christianity*, 95–128.
19. Gaca, *The Making of Fornication*.

concluded in her groundbreaking study, "Foucault and others are therefore mistaken in maintaining that 'the codes in themselves did not change
a great deal' between Greek and Christian Greek sexual principles. Paul's
unconditional imperative to flee fornication was radically new to the Greeks
and other Gentiles, and its aim was to supplant religious sexual existence as
they lived it, or, in the case of the philosophers, as they conceived it should
be lived."[20]

The impulse of reason at the service of understanding faith also gave
strong impetus to the emergence of the university.[21] Hence the university
was a distinctively Catholic invention that evolved from cathedral schools
established to train monks and priests. As Stark writes:

> [The university] was not a monastery or place for meditation.
> Rather, as Marcia L. Colish put it, "The scholastics who created
> this heady educational environment rapidly outpaced monastic
> scholars as speculative thinkers." The key word here is "*specula-
> tive*." The medieval universities were unlike Chinese academics
> for training Mandarins or a Zen master's school. They were
> not primarily concerned with imparting the received wisdom.
> Rather, just as is the case today, faculty gained fame and invita-
> tions to join faculties elsewhere by *innovation*.
>
> The results were entirely predictable: factions formed and
> reformed; new schools of thought abounded; controversy be-
> came the dominant fact of scholarly life. In a world over which
> One True Church claimed exclusive doctrinal authority, the
> spirit of free inquiry cultivated in the universities made theol-
> ogy the *revolutionary* discipline. As increasingly large numbers
> of learned scholars pored over scriptures in search of original
> insights, inevitably they often reached contradictory conclu-
> sions, some of which prompted serious religious conflict and
> dissent.[22]

The medieval university was the first organized institution in the world that
showed consistent interest in the cultivation and preservation of knowledge.
The lineage of modern universities can be traced back to medieval universities such as Bologna, Paris, Oxford, and Cambridge, not to Greece or Rome.

The emphasis on God and reason also helped spur the rise of modern
science. Historians now almost universally recognize that the modern scientific revolution would have been manifestly impossible without deeply

20. Ibid., 293.

21. Riches, *Education and Culture in the Barbarian West*; Leclercq, *The Love of
Learning and The Desire for God*.

22. Stark, *For the Glory of God*, 63.

embedded Catholic presuppositions in those societies where science originated.[23] Though we might take science and the orderly nature of creation for granted today, the belief in a rational Creator who endows the creation with orderly laws provided the fathers of modern science with the necessary intellectual resources to analyze the universe. At the time Western Europe was deeply influenced by the rational theology of the scholastics and the university's emphasis on speculative thinking.

In Catholicism all creation is seen to reflect the mind of the Creator. Science developed because of the belief that creation is a cosmos (being orderly), not chaotic or animistic as in some other religions and cultures. Scripture lent support to the rationality of the universe in late antiquity, and this subsequently laid the foundations for understanding the world in a certain way. Cultures affected by other religions did not have the intellectual resources needed for science to develop, traditionally understood.

Stanley Jaki and many others have argued that these civilizations worked out of conceptual frameworks that hindered the growth of science. Jaki extended his thesis to several civilizations as test cases and demonstrated that in each of them science was unable to develop as a result of non-Christian conceptions of reality: Arabic, Babylonian, Chinese, Egyptian, Greek, Hindu, and Mayan.[24] It seems that the decline of Christianity in the West will gradually harm the advancement of science (especially the biological, chemical, and physical sciences). As physicist Peter Hodgson recognizes: "While there are many causes for the decline of science, the decline of Christian belief must be among them."[25]

Belief in God is one of the most influential beliefs in Western civilization. Science itself seems to vindicate this conclusion. Over the last few years, a cumulating amount of research has confirmed the notion that spirituality has a positive influence on human well-being and longevity. Believers are happier, healthier, and live longer than their unbelieving counterparts. Affirmed with consistency in the medical community, researchers maintain that belief in God and human health grow in direct, not in inverse proportion with one another.[26] W. R. Miller and C. E. Thoreson assert: "It is hardly news that spirituality and religion can have an important influence on

---

23. Grant, *The Foundations of Modern Science in the Middle Ages*; Hooykaas, *Religion and the Rise of Modern Science*; Lindberg, *The Beginnings of Western Science*; Gaukroger, *The Emergence of a Scientific Culture*; Osler, *Reconfiguring the World*.

24. Jaki, *Science and Creation*.

25. Hodgson, *Theology and Modern Physics*, 221.

26. Vitz, *The Faith of the Fatherless*; Pargament, *The Psychology of Religion and Coping*; Koening and Cohen, *The Link between Religion and Health*.

human health and behavior. Religious resources figure prominently among the methods that people call on when coping with life stress and illness."[27]

The causal relationship between religion and health is occasionally challenged by projection theorists and their forebears (Freud, Marx, and Feuerbach), but these challenges do not square with the prevailing clinical evidence. As Miller and Thoreson recognize:

> In the spirit of two-tailed tests, clearly research on religion should examine both its positive and its negative potential effects on health. Certainly misuses and abuses exist within religion, as they do in any significant social institution. Apart from such distortions of religion, however, it is entirely possible that certain religious beliefs or practices are associated with adverse health effects. At present there is no substantial base of empirical evidence regarding negative effects of religion on health (Thoresen et al., in press). If research on health benefits of religion has been widely avoided within mainstream psychology, well designed studies of its potential adverse effects appear to have been even more shunned.[28]

It should be kept in mind that "the projection theory" is not science, but a philosophical contention. Freud himself said: "Let us be quite clear on the point that the views expressed in my book [*The Future of an Illusion*] form no part of analytic theory. They are my personal views."[29] Freud had very little acquaintance with patients who believed in God. Nor did he ever publish a report based on hard evidence garnered from working with believers.

Yet another area of research should focus on the emergence of charitable organizations, health care, and organized hospitals in the patristic and medieval periods.[30] Jesus' teaching on unconditional love shaped countless forms of charitable organizations during the patristic era. Part of the reason for the emergence of monastic orders during the medieval period was to help the poor survive and help the sick recover from disease.

27. Miller and Thoreson, "Spirituality, Religion, and Health," 24; see Weaver et al., "A Systematic Review of Research on Religion and Spirituality in the Journal of Traumatic Stress, 1990–1999," 215–28.

28. Miller and Thoreson, "Spirituality, Religion, and Health," 32.

29. Meng and Freud, eds., *Psychoanalysis and Faith*, 117.

30. Ferngren, "The Imago Dei and the Sanctity of Human Life," in Englehart, McMillan, and Spicker, eds., *Euthanasia and the Newborn*, 23–47; Amundsen and Numbers, eds., *Caring and Curing*; Ferngren, "Medicine and Compassion in Early Christianity," 1–12; Porterfield, *Healing in the History of Christianity*; Ferngren, *Medicine and Health Care in Early Christianity*.

Critics have argued that early Christianity was characterized by magical means of healing and other superstitious practices. But this contention is now challenged by more recent scholarship. Today many scholars maintain that the Christian churches relied on the best available naturalist sources of healing in the early medieval period. Moreover, the origin of the medieval hospital was influenced by Catholic ideals such as compassion for the patient. As Gary Ferngren, an expert in the rise of early medicine, explains:

> Throughout the Hebrew scriptures one finds the popular view enunciated that illness and disease are God's punishment for sin and wrongdoing. . . . Pagan culture [on the other hand] discouraged all attempts to deal with the sick as a societal problem, in part, because it assumed that the sick were suffering deservedly; in part, because of the pessimism that regarded society as incapable of significant improvement; and, in part, because of a quietism that rejected the desirability of attempting real change in society. The resulting passivity accounts for the failure of state officials to undertake public relief during times of plague and reflects the ease with which ancient societies accepted suffering without undertaking efforts to ameliorate it. Underlying it as well was the belief that plague was retributive, a punishment by the gods on society for some failure of an individual or magistrate that could be removed only by their propitiation.
>
> Unlike the classical world, Christianity rooted its attitude to philanthropy in theology. The impulse behind Christian philanthropy was the encouragement of a self-giving love of one's fellow human beings that reflected the love of God in the Incarnation of Christ and his death for the redemption of the world. . . . The Incarnation of Christ had changed and elevated the human body, including that of lepers. Their bodies transmitted their holiness to those who had cared for them.[31]

The Church's interest in physical healing was intimately linked to its concern to fulfill the Great Commission. The rise of Christian faith helped spur the emergence of health care and medicine.

On another front, believers have depicted the created world and the events of salvation history in different forms of artistic expression across the ages.[32] Since belief in the incarnation is taken to mean, in part, that God has elevated the creation to a new level, creation should be appreciated. One would be hard pressed to find any art historians who would deny the positive influence of Catholicism upon the arts. Despite the repeated attempts

---

31. Ferngren, *Medicine and Health Care in Early Christianity*, 142, 144, 143.

32. Saward, *The Beauty of Holiness and the Holiness of Beauty*.

of iconoclasts, the Church consistently defends art as a form of spiritual expression (by referring to theological principles).[33] Inspired by the conviction that the world is orderly and capable of being pondered, Catholic artists seek to construct their work according to "measure, number, and weight" (Wis 11:21).[34]

Many examples immediately come to mind: the Sistine Chapel, Da Vinci's *The Last Supper*, Michaelangelo's *Pietà*, and Rembrandt's *Christ at Emmaus* and *Simeon in the Temple*. Veronese, Titian, and Tintoretto are responsible for painting some of the best murals in Europe. These can all be found in Venice. Who can ignore Handel's *Messiah*, Mozart's *Requiem*, and the music of Johann Sebastian Bach? Not to be overlooked, the centerpiece of medieval art is the Gothic cathedral. As Paul Johnson writes: "The medieval cathedrals of Europe . . . are the greatest accomplishments of humanity in the whole theatre of art."[35]

No impartial historian denies that some of the most memorable works of literature have also come from such Christians as Dante, Shakespeare, and Milton. Christian and Catholic beliefs provided these geniuses with a distinctive way of expressing themselves. Their influence has been so monumental that even critics of Christian faith have, in many cases, borrowed their themes to convey the points they wish to make. Take Goethe's *Faust* as an example. His allegory of suffering is derived from Catholic views on suffering.

Negative Apologetics and the *Via Empirica*

One criticism of the *via empirica* is that high levels of morality (and human benefits) can be found outside the influence of the institutional Church. As the atheist sociologist Phil Zuckerman reports, "nations marked by high levels of organic atheism—such as Sweden or the Netherlands—are among the healthiest, wealthiest, best educated, and freest societies on earth."[36]

33. For a discussion of the Church's response to iconoclasm, see Davis, *The First Seven Ecumenical Councils (325–787)*, 290–305. For a contemporary Catholic endorsement of art, see John Paul II's *Letter to Artists*. Also relevant is Benedict XVI's meeting with artists on November 21, 2009. These documents can be found on the Vatican website.

34. Baldwin, *The Scholastic Culture of the Middle Ages 1000–1300*, 107; Scott, *The Gothic Enterprise*, 124–25.

35. Johnson, *Art*, 153.

36. Zuckerman, "Atheism," in Martin, ed., *The Cambridge Companion to Atheism*, 57. It should be noted that Danes and Swedes do not consider themselves "atheists" in

Setting aside the difficult contention of showing that these societies have never been affected by Christianity, the more important thing to remember is that Christian beliefs and the concrete expression of the marks of the Church do not always go hand in hand. Vatican II does not endorse the "exclusivist" viewpoint in the strict sense of the term. Catholic teaching does not hold that holiness can be found only in those cultures influenced by the Church. Since grace is not a quantitative thing, holiness can be found outside the influence of Catholicism.

So, if the *via empirica* were to claim that holiness can be found only in those societies influenced by the Christian world-view, then of course Zuckerman's findings seem to gain some force. Unlike fundamentalist advocates of Christian faith, Catholic theologians do not argue that holiness can exist only in Christian communities and societies. Zuckerman repeatedly caricatures the "Christian view" as a strict exclusivism.[37] But the *via empirica* claims that, all things being equal, Christianity will make a moral difference. Above I presented four philosophical arguments to elucidate that contention, and it is confirmed by recent findings in the social sciences. What is more, this evidence is not all that controversial among scholars who study the relevant topics. Zuckerman himself notes the positive effects of the Christian faith upon the world.

Catholic theology affirms that human beings are the only creatures that God has willed for their own sake. Hearing the gospel is merely an outward sign that God is calling its hearers to a greater relationship with himself, not that he loves those who hear the message more than those who remain cognitively ignorant of it. Nor does Church teaching deny that God is not working for the betterment of persons in societies outside Christianity. If there are degrees of holiness among Christians, then we would assume that these same degrees may be actual also among those who, because of their historical situation and through no fault of their own, cannot have explicit faith in Jesus Christ. God truly wills the salvation of every member of the human race, not just those who happen to be born at the right time and in the right place.

What, then, is the benefit of the institutional Church given the multifaceted nature of God's grace? Accepting God's revelation in Christ, believers can point to something tangible in history to substantiate God's love for the human race. Christ confirms divine revelation and gives it a historical,

---

the sense of "explicit denial of the existence of God." Instead most of them believe that something exists beyond the physical world, but do not articulate what it is; as admitted by Zuckerman, *Society Without God*, 163.

37. Zuckerman, *Society Without God*, 4, 6, 13, 17–20, 29, 31, 128, 151, 162, 167.

concrete expression.[38] Therefore, God is working outside the formal influence of the Church, but is explicitly known and reinforced through the
Church's teachings. God's grace is not bound to Catholicism, but Catholicism is bound to God's grace, which is for Catholic faith Christ's grace as
well. As such, explicit Catholic Christianity is the full realization of God's
grace. Being a part of the Church enables one to have the highest potential
for living out the grace of God. By no means is this opportunity always actualized by Catholics. Likewise, many individual unbelievers do not follow
the light of conscience and become Catholic.

We should expect to see some positive contributions to some societies in non-Christian contexts which lack the outward sign of grace we call
"the Church." However, full spiritual vitality and Christ oriented institutional integrity can be found only in the Catholic Church. God's grace can
be detected in places not influenced by institutional Christianity. Grace is
not limited to Christians, but is manifested in the world in different times,
locations, and degrees. By the grace of God, some "non-Catholic" cultures
may outshine the "Catholic" ones. Grace can be indirectly felt in societies
affected by the Church, but it is not limited to Catholic circles alone.

Conclusion

When one thinks of the terrible incidents in Church-related persecutions,
and recalls the pettiness and inadequacies of so much daily Church life, it
becomes easy to doubt the vital work of the Spirit. Nevertheless, the four
marks exert a special attraction for evangelists, ecumenists, and apologists
today. The encounter with communities that are authentically one, holy,
catholic, and apostolic can bring about conversions. By *their* fruits they
will know *God*. The ordinary person is not usually persuaded to believe in
Christ through arguments as much as they are concerned to see God's work
in people. As John Henry Newman said, "as 'the heavens declare the glory
of God' as Creator, so are the saints the proper and true evidence of the God
of Christianity, and tell out into all lands the power and grace of Him who
made them. . . . They are the popular evidence of Christianity."[39]

Although the *via empirica* is not strictly based upon a direct encounter
with human holiness, it has tried to rationally elucidate some of the positive
changes that Christian cultures have left in this world. These changes can
be highlighted to reinvigorate an almost forgotten argument in the Church
known as the *via empirica*. Notwithstanding the positive changes in cultures

38. Vatican II, *Dei Verbum*, 4.
39. Blehl, *The Essential Newman*, 334.

unaffected by institutional Christianity, the *via empirica* can be defended on behalf of the Divine Founder.

— 12 —

Does Christianity Cause Violence?

ONE OF THE PRIMARY arguments in atheist literature against Christianity is that it causes violence. Such an argument is relevant to the *via empirica*, or the argument from the transformative influence that Christianity has slowly had upon any culture which has embraced it. If Christianity literally causes violence, then this would serve as an indirect argument against the unique identity and teachings of Jesus himself. Conversely, if Jesus was God incarnate, we would expect his teachings to influence the world for good, not for evil.

Steven Pinker is representative of the atheist viewpoint against the *via empirica*: "religions have given us stonings, witch-burnings, crusades, inquisitions, jihads, fatwas, suicide bombers, and abortion clinic gunmen."[1] He says that humans once believed God commanded them to "massacre Midianites, stone prostitutes, execute homosexuals, slay heretics and infidels, throw Protestants out of windows, withhold medicine from dying children, and crash airplanes into skyscrapers."[2] Let us be clear about the atheists' claim: the argument is not that violence results when Catholics engage in war because the right conditions are in place for a defensive strategy to justify political ends (as proponents of the just war have traditionally maintained), but that Christianity itself is one of the primary reasons why violence breaks out in the first place.

Attributing violence to the fundamental teachings of the Church—in either a direct or indirect manner—is tantamount to affirming that God is a malevolent God who works through his people to spread evil and suffering in the world. On this view, the Christian God is nothing other than an evil god, not an omnibenevolent deity who is concerned with the welfare of the human race. There might as well be no god at all. Steven Weinberg pulls

1. Pinker, *How the Mind Works*, 555.
2. Pinker, *The Blank Slate*, 189.

no punches: "Good people will do good things, and bad people will do bad things. But for good people to do bad things—that takes religion."[3]

Christians who have become violent in the name of the Savior have either knowingly or unknowingly allowed reductive ideologies into religious justification to control their thinking and choices. Christianity does not cause violence, but violence that is committed under the banner of Christianity is actually a distortion of Christian faith. This chapter must be interpreted as a piece of negative apologetics; it is concerned with refuting and/or diminishing claims that have been pronounced against the fundamental teachings of the Christian faith. Another task of negative apologetics exposes the weaknesses within those criticisms. The last chapter was a work in positive apologetics, which attempts to undercut atheist claims by overwhelming them with positive evidence showing the cultural impact of Christianity.

The New Atheists and Moral Absolutism

Different groups of new atheists propose different types of negative arguments against the *via empirica*. Richard Dawkins claimed that the notion of absolute truth predisposes Christians to engage in violence, and, to a more intense degree, war. When asked to explain his contempt for religion, Dawkins responded that it is a sure spawning ground for violence: "Certainly [belief in God] can be positively harmful in many ways," he replied, "obviously in causing wars, which has often enough in history . . . causing people to do ill to one another because they are so convinced that they know what is right. Because they feel it from inside—they've been told from within what is right—anything goes—you can kill people because you know that they're wrong."[4]

Dawkins has a significant point here (as I will explain later on): a rigid understanding of truth is a sure sign that one's faith is becoming corrupt. What Dawkins seems to forget is that absolute truth is undeniable, regardless of one's worldview. For example, he argues that Christian doctrines are, to paraphrase him, false;[5] and he also upholds the so-called "truth of atheism." But these are two absolute claims. To put this in other terms, if inner-

3. Weinberg, "A Designer Universe?" 48.

4. Source unknown (per David Martin, this interview was taken from Dawkins' conversation with Sue Lawley on "Desert Island Discs" in spring 1995). Taken from Martin, *Does Christianity Cause War?* 24.

5. Dawkins, *The God Delusion*, 250, 253, 258, 307, 313, 318.

religious clashes between Christians and Catholics causes violence because of doctrinal and moral differences, then wouldn't Dawkins' differences with Christians put him at risk in becoming violent toward them?

Epistemologically speaking, the issue is not whether Christians set themselves up to become violent by thinking they know the truth, but in how rigid their understanding of truth might be. In Catholicism, truth is one. Unity arises between people as they come to know it more clearly. Unity in the truth, however, does not automatically entail uniformity in the truth. A rigid view of absolutes can lead to intolerance and violence. But this is not how the Catholic Church understands truth. There is supposed to be a legitimate pluralism within the bounds of Catholic orthodoxy.

Although Catholics can and must learn to "put up with" what we think are erroneous beliefs in other worldviews, we must strive to respect everyone's right to think and choose differently. This conviction can and must be upheld, especially in light of the fundamental conviction that all people are created in the image of God. Indeed, disagreement can and must coexist with respect. When I say "respect," I mean that Christians are in fact called to peacefully acknowledge that others can disagree with them without resorting to force in the process. To put this in other terms, the fact that we can agree to disagree about our fundamental beliefs can actually become an opportunity for us to keep our fundamental questions and interaction about God alive and even renewed. Despite our differences in a pluralist society, Christians can contribute to promoting the common good with others who do not agree with them without advancing violence.

Theologians stress that all people can apprehend the absolute truth about God and humanity. But Catholic theology is a little bit more nuanced than this and holds that every person can see and articulate this absolute truth in different ways.[6] This does not lead to outright pluralism, but to an inclusive faith that maintains the unique status of Jesus Christ.

In many cases the atheist charge of absolutes is closely linked to biblical injunctions in the Old Testament. A widespread argument of the new atheists is that the God of the Old Testament once commanded the extermination of certain groups.[7] For them the God of the Old Testament is a God of war. Many atheists are fond of saying that the Old Testament is filled with atrocities committed in the name of God.

Instead of arguing on a literalist point-counterpoint basis with atheists, one must provide a more nuanced response. The Old Testament must be seen as a collection of individual books from different cultural traditions,

6. For a discussion, see Nichols, *The Shape of Catholic Theology*, 263–356.
7. Dawkins, *The God Delusion*, 31, 238, 242–43.

written at different times. All of these books shed light on how the nation of Israel perceived what they thought was God's providence for them at the time. Since the Church's understanding of revelation continues to develop as time goes on, our understanding of it today should clarify the meanings of these older texts.

Today the correct interpretation of the Old Testament must be seen through the lens and prism of the life and teachings of Jesus (cf. Matt 5:17–18). Christians have always used a variety of methods of interpretation when viewing the Old Testament with that lens in focus. When the literal method of interpretation becomes the sole method of interpretation, it is easy to infer that the God of the Old Testament is a violent God who has timelessly commanded his people to kill those who would oppose him.

As such, a Catholic understanding of the Hebrew Scriptures should not only include the literal sense of interpretation, but also the spiritual sense. As John Paul II declared, the magisterium of the Catholic Church, in addressing biblical exegesis, "rejects a split between the human and divine, between scientific research and respect for the faith, between the literal sense and the spiritual sense."[8] Later on in this document, he writes, "exegetes have to make use of the historical-critical method. They cannot, however, accord to it a sole validity. . . . Exegetes should also explain the Christological, canonical, and ecclesial meanings of the biblical texts."[9] The Scriptures are also shaped by the community and historical and social contexts through which individuals engage, internalize, and act upon these texts. In order to understand them accurately today, one must interpret them within and in the light of the community that was responsible for originally writing them down.

Uncontroversially, Catholics hold that all Scripture is inspired by God. But this does not mean that everything reported in Scripture should be taken at literal face value (which is how a historical-critic will tend to view them). For it is widely recognized that the books of the Old Testament are not mere historical reports, but are highly colored by theological motifs and developing cultural convictions. This is another reason why historical-critical exegesis cannot be the sole means of interpretation. It will fail to do justice to the texts to understand them correctly. When many methods are used through the lens of Christ's life, the picture of God that emerges is not a God of war, but a merciful God who demands justice, urging his people to remain faithful to the covenant.

8. John Paul II, "Address on the Interpretation of the Bible in the Church," 6, in Pontifical Biblical Commission, *The Interpretation of the Bible in the Church*, 16.

9. Ibid., 106.

New Atheists as Doctors of Modernity

Harkening back to Karl Marx's view of religion, Christopher Hitchens complains that belief in the afterlife predisposes believers to not care about what happens in this lifetime. The more and more believers project their cares onto the next lifetime, the less and less they will care about what happens in this lifetime. They will not care whether they die, or whether they die in battle or in suicide attacks. In many cases belief in the afterlife predisposes believers to become violent.

Now this is an understandable conclusion for Hitchens and others (like John Lennon, for instance, who sang "Imagine there's no heaven" with a promise that this would leave us with "nothing to kill or die for") to make if they deny the continuity between this lifetime and the next. It is also understandable if these atheists think that Catholicism teaches that all people will go to heaven. But in the Catholic view, there is a one-to-one correspondence between the person who dies and the person who rises. Catholic theology has always maintained that hell is a real state of final existence.

The individual fate of each individual person—whether it ends in the bliss of heaven or the justice of hell—is ultimately determined by the way in which we shape our characters in this lifetime. According to Catholic theology, the doctrines of heaven and hell invest every moral decision in our lifetime with eternal significance. Life is filled with meaning because good actions are worthy to perform in and of themselves. Immoral actions must always be avoided.

In Christian view of the world, human beings continue to live into the afterlife. Thus everyone is held accountable for their actions in this lifetime. A greater good will prevail over evil. In turn, every decision that is made by Catholics in this lifetime has eternal significance because there is something to hope for in the end. Catholics can make decisions that, albeit painful, are performed for the greater good.

Catapulted by the Paschal Mystery, the first Christians were led to care more about earthly life, including the goodness of creation itself. Belief in the incarnation demanded this kind of attitude. Again, God entered into creation and became human. Not caring about one's embodied life and the creation itself is diametrically opposed to the very meaning of believing in the incarnation. At most, Hitchens argued against a false conception of what it means to be a Catholic. Like the other arguments surveyed here, this one is completely unsuccessful.

Celestial escape from worldly affairs is brought to the fore by Dawkins in Freudian terms. According to Richard Dawkins, Christianity is actually bad for people—it is a "kind of mental illness."[10] In this view, belief in God is a kind of mental virus that infects what is otherwise a healthy mind. The more and more people succumb to religion, they more they become inclined to do things normal people would not do. This includes violent behavior.

Dawkins' argument is basically a newer version of Feuerbach, Marx, and Freud's projection theory against belief in God. In their view, God can be merely explained in terms of sociological, psychological, and/or anthropological categories of the mind. When individuals begin with this atheist presupposition, the projection theorist has a strong point in arguing that faith leads people down the path of self-destructive behavior. But until good arguments are first given for atheism, the projection theorist simply begs the entire question. Basically what Dawkins is saying is that because God does not exist, how could there be such a thing as religion, or religiously related violence? But this starting point is the very thing that needs to be challenged. In contemporary theology and philosophy, arguments in favor of theism are often seen as cogent—arguments that are often unaddressed in the new atheist literature.

Similarly, the atheistic projection theorist seems to commit the genetic fallacy. They confuse how one comes to believe in God with whether the belief in question is true. Certainly, the psychology of belief is not the same thing as the rationality of belief; how one comes to believe in God may not have anything to do with whether the belief in question is true.

Moreover, the idea that God is a projection of our minds to keep us safe from the unrelenting forces of nature and society is somewhat idiosyncratic. To be sure, the God of Christian tradition is merciful, but he is also seen as retributive. This kind of God makes it difficult to understand why anyone would want to project him. This is a point that even Dawkins concedes in his book. Christians and Catholics might ask the atheists in response: is it really a bad thing to say that belief in God brings satisfaction and peace of mind to those who need it? All people need to be comforted with a variety of things—food, shelter, and friendship. All of these are real human needs. Perhaps there is a real human need for God.[11]

It should be remembered that there is nothing wrong with coming to God for help in our time of need, but in Christian worship we also adore God for who he is. In Catholic theology, salvation becomes more demanding for anyone exposed to the Savior, not easier to attain. It must be admitted that believers do sometimes project things about an incomprehensible God. But some false projections do not entail that all beliefs about him are

10. Dawkins, *The Selfish Gene*, 330; Dawkins, *The God Delusion*, 186, 188.

11. Kreeft, *Heaven*.

false. Growing in discipleship and knowing God is an ongoing, daunting process. Lastly, the atheists might also be confusing the Catholic call to a lead a simple lifestyle with psychological weakness.

On another front, the issue of belief in God has very little to do with electro-chemical and neurobiological processes in the brain. It is has everything to do with how the scientific evidence is interpreted. Some will interpret the evidence and argue that belief in God can be merely reduced to complex physical mechanisms. Others will argue that all human experience has, in fact, a neurobiological component to it. Seen in this way, brain processes are the proximate cause of how people experience God, but the ultimate cause is the extra-mental reality of God himself. Until Dawkins can explain why a single layered explanation of the evidence should be preferred, this interpretation remains a valid one.

In addition, there is a growing amount of well-established scientific evidence that indicates a direct causal link between religious commitment and well-being. To my knowledge, Dawkins is either completely unaware of these findings or chooses to ignore them. Daniel Dennett, it may be added, who is an avid reductionist in the biological sciences, admits that this conclusion about the relationship between religion and health is sound.[12] In fact, he says, one of the advantages of religion in the long struggle of evolution was that it helped human beings to live in communities without fighting and killing one another![13]

Christianity, Atheism, and the Testimony of History

The testimony of history clearly reveals that Christians have committed many heinous crimes. Whether it is the Crusades, the Inquisition, the fighting between Catholics and Protestants, the justification of slavery, the slaughter of those who refused to convert, or the fighting in Northern Ireland, history conclusively shows that Christianity can be a violent religion. Monotheism seems to have brought a violent legacy to the West.

Now there is no question that many Christians have committed many crimes. But the thing to keep in mind is that this objection must show that *Christianity itself* causes violence. With this extreme difficulty in mind, this argument from "historical observation" does not demonstrate that

12. Dennett, *Breaking the Spell*, 55, 272–77. Cf. 190.
13. Ibid., 172. Cf. 179.

Christianity causes violence, but has more of a descriptive character to it, exposing the very problem that needs to be addressed.

Even though historians can give many examples showing where the faith has been correlated with violence, it is difficult to deny on those same grounds that Christianity has been associated with a tremendous amount of good. As Michael Shermer has admitted, "for every one of these grand tragedies there are ten thousand acts of personal kindness and social good that go unreported. . . . Religion, like all social institutions of such historical depth and cultural impact, cannot be reduced to an unambiguous evil."[14] All of the good and the bad must be weighed and assessed together, not just the bad track record that is associated with Christianity. But considering the bad and ignoring the good is exactly what many of the new atheists have done.

These examples of Christian violence indicate that we are dealing with highly ambiguous scenarios that are open to interpretation on a variety of levels. Given this ambiguity, it becomes difficult to demonstrate that Catholic teaching was responsible for driving believers down the narrow path of committing such awful crimes. The causal factors involved with war, for instance, are usually explained in terms of social, political, and economic causes—not religious ones.

To make matters even more complicated, the problem of identifying the true causes of war and violence comes in the attempt to identify and explain what actually counts as good and bad. For example, many persons all over the world viewed Mother Teresa as doing much good for the destitute in the streets in India. Others saw her as having a bad social effect on the Indian political system. They believed that her resources could have been utilized for better reasons. So the problem of defining what is good and evil (which must be distinguished from the very fact of good and evil, which is universal) usually varies from one culture to the next. The point is that this often makes it difficult for anyone to identify that Catholicism causes violent acts.

To bring this point home, the argument from "historical observation" is no more effective than saying *atheism* causes violence. After all, some historians have said that atheist politicians such as Lenin admitted to using "protracted violence" to eliminate religion off the face of the earth. The same could be said with respect to politics. In Latin America, tens of thousands of people "disappeared." In Cambodia, Pol Pot was responsible for killing millions in the name of socialism. But surely it is safe to conclude that *politics* is not evil. The same could be said about science. Surely no atheist would claim that *science* is evil simply because some scientists were responsible

14. Shermer, *How We Believe*, 71; cf. Dennett, *Breaking the Spell*, 253.

for creating weapons to torture people—like napalm.[15] The main point is that every single human institution can be utilized for evil when it is abused. "All ideals—divine, transcendent, human or invented—are capable of being abused. That's just the way human nature is. And knowing this, we need to work out what to do about it rather than lashing out uncritically at religion."[16]

Many of the examples that are often mentioned should be contextualized to get a better idea of the causal factors that may be involved. Historians have shown that many of the crimes of Christian violence are simply not as bad as commonly thought (for example, the amount of people killed in the Spanish Inquisition,[17] or the amount of people killed in the witch hunts in Salem).

Reductivism as a Catalyst for Religious Violence

One of the strengths of the new atheism is that they expose a correlation between Christianity and violence. No one should doubt the importance of exposing this problem. This ought to drive Christians to identify the root cause(s) of the violence performed in the name of Christ to correct these problems accordingly. We are still left with having to explain why Christians become violent in the name of Christ. In order to accomplish this task, I will explain and describe the thought patterns and/or ideologies that influence believers to engage in these acts. When one or more of these patterns of thinking are in place, this can alert us of the seeds that can potentially sprout into violence. At the same time, we can look back in history and see that when Christians and Catholics used force, these thought patterns were already operative and in place.

Religious believers who think in terms of black and white may unknowingly feed attitudes and actions to justify violence that is literally opposed to the teachings of the Church. The issue is not about renouncing the notion of absolutes (a metaphysical reality), but about a specific interpretation of them (a one-sided epistemology)—one in which truth demands uniform consent from everyone. In this rigid view of truth it becomes easy to view non-Catholics as outsiders, and, to a more extreme degree, as enemies

---

15. As Weinberg, *Dreams of a Final Theory*, 259, recognizes, scientific atheism "has made its own contribution to the world's sorrows," but "where the authority of science has been invoked to justify horrors, it has been in terms of perversions of science."

16. McGrath and McGrath, *The Dawkins Delusion?* 81.

17. Kamen, *The Spanish Inquisition*, 10, 17–18, 30, 41, 59–60, 305.

who deserve punishment.[18] The official Catholic position does not do away with absolutes, but allows for a variety of interpretations along an orthodox spectrum. Truth should lead to a symphony of voices in unity, not stagnant unison. Epistemological subjectivity is compatible with metaphysical objectivity.

Historically speaking, the rigid view of truth probably led the crusaders to see their Muslim opponents as disobedient to the gospel—simply because they were Muslims and not Christians. This led them to slaughter the Muslims by the thousands. Fundamentalists in our own day have also fallen prey to this one-sided ideology in murdering doctors who performed abortions (for example, the reverend Paul Hill). They claimed that their interpretation of the Bible was the *only* right one. According to Hill, whoever opposed his interpretation deserved to die.

Second, when Christians limit the freedom and intellectual engagement of faith, this can make them and others prone into taking directions that lead to violence in an uncritical fashion. These individuals think that they know what God wants for them and everyone else (put this together with epistemological absolutism, and the recipe for violence increases exponentially). For example, it is a known fact that David Koresh and Jim Jones ordered the women in their groups to have sex with them. These women completely bypassed the voice of common sense and conscience and, in blind faith, did what they were told—all in the name of "faith." "When people embrace this orientation," say Charles Kimball, "their brains often appear to stop working properly; they no longer rely on their judgment and common sense."[19] Catholic faith is supposed to affect the whole of human nature, including the mind.

Third, reductive interpretations of the Bible can induce believers to become violent. This violent approach usually occurs when the literalist method of historical-critical interpretation is used at the expense of other methods when reading certain passages in the Bible that seem to suggest that God wants his people to fight and kill others.

Many Christians have fallen prey to this Bible-based fallacy. Without interpreting the Scriptures correctly, using a variety of methods, many

---

18. Dawkins, *The Selfish Gene*, 330, correctly holds that rigid understandings of absolutes can lead Christians to become violent. As he puts it, "If a man believes in a different god, or even if he uses a different ritual for worshipping the same god, blind faith can decree that he should die—on the cross, at the stake, skewered on a Crusader's sword, shot in a Beirut street, or blown up in a bar in Belfast." What Dawkins correctly notes is that a rigid faith can lead one to brutal acts of violence. But this contention would not include balanced forms of Christian faith.

19. Kimball, *When Religion Becomes Evil*, 88.

Christians have irresponsibly used prooftexts in support of slavery, discrimination against women, racial minorities, homosexuals, and Jews. It has also led married couples to think that God was going heal their children without using the necessary medicine; after all, they argued, God works miracles for those who have "enough faith." It has also been used by Christians who sincerely believed that Mark's Gospel sanctions the use of snake handling. Lopsided readings can lead many uninformed interpreters into thinking that certain behaviors are fine without recognizing at the same time that these actions can lead to dire consequences.

Fourth, psychological debilitations make it easy to perceive one's situation as bleak, catapulting people down the path of destructive behavior.[20] When believers are in need of psychological help, it becomes easy for them to say or do things in the name of the Savior that they would not ordinarily do. When certain ends are heightened at the exclusion of others, this can lead Christians into becoming violent toward those who get in the way of them being able to fulfill their obligations. Charles Kimball suggests:

> In authentic, healthy religion the end and the means to that end are always connected. But it is often easy for religious people to lose sight of the ultimate goal and focus instead on one component of religion. When a key feature of religion is elevated and in effect becomes an end, some people within the religion become consumed with protecting or achieving that end. In such cases, that component of religion functions like an absolute truth claim, and zealous believers become blind in their single minded defense of it. As we will see, this corruption takes many forms, but the pattern is unmistakable. The end goal of protecting or defending a key component of religion is often used to justify any means necessary.[21]

Sometimes this mentality manifests itself in trying to defend sacred spaces, or in maintaining religious life or a group identity. In history we see the concept of the end justifying any means in Catholics who defended their group identity so intensely that they ended up demonizing others in the process—Jews, Muslims, women, and other classes and races.

Another example appeared when some bishops in the Church hid and shifted pedophile priests from one parish to another. For these bishops, the moral end of trying to maintain the Church's reputation ended up superceding the other moral end of being honest and preventing further harm to

---

20. Committing pedophilic acts is not due to the practice of celibacy, but to psychological factors.

21. Kimball, *When Religion Becomes Evil*, 129.

innocent children. When Christians consider certain goals sacrosanct and above all else, it is easy for them to do whatever it takes to make sure these ends are met—even if it takes violent action to do so.

Fifth, Christians have often used religious rhetoric to cover up their secular and/or political purposes to engage in war. Keith Ward observes: "It is when religious institutions are blended with political institutions that religion can be enlisted in the use of force—and even then it is just one identifying marker among others."[22] The issue of political power was at least one of the markers in the case of the crusades. The concern for spreading Christianity may have played some part in advancing these terrible battles by stoking them with religious overtones, but the fundamental motivating factor was the hunger for power and wealth. The wars of religion (between Catholics and Protestants) are another perfect example when political leaders used religious categories to advance their cause, but actually their decisions were shaped more by geo-political and economic factors.

Above I have identified the various thought patterns that dispose individuals to engage in brutally violent acts. Reductionism pervades these individuals' mindsets. By recognizing these warning signs, Catholics and Christians can begin to root out the causes of violence that is performed in the name of faith before it actually happens.

Some critics will argue that Christians can be just as vicious as the worst unbelievers. This would also militate against God's work in the Church, calling the ecclesial attributes of unity and holiness into question. But this may only show how much worse true Christians would be without their faith. This allegation is not a definitive refutation of holiness. For we should expect this holy alteration from unbelief to belief to effect changes in habits of action. But we should not expect these changes to be radical in new believers who already possessed a significant amount of virtue. The change is always relative, depending upon the person. It continues to be highly relative within the believing community.

As such, sin is not a genuine effect of believing in Christ, but the result of having a reductive understanding of faith. Sometimes this reductionism is so extreme that it can only be equated with unbelief. The Church includes all that is holy, even that which is holy in her sinful members. But she excludes whatever is impure—even that which is unholy in her morally holy members. As Avery Dulles acknowledges: "Sin, therefore, cannot be attributed to the church when considered in its formal principles, but only when considered materially, in its guilty members. They exhibit not the true nature but the 'un-nature' of the church. Nevertheless it is true that, . . .

22. Ward, *Is Religion Dangerous?* 79.

[i]n all its historical forms the true nature of the Church is accompanied, like a dark shadow by its 'un-nature;' the two are inseparable."[23] Critics must be able to demonstrate that Catholic Christianity is responsible for causing sin, not that it is merely correlated with it.

Conclusion

If Catholicism is true, then we would expect it to make a positive difference in the lives of those who believe in it. Such a contention was argued in the last chapter. Human beings have a need grounded in human nature that demands that we know how life is supposed to be lived. It thus makes sense that God will intervene in human history to enable people to become the persons they were meant to be. Although the evidence for the positive impact of the Christian faith upon the world is relatively indisputable, one of the first and immediate objections to the *via empirica* is that Christianity produces violence.

"Violent Christian acts" are not due to the teachings of Jesus, but to human beings who are in continuous need of God's saving grace. Francis Sullivan put it this way, "to put it more acutely, the mystery is that the church is the people of God which, as consisting of real *people*, is inevitably marked by sin, but, as people *of God*, cannot fail to be holy."[24] All Catholic Christians who have become violent have allowed certain ideologies such as oppressive political, economic, and psychological forces to control their religious thinking and/or choices. So long as Christ is followed by sinful persons, the faith inspired by Christ will be "corrupted" to some extent. Here it should be noted that believers are not the only ones to share the burden of sin. But "true believers" will always partake against the struggle to fight against sin. And this is precisely the reason why God took on flesh and came into our world—to redeem us from violence (Luke 24:34). God continues to renew Christians in the Spirit who have yet to reach the fullness of the Kingdom.

23. Dulles, "The Church as 'One, Holy, Catholic, and Apostolic,'" 21.
24. Sullivan, *The Church We Believe In*, 67.

PART FIVE

Jesus Christ and the Religious Others

— 13 —

The "Scandal of Particularity"

IF GOD RAISED JESUS from the dead, then we would expect to see Christianity make a positive difference in the lives of believers. In the last two chapters we encountered one version of the *via empirica*, defending it against the secular allegation that Christianity serves as a force for evil. Given the conclusions tentatively established thus far, one might be inclined to ask: why hasn't everyone had the opportunity to hear the good news? Considering that the gospel answers the deep questions that human beings ask, doubters might wonder why the Church's missionaries have been unable to reach every human being with the good news.

Added to the challenge is the Church's longstanding claim that she is the "one true religion." Many individuals find the Church's contention highly disputable, and it allows doubters to call into question the other fundamental teachings of Christianity as well. For if the Church is wrong in one major area, then she might be wrong about other fundamental teachings.

These doubters highlight a tension between the omnibenevolence of God and inculpable ignorance of the gospel. One way that Catholics might answer these challenges by laying out the relevant biblical testimonies and the magisterium's teaching on the challenge of "no salvation outside the Church."[1] By establishing these parameters, one is allowed to construct certain kinds of apologetical arguments.

Jesus Christ and the Church as the Ark of Salvation

God created human beings as body-soul unities. Human beings express themselves in and through their bodies. Thus communication and deep

1. For an excellent discussion, see Sullivan, *Salvation Outside the Church?*

communion with others is always performed in the body. In order to communicate effectively with his creatures, Christianity teaches that God the Son became human and dwelt among us (cf. John 1:1, 14). God's universal mission in reaching human beings in their need is not restricted to the spiritual, but includes the physical. Just as Jesus gave his flesh for the life of the world (John 1:29), so also does he want to unite himself to contemporary persons as the risen Lord. The earthly Jesus is with human beings through the power of the Holy Spirit.

During his public ministry, Jesus laid the foundations of the Church by selecting Twelve apostles.[2] Just as Christ was sent by the Father, so Jesus sends out the Twelve (Luke 10:16): "Whoever listens to you listens to me. Whoever rejects you rejects me. And whoever rejects me rejects the one who sent me." The biblical testimony indicates that Christ endowed the apostles with his own authority, and gave them the mandate to teach, govern, and sanctify in his name.

Salvation, then, correlates with an acceptance of apostolic teaching (cf. Matt 16:18; 18:18; Eph 2:20; 1 Tim 3:15). The risen Christ is therefore mystically connected in and through his body on earth, the Church (Eph 1:15–23). Therefore, to reject the distinctive teachings of the Church is to reject the risen Christ. Jesus' presence and activity is extended throughout the ages by visible means: sacramental signs, magisterial teachings, and the community of the faithful. The Church is not merely an invisible entity, but includes visible elements as well.

With the help of the Holy Spirit, the apostolic writings (the Scriptures) accurately testify to Christological truth. Gerald O'Collins summarizes the Scriptural witness on Jesus' uniqueness:

> From its earliest to its later books, the New Testament does not waver in acknowledging Christ as the one Saviour for all people. As the First Letter of John puts matters, he is 'the expiation for our sins and not only for ours only but also for the sins of the world' (1 John 2:2). The first Christians recognized his redemptive role to be universal (for all without exception), unique (without parallel), complete (as One who conveys the fullness of salvation), and definitive (beyond any possibility of being equaled, let alone surpassed, in his salvific function). . . . The New Testament sense of Christ's indispensable and necessary role for human salvation could be summarized by a new axiom:

---

2. For a discussion on Jesus as Founder of the Church, see O'Collins, *Rethinking Fundamental Theology*, 265–91; see also International Theological Commission, *Select Themes of Ecclesiology on the Occasion of the Twentieth Anniversary of the Closing of the Second Vatican Council*, 1.

extra Christum nulla salus (outside Christ no salvation). . . . The
same holds true of those who have not yet received the message
of the incarnation, death, and resurrection of Christ. Christ is
hidden, yet uniquely active, among the peoples of the world.[3]

Correspondingly, the modern day successors to the apostles (the bishops)
do not arbitrarily formulate doctrinal positions, but are guided by the Holy
Spirit to accurately interpret the deposit of faith which has been handed
down from the time of Christ himself.[4] The successors also refer to the
Scriptures to assist them. Correlatively, because Jesus is the supreme mediator, these characteristics apply, in an analogous sense, to the Church itself.[5]
Just as the Spirit guided the composition of the biblical books, so the Spirit
is guiding the Church. The Church is therefore necessary for salvation. The
apostolic Scriptures, which were written under the influence of the Holy
Spirit, are referred to as the written Word of God (1 Tim 3:16–17; 2 Pet
1:20–21). The Church is indefectible, and guided with the special charism
of infallibility for interpreting the written Word.[6]

After the New Testament documents were written, collected, and dis-
tributed among the earliest Christian communities, believers continued to
defend their belief in the mysterious link between Christ and his Church.
Cyprian, Jerome, Augustine, and Fulgentius regard the Church as the saving
Ark of Noah. Their missionary zeal was matched by their insistence that
"outside the Church, there is no salvation." This axiom continued to be promoted and interpreted in different ways throughout Church history.[7]

Doctrinal Development and
"Outside the Church, No Salvation"

Distancing itself from a strictly exclusivist stance on the possibility of salvation outside her visible confines, the teaching authority of the Church is

3. O'Collins, *Christology*, 315–16, 325.

4. This point is disputed by Protestant Christians. Guided by the "Scriptures
alone," Protestants deny the binding teaching authority of the pope, and the bishops
in communion with him. For a Catholic response to "Scripture alone," along with a
defense of Sacred Tradition, see O'Collins, *Rethinking Fundamental Theology*, 190–215.

5. The Church itself is seen as a type of "sacrament," a sign and instrument of
salvation. Vatican II, *Lumen Gentium*, 1, 2.

6. The charism of infallibility does not mean that the pope, bishop, and the laity
are impeccable. Nor does it mean that every teaching of the Church is infallible. But the
Holy Spirit ensures that the Church will teach and receive Christological truth infallibly. See Dulles, *Magisterium*.

7. Sullivan, *Salvation Outside the Church?*

considered inclusivist about who can be saved.[8] Here the term "inclusivism" means that outsiders to Catholicism can be saved. Apropos the question of who will be saved, one should be agnostic on either the identity or number of the saved outsiders.[9] Catholic teaching is compatible with either view. The doctrinal development has more to do with the way the Church's teaching has been presented, understood, and expressed, not with whether the content of doctrine has changed. Nor is the question concerning the number or identity of the saved outsiders an important one to answer (cf. Luke 13:23–30). John Paul II suggested: "In Matthew's Gospel He speaks clearly of those who will go to eternal punishment (cf. Matt. 25:46). Who will these be? The Church has never made any pronouncement in this regard. This is a mystery, truly inscrutable, which embraces the holiness of God and the conscience of man. The silence of the Church is, therefore, the only appropriate position for Christian faith."[10]

Some commentators have incorrectly assumed that the Catholic Church was an exclusivist[11] before Vatican II. Consequently, the typical caricature is that the Church changed her overtly restrictivist stance to a more open position.[12] Unlike preconciliar theology, these critics affirm that the Catholic Church is now open to the possibility of salvation outside her visible confines. A careful reading of the Catholic Church's teaching reveals that this assessment is incorrect.

The magisterium has limited itself to a handful of statements on the necessity of belief in Jesus Christ for salvation. One of the first noteworthy passages was found in the Fourth Lateran Council (1215): "There is but one universal church of the faithful, outside of which no one at all can be saved." The Council of Florence (1441) reaffirmed the same axiom: the Church "firmly believes, professes and preaches, that none who are outside the Catholic Church, not only pagans, but also Jews and heretics and schismatics, can partake of eternal life, but they will go into eternal fire." Other passages from the magisterium could be cited.

---

8. Though many theologians shy away from using the categories of exclusivism, inclusivism, and pluralism for understanding the necessity of Christ for salvation, the tri-polar categorization can still be responsibly defended. For a discussion, see Schmidt-Leukel, "Exclusivism, Inclusivism, and Pluralism," in Knitter, ed., *The Myth of Religious Superiority*, 13–27.

9. Dulles, "The Population of Hell," 36–41.

10. John Paul II, *Crossing the Threshold of Hope*, 185–86.

11. Exclusivists insist that the religious outsiders, regardless of their circumstances, cannot be saved.

12. We will discuss one theologian who advances this reductive theological view in the last chapter of this book.

When these passages are interpreted within their historical context, it cannot be denied that a type of exclusivism is endorsed: "outside the Church, there is no salvation." However, it is widely acknowledged by contemporary commentators that the Church applied its exclusivist stance to those who were accountable to accept Christ and his body on earth, the Church. Moreover, this contention is not all that controversial among scholars writing on the subject today.

Although the Church taught that she was the one true Christianity before Vatican II, outsiders could still be saved. Hence it could be argued that the Church was ambiguously exclusivist. As Joseph Fenton, a staunch defender of Catholic orthodoxy, once explained:

> Any person who is at all familiar with what the great mass of religious and theological writings of our times have had to say about this dogma is quite well aware of the fact that, in an overwhelming majority of cases, these writings have been mainly, almost exclusively, concerned with proving and explaining how this dogma does not mean that only members of the Catholic Church can be saved. This, of course, is perfectly true. The ecclesiastical magisterium, in teaching and guarding this dogma, insists that there is no salvation outside of the Catholic Church and at the same time likewise insists that people who die without ever becoming members of the Catholic Church can obtain the Beatific Vision.[13]

The only way for culpable individuals to receive salvation is for them to accept Christ and his Church. Conversely, those who are not culpable in failing to accept Christ can be saved. Though we are unable to identify who is "culpable" and who is not, an agnostic outlook should not prevent Catholics from holding that the Church is the one true ark of faith. This longstanding teaching was carried on for centuries before the advent of Vatican II.

Admittedly, some Catholics may have held to an exclusivist emphasis during the preconciliar period, but this should not be equated with a bare exclusivism. A "bare exclusivism" would automatically render each and every "outsider" as part of the reprobate (these "outsiders" would include the inculpably ignorant, the mentally handicapped, and children who die before the age of reason). Nowhere was the refutation of the "bare exclusivism" made more apparent in the preconciliar period than in the famous letter sent by the Holy Office to Fr. Feeney in 1949. Feeney mistakenly held that "outside the Church, there is no salvation" meant "bare exclusivism."

13. Fenton, *The Catholic Church and Salvation*, ix, x.

But in so doing, he found himself outside the Church (he ended up being excommunicated for holding to a bare exclusivism!).

By way of summary, the Church was "exclusivist" by affirming that redemption only comes only through Christ. But she was clearly "inclusivist" in refusing to limit the grace of God to the confines of the Church. She may even be considered "pluralist," although she hesitates to regard everything in the other religions as salvific.

Saying that the Church is necessary for salvation does not strictly encompass only those individuals participating in the Church's liturgical and sacramental system. That interpretation would have been guilty of upholding a "bare exclusivism." When understanding the maxim "outside the Church, no salvation," communion with the Church was not relegated to describing one's theological and juridical agreement with the doctrines of the institutional Church. Rather it was primarily used to describe those inculpable individuals who were mystically connected to Christ, whether they were conscientious of this spiritual connection or not. By including the spiritual element, inclusivism can be ascribed to Catholicism.

The Church as the Universal Sacrament of Salvation

Today no one can formulate an adequate Catholic theology of religions without reference to Vatican II.[14] The Council Fathers taught the Church rejects nothing that is true and holy in non-Catholic religions.[15] Positively speaking, the good in these other religions can serve as a preparatory means to help individuals receive the fullness of the gospel. In *Lumen Gentium* 16, we read: "Nor does Divine Providence deny the helps necessary for salvation to those who, without blame on their part, have not yet arrived at an explicit knowledge of God and with His grace strive to live a good life. Whatever good or truth is found amongst them is looked upon by the Church as a preparation for the Gospel."

Instead of openly criticizing theological views that are contrary to Catholic doctrine, the Council recognizes there are elements of truth and goodness to be found outside the Church. *Lumen Gentium* 17 teaches that "whatever good is found sown . . . in the particular rites and cultures of peoples" can be "healed, elevated, and consummated" by the gospel and

14. For book length treatments of Vatican II on the salvation of the religious others, see Ruokanen, *The Catholic Doctrine of Non-Christian Religions*; O'Collins, *The Second Vatican Council on Other Religions*; D'Costa, *Vatican II*.

15. Vatican II, *Nostra Aetate*, 2.

Catholic teaching. This statement, with its three verbs, was repeated in *Ad Gentes* 9. Vatican II teaches that God has sown some truth and goodness among the religious others. The strikingly new stance of the Council did not lie in its affirmation that non-Christians could be saved, but in its refusal to call non-Catholics "pagans," "heathens," "idolaters," and the like.

Unlike the Protestant Reformers, the Church has never held that the human is totally depraved apart from revelation and faith. For the first time in *conciliar history*, a positive statement is ascribed to other religions (albeit positive ascriptions are made by individual Catholics before Vatican II). Salvation can be found *in* the other world religions, but is not completely *of* those religions.

Similarly, *Nostra Aetate* speaks about elements that are "true and holy" in other religions.[16] It also said that other religions' "precepts and doctrines often reflect a ray of that Truth which illuminates all human beings." This clearly refers to some kind of presence, albeit hidden and mysterious of the Word of God in those other religions, the true Light that enlightens everyone coming into the world. The Light of the world (revelation) is also the Life of the world (salvation). Although the inculpably ignorant can be saved, these positive elements ultimately serve as a preparatory means for receiving the fullness of Christ. "Whatever the implications of this important development," says Gavin D'Costa, "it still means that the religious elements being highlighted and praised are, . . . no more or less than preparations for the fullness of truth who is Christ."[17]

Moreover, conciliar statements about truth and goodness in other religions should be put in their proper context. Although the ancient maxim, "outside the Church, no salvation," is not explicitly mentioned in the Council, the bishops reaffirm that Catholicism is the truest or fullest expression of Christianity. If one is culpable for accepting Christ as a member of the Catholic faith, then one must actively pursue their questions in the best way that he or she can. Although the presence of the Holy Spirit is found outside the Church, this does not nullify the Church's longstanding claim that she is the one true religion.

Some commentators mistakenly hold that the bishops changed the basic content of Catholic teaching. While Vatican II updated the Church's teaching, it would be an egregious mistake to contend that theologians, under the guidance of the magisterium, should affirm that the inculpable cannot be saved. One cannot read the documents of Vatican II and hold that ecclesiastical or religious relativism is constitutive of Catholic teaching.

16. Ibid., 2.
17. D'Costa, *Vatican II*, 107.

Further, even if there are other some elements of truth and holiness in other religions, there must still be at least some false beliefs or practices in them. These false beliefs do not come from the Holy Spirit; they serve as an impediment to salvation. Although the bishops stressed the importance of respecting religions, spiritualities, and cultures that are different from Catholicism, Vatican II does not endorse "false irenicism" or religious indifferentism.[18] In paragraph 16 of *Lumen Gentium* it is said:

> But very often men, deceived by the Evil One, have become vain in their reasonings and have exchanged the truth of God for a lie, serving the creature rather than the Creator. Or some there are who, living and dying in this world without God, are exposed to final despair. Wherefore to promote the glory of God and procure the salvation of all of these, and mindful of the command of the Lord, "Preach the Gospel to every creature," the Church fosters the missions with care and attention.[19]

In *Lumen Gentium* 17, the Council teaches that the Church helps individuals from other religions to be saved from "the slavery of error." *Ad Gentes* 9 adds that the Church has the responsibility to purge "evil associations" from the "elements of truth and grace that are found among peoples." The religious others bring some truth and goodness with them, but there is some evil and error. Though false doctrine or disciplines might be found deep within the Catholic Church, these are not found at the foundational level in the hierarchy of truths.[20]

Here some Catholics might worry about undercutting the motivation that is required to evangelize the formal outsiders if the latter can in fact be saved. That being said, mission work should not be promoted by fooling oneself that it is strictly the Church's duty to bring salvation to the nations. Yves Congar said, "the apostles were pressed, impelled, not so much by their love for Christ as by Christ's love which, imparted to them, dwelt in their hearts and reinforced their devoted lives, seeking through them to be spread over the world: 'It is fire that I have come to spread over the earth (Luke xii. 49).' There is no need to look for reasons to justify love: it is in itself able to impart good."[21] Catholics will in fact participate in the Great Commission when they truly grasp and receive God's love for humanity, which is expressed concretely in Jesus Christ. It is only natural for Catholics and other

---

18. Vatican II, *Nostra Aetate*, 2.

19. Vatican II, *Lumen Gentium*, 16.

20. The challenge of corruptions in the Catholic Church is addressed in chapters 7, 11, 12, and 15.

21. Congar, *The Wide World, My Parish*, 131.

Christians to become evangelical when they are truly "born from above." The only way that faith will increase in oneself is when it is given away to others.

Admittedly, the Church does not always embody the four ecclesial attributes (one, holy, catholic, and apostolic) perfectly. Rather, as the objectively fullest expression of Christianity, Catholics have the greatest potential to live out the marks. All other things being equal, Catholics can take greater advantage of the gifts they have been given within the formal boundaries of the Church. Grace cannot be quantified; it is not limited to Catholics alone; rather, it is qualitative, dynamically and efficaciously working in other Christian churches and religions.

Other Christians and members of the world religions who take advantage of the gifts and callings they have received can become more one, holy, catholic, and apostolic than Catholics: all inculpably ignorant Christians and other religionists can in fact attain an equal if not higher degree of sanctity than Catholics. The documents of Vatican II did not change the Church's thinking about the possibility of the outsiders being saved, but formulated the doctrine in positive language. Instead of saying "outside the Church, no salvation," for instance, Catholic theologians would rather speak of "the Church as the universal sacrament of salvation."

Catholic Theologians and the Implementation of Vatican II

The postconciliar period has witnessed a surge in theological writings on Catholic uniqueness. No serious theologian in the postconciliar era denies that the formally unevangelized can be saved, but when it comes to figuring out how these individuals receive salvation, there has been some considerable debate among theologians.

One group of theologians have argued that revelation has been given exclusively to Israel, culminating in the person of Jesus Christ. Non-Catholic worldviews, then, are not seen as objectively salvific as Catholicism. "Natural Christians," as the popes categorize the religious others, are not saved because of their religions or life-views, but are saved in spite of the false teachings in them. Thus, God does not will the distinctive teachings (that are erroneous) in the other religions, but the salvation of each individual person in those religions through those teachings that overlap with Catholic truths. These theologians want to preserve the older scholastic distinction between nature and grace. Catholicism is seen as the "fulfillment" of world religions.[22]

22. One exponent of this view might be the Lutheran theologian Ruokanen, *The*

Another group of theologians have stressed that a revelatory dimension can be found in other world religions. According to this theological contention, the other religions can serve as salvific vehicles of grace.[23] Proponents of this model wish to connect nature and grace more closely together. Inspired by the theology of Karl Rahner, these theologians have argued that God does not operate in a purely individualistic manner. Grace always takes a sacramental, social shape and is always manifest in the concrete world, even in the institutions of religious traditions.

Although these models are distinct, they complement one another. Catholics cannot maintain that every teaching in the other religions preserves revelatory truths that complement and/or run parallel to the revelation that was given in Jesus Christ.[24] Some type of "fulfillment" is necessary for any comprehensive Catholic theology of the religions. This contention is not to say that the invincibly ignorant must come to know Christ explicitly to be saved. By definition, someone who is inculpably ignorant cannot come to know Christ explicitly. Moreover, an inculpable individual who is unaware of Christian truth may be culpable for accepting and living out a truth in and through his or her own religious tradition (refuse to abide by those truth), and not be saved.

The Church itself has settled this issue between the two formally distinct models. Christ's revelation is different in *kind* and not just in *degree* from other special, divine disclosures. John Paul II reaffirmed the uniqueness of Christ by affirming that he is "the essential point by which Christianity differs from all the other religions, by which human search for God has been expressed from earliest times."[25] Elsewhere, the pope said that the Holy Spirit operates outside the formal, canonical boundaries of the Church.[26] The continuity and similarity between the Christian revelation and the world's other religions is equally marked by a radical discontinuity and dissimilarity.[27] The Spirit is not absent from whatever is true and holy in the world religions, but the pope's statements do not mean that all religions are objectively equal to one another.

The documents of Vatican II are also confirmed by the controversial document *Dominus Iesus*. Although some theologians disputed secondary details in the document, it forthrightly settled the teaching of the Church:

Catholic Doctrine of Non-Christian Religions.

23. For an account, see Dupuis, *Toward a Christian Theology of Religious Pluralism.*

24. Congregation for the Doctrine of the Faith, *Dominus Iesus*, 6, 12, 14, 21.

25. John Paul II, *Tertio Millennio Adveniente*, 6.

26. See the encyclical of John Paul II, *Dominum et Vivificantem,*

27. Dupuis, *Toward a Christian Theology of Religious Pluralism*, 173.

"one can and must say that Jesus Christ has a significance and a value for the human race and its history, which are unique and singular, proper to him alone, exclusive, universal, and absolute."[28] Undoubtedly, *Dominus Iesus* was consistent with Vatican II on the possibility of salvation outside the institutional Church.[29]

One of the main objections to *Dominus Iesus* had to do with the statement that "formal outsiders" were in "a gravely deficient situation in comparison with those who, in the Church, have the fullness of the means of salvation."[30] But a careful look at the statement reveals that it was merely referring to the objectivity of inculpable ignorance. Even though some "outsiders" are considered in a gravely deficient situation compared to that of the "insiders," the former may in fact be subjectively closer to the risen Christ. These critics fail to recognize that the document went on reiterate the teaching of *Lumen Gentium* 14: salvation becomes more demanding for those exposed to Catholic truth, not easier to attain.

The metaphysical, objective truth of Christ is compatible with the epistemological relativity of different individuals in response to the divine light given to them. On the one hand, an emphasis on the "truth of Christ" at the expense of subjective factors leads to a bare exclusivism. On the other hand, stressing the relative nature of religious belief leads one down the path of an unwarranted pluralism. Like the mainstream Catholic tradition, *Dominus Iesus* accepts and balances both crucial elements for formulating and defending Catholic teaching.

Conclusion

Catholic theologians and other intellectually engaged laymen seek to reconcile the uniqueness of God's revelation in Jesus and the nature of God in the face of contradictory religious claims and secular outlooks. Catholic theologians also have the responsibility to keep abreast of current challenges that might be raised in the Catholic community in response to issues related to religious diversity.

One significant challenge has to do with balancing the universal love of God and the particularity of Jesus. Some have claimed that Vatican II

28. Congregation for the Doctrine of the Faith, *Dominus Iesus*, 15.

29. For additional confirmation, see Heim, "A Protestant Reflection on Ecumenism and Interfaith Issues," in Hefling and Pope, eds., *Sic et Non*, 68. Also see the essays by Imbelli, "The Reaffirmation of the Christic Center," 96, 99, and Akinwale, "A Timely Affirmation and Clarification of Vatican II," 169–78.

30. Congregation for the Doctrine of the Faith, *Dominus Iesus*, 22.

substantially changed the content of the Church's teaching. Such a contention cannot be responsibly sustained in the light of a careful reading of Catholic tradition and the Council documents. The content of Catholic teaching should be distinguished from the way it is received, understood, and expressed by different people.

— 14 —

The Soteriological Problem of Evil

Now that we have already discussed the relevant magisterial documents on "the Church as the universal sacrament of salvation," it is time to address why some critics attempt to undermine the Church's teaching on believing in Christ as the universal Savior. These critics cannot help but wonder why God would allow so many individuals to be born into circumstances that prevent them from explicitly knowing Jesus Christ and his body on earth, the Catholic Church. Jacques Dupuis puts the challenge in stark terms:

> Could not God have provided more generously for the salvation of the bulk of humankind? Did a disposition that would unilaterally favor a Christian minority—currently one billion and a half out of six billion human beings—in terms of the possibility of salvation in Jesus Christ seem just and worthy of a God of universal love? And could it sincerely be thought that God's 'universal will' that all persons be saved, clearly affirmed in the New Testament . . . was serious and efficacious?[1]

Unsatisfactory answers to the kinds of questions that Dupuis raises have enabled some pluralists to formulate powerful objections to Catholic uniqueness. A closer look at the nature of these questions reveals that the person who is asking them is concerned about the problem of natural evil. In this particular case, the natural evil is that certain individuals are unable to overcome their ignorance of the gospel because of circumstances outside their control. Even missionaries are unable to reach these individuals with the gospel of Christ. Everyone is called to respond favorably to the gospel. It follows that the invincibly ignorant are somewhat deprived of being allowed to become the persons they were meant to be in Christ.

---

1. Dupuis, *Christianity and the Religions*, 3.

No matter how one might formulate their response to these challenges, Catholic theologians should hold that it is better to hear and respond favorably to the gospel than to be completely ignorant of it. John Paul II affirmed: "No believer in Christ, no institution of the Church, can avoid this supreme duty: to proclaim Christ to all peoples."[2] Although the inculpably ignorant can have veridical experiences of the risen Christ, these encounters do not diminish the fact that the "saved outsiders" remain cognitively ignorant of the Savior.

One must have an adequate philosophy of God and natural evil in order to construct a broader framework that enables one to address the problem. Let me call the problem the "soteriological problem of evil." This philosophical discussion on God and evil has been practically nonexistent in Catholic reflection on the theology of religions. If one understands Thomas Aquinas' philosophy of God and how it relates to the challenge of natural evil, one should argue that reconciling Christ's uniqueness in the face of inculpable ignorance become a nonstarter—if not a meaningless issue for Catholic apologists to answer.

Aquinas, Evil, and Modern Philosophy

Some philosophers have argued that the presence of evil disproves the existence of God. The objection usually runs something like this: (1) God is the creator of everything (other than himself); (2) evil is something; (3) therefore, God created evil. Because a good God would not create evil, the critic argues, God does not exist.

Now, although Thomas Aquinas takes the reality of evil seriously, he demolishes the argument because the second premise is highly dubious. For Aquinas, evil is not a substance, but the privation of something. Aquinas concedes that evil is not an illusion or a self-subsistent entity. Rather, evil is "a deprivation of some particular good inhering in an object."[3] Therefore Aquinas successfully avoids the trap in the argument by refuting the minor premise in the argument. Evil is the privation of some good that ought to be present in an object. Evil is like rot in a tree or a wound in someone's arm. In the case of the wound, the person's arm lacks physical health.

Thus evil is not merely an absence of something (for example, the absence of life in a stone would not be considered evil), but the privation of some good that should be present in an object. From this conclusion it follows that good can exist in the absence of evil (for example, God can

2. John Paul II, *Redemptoris Missio*, 3.
3. Aquinas, *Compendium of Theology*, 114.

exist in the absence of anything). Evil is not an eternal principle that competes with good (as in Manichean dualism). Neither is evil an illusion (as in pantheism). Evil is real. It is the real lack in something. To be sure, a blind person is aware of the fact that he lacks eyesight! It follows that no object is completely evil. In brief, "nothing can be totally an unmitigated evil."[4] If something was completely evil, then it would destroy its own existence (which is a good). Evil is always parasitical on what is good.

One type of evil is known as "moral evil." Moral evil occurs when someone chooses an action that is contrary to human nature. God allows for the possibility of evil, but humans are responsible for moral evil (privation in relationships). As Aquinas says: "God therefore neither wills evil to be done, nor wills it not to be done; but he wills to permit evil to be done, and this is good."[5] The other type of evil is known as natural evil (privation in substances).

Natural evil is a failure, defect, or absence in the structure or process of a thing. Some examples of natural evil include premature death, disease, hunger, and sufferings related to the evolutionary struggle for survival. As in the case of moral evil, these evils are "sought indirectly, namely because it is the consequence of some good."[6] What is good for higher forms of life is evil for lower forms. For example, cancer growths survive in a person's body, but the person suffers and dies. The former is good for the cancer, but is evil for the person. Sometimes a drowning person (evil) inspires acts of bravery (good) from a lifeguard. However, God is causing only what is good. As a result of God's will in creating good things, evil occurs *per accidens*. Evil may serve as the *occasion* for good, but it never serves as the *cause* of good.

Many modern philosophers, by contrast, have held that God has a "purpose" in allowing evil for the generation of good. Because human beings are limited by their cognitive faculties in discerning the will of God, these theists have insisted that we should not accept the reality of "gratuitous evil." Nontheists have sharply reacted to the theists' moral exoneration of God by arguing for gratuitous evil. The modern theists, by contrast, are left justifying God's ways by explaining the deity's "morally sufficient reasons" for allowing evil. Such a task is heavily burdensome for the theist, if not completely misguided from the start. For Aquinas, both views begin on the wrong premise. In Aquinas' view, we cannot know what God is. We can only know what God is not.

4. Aquinas, *Summa Theologiae*, 1.19.3.
5. Ibid., 1.82.1.
6. Ibid., 1.22.2.

For one thing, it seems like the world contains pointless evil. This can be seen in many low grade evils such as receiving a paper cut, being bitten by a mosquito, or stubbing one's toe. By holding to an overdetermined philosophy of the world, the modern theist has argued that "hidden benefits" must appear at some point in the world by connecting them to previous evils. To give an example, every time a fawn is killed by brain tumors, God rewards a beneficiary (who might be completely unaware of what is happening to the fawn) in some other location. Notwithstanding this speculative possibility of positing the greater good, one is *prima facie* justified in holding to the reality of gratuitous evil.

By denying the reality of such evils, many modern theists are forced to argue that God *uses* evil as a *necessary* means to establish a greater good.[7] This contention is in opposition to Aquinas' philosophy. In Aquinas' view, evil is never willed by God, but only occurs accidentally. As Charles Journet rightly said: "Must it be said that all these evils 'contribute to the perfection of the universe?' This is strongly denied by St. Thomas. This would be to make them a part of the universe and to see in them the causes of the good things to which they are attached."[8] Thus many theists under the influence of modern philosophy are forced to hold that there are certain means by which God is constrained while aiming to do what is morally good. Notice that in this view, God is said to "abide" by the dubious moral principle that "the end justifies the means". The logic of theodicy says that many persons must end up being used for the sake of someone else's good. This approach unduly anthropomorphizes God and categorizes him as a moral agent.

The origins of the so-called "the greater good defense" can be traced back to the theology of the Protestant Reformers, and philosophers such as Gottfried Leibniz (1646–1716). The reformers' emphasis on God's sovereignty, for instance, facilitated the use of theodicy. Reformed theologian John Calvin (1509–64) rejected the distinction between divine "willing" and "permitting," and held that every event has been divinely ordained. As an example, let us say that a child is raped. On Calvin's view, God literally ordained this horrible tragedy so that he might bring about a greater good. Sin becomes the instrument by which virtue is generated. In this way, God ordains acts that would otherwise be condemned by him. This view of God's control differs from sovereignty as understood in terms of autonomy and governance. On the latter view, God's counsels are the result of his free decision; thus God does not consult a moral standard above himself before he acts.

---

7. Swinburne, *Providence and the Problem of Evil*; Hick, *Evil and the God of Love*.

8. Journet, *The Meaning of Evil*, 80.

Thomists split the horns of the dilemma and argue that modern theists and atheists are beginning from the wrong premise: namely, that pointless suffering should determine whether one should accept or deny God's existence. Aquinas rejects this starting point. For him, a good God exists—and there are gratuitous evils. God, in Aquinas' philosophy, does not cause evil. Aquinas' position is a hugely beneficial path to take in the current theist-atheist debate, for it does not place the burden of proof upon the believer to demonstrate that evil will be used for a greater good. God's existence is known through other means, not through the weighing and assessing of proposals given by theodicists and their opponents. According to Brian Davies:

> Some have suggested that the reality of evil is reason, on moral grounds, to say that God either certainly or probably does not exist. Others have maintained that God's existence can be defended in the light of evil since God is morally justified in allowing the evils that occur. . . . Aquinas sides with neither of these positions. He affirms that God exists and that God is good, but he does not try to defend God's goodness on moral grounds. So, though he thoroughly disagrees with those who reject belief in God, he is not a theodicist. If we take the problem of evil to be expressed by the question, "How can God justify morally for the evil that exists?" Aquinas would dismiss it as a pseudo-problem. . . . With that understanding in mind, Aquinas would clearly take the problem of evil, as just construed, to be a bogus one.[9]

God does not so much do away with evil in heaven as much as he overwhelms the privations of the world with his definitive and immediate presence. In heaven the elect always do what is good without being affected by the pains of natural evil.

Some evils resist reprocessing. The world was not made with the potential to redeem every evil. Even so, there is no reason to defend or reject God's existence. For God is *not* a moral agent to be excoriated by atheists or exonerated by theists. God does not have to answer for his actions in creating what was otherwise a good world. If one understands what is being talked about when referring to God (through the use of the *via negativa*), then the "problem of evil" should not be considered a problem. God not "use" evil as an instrument to foster virtue. With this understanding of God and evil in the background, let us turn to some challenges that theologians and philosophers face when discussing Christian uniqueness in a world of religions.

9. Davies, *Thomas Aquinas on God and Evil*, 113.

Catholic Theologians and Divine Revelation

Many theologians have argued that there is a revelatory dimension to be found outside the boundaries of Christianity. Unless God reveals something of himself to the formal outsiders, then these individuals could never be saved. So there is a sense in which God wills the existence of other religions. Gerald O'Collins, for instance, speaks freely of people being saved *through* the other religions.[10] Many theologians would welcome the language of "being saved through the other religions."

Correlatively, it must be said the formal outsiders are also saved despite the non-Catholic teachings in those other religions. As indicated in the last chapter, some sort of fulfillment is required for a Catholic theology of religions.[11] For, God does not will *everything* in other religions. God only causes what is good, and never uses evil (and/or falsehoods) as a means to save and sanctify the lost. Likewise, God saves Catholics despite whatever false teachings may be in their Church. Not every teaching in the other religions is salvific, and to the extent that these teachings contradict established Catholic doctrine (the incarnation, Trinity, etc.) there is an impediment to salvation.

Notwithstanding the fact that God is revealing himself outside of Christianity, Catholic teaching may remain vulnerable to the skeptical challenge: "Why hasn't God enabled everyone to hear the message of Christ explicitly?" Even though outsiders may know Christ to a more intense degree and in a different way than Catholics, the fact remains that the outsiders are unable to know Christ in an explicit way. Although salvation becomes more demanding for believers, it cannot be denied that it is better to hear the gospel and respond to it than be completely ignorant of it. Love grows in direct, not in inverse proportion with truth. If God loves everyone, the skeptic says, then God and his Church should be able to explicitly relay the gospel to all of humanity. To hear and respond to truth complements and fulfills the religious experience of being loved.

Again, the skeptic can easily ask: "Why must everyone must face different circumstances and presentations of the one metaphysical truth of Christ?" Notice at this point that the problem should become a concern for Thomas and his philosophy of God and natural evil. Why would some individuals have certain capacities that others cannot access (say, because of premature death, or because of some other debilitating handicap)? Why, again, would certain individuals be born in a time and place where the gospel

---

10. O'Collins, *The Second Vatican Council on Other Religions.*

11. Vatican II, *Lumen Gentium,* 16.

is unavailable to them (say, because Christianity is illegal in their country, or because the Church had not influenced the surrounding culture yet)?

Thomist Philosophy and Its Implications for the Soteriological Problem of Evil

Paleontologists have estimated that the human race had been on earth for literally tens of thousands of years before the advent of either Judaism or Christianity. Although the statistics suggest that more than 98 percent of the human race have appeared after Jesus Christ, the sobering fact still remains that there are millions of people who remain cognitively ignorant of the gospel. We may be comforted by the fact that a provident God sent his Son at a time where millions of people eventually had the chance to hear and respond to the gospel, but these statistics do not considerably increase the case for Catholic Christian uniqueness. So long as one person has been found inculpably ignorant, God's universal love for humanity seems to be cast into doubt.

Nonetheless, the issue of why each and every person was been born into circumstances with limited capacities outside their control does not pose a threat to the theologian who takes a Thomist approach to God and natural evil. Thomists might argue that although God wills the salvation of every person, it is frankly irrelevant (and, illicit) for critics to ask: "Why didn't God arrange the necessary preconditions for everyone to hear and respond to the gospel in a persuasive manner?" Such a concern assumes that God is a "moral agent," similar to that of humans. Further, to assume that God is a moral agent is to misunderstand what is being talked about in reference to God. As Davies says, "God is nothing in the world and is not one of a kind among others of the same kind."[12] He continues:

> To start thinking about this topic [of evil] while presuming that we know what God is seems to me misguided. Yet discussions of God and evil frequently proceed on the contrary assumption. They often begin by supposing that we do have a pretty good understanding of God. This supposition usually takes the form as regarding God as something familiar to us. It reaches its peak in the claim that God, if he exists, is a moral agent.[13]

If Catholic theologians and their modern interlocutors take a modern philosophical approach to God, then you would expect their treatments of

---

12. Brian Davies, *The Reality of God and the Problem of Evil*, 79. Cf. 58, 92.

13. Davies, *The Reality of God and the Problem of Evil*, 80. Cf. 103–5.

these topics, in Davies' words, "to home in at once on questions of the form 'Is God morally justified in . . . ?'"[14] One might fill in the space that was left blank by Davies: in "allowing millions of people to not hear of Christ and his Church."

Moreover, the critic assumes that God could have done a "better job" in creating the world so that everyone might have the chance to hear the gospel. But, in the Thomist view, God is not subject to a moral standard. How, then, can God do a "better" job? Neither can God be morally exonerated by theodicists. By saying God cannot do anything about the unintended effects of natural evil in creating the universe is not to say God is semipotent or even limited in goodness.[15] Thus the question of "Why didn't God ensure that everyone would hear the message in the same way?" cannot be meaningfully posed by the skeptic, let alone answered by an apologist.

Let us turn to an analogous scenario that might shed light on the discussion. We now know that the universe is approximately 13.72 billion years old. The age of the universe is only matched by its extraordinary size. Awareness of these astronomical facts has enabled many skeptics to doubt the existence of God. They protest: "Surely the universe is an empty waste of time and space!" If this challenge was not difficult enough for some believers to answer, a handful of other questions make it more difficult for them: "Why couldn't God create the earth right from the outset, arranging the world in such a way that enables the gospel to be persuasively heard by everyone at least once during their earthly life? God can do all things, right?" Such questions can leave a believer reeling in crippling doubt about his or her own faith.

Let me respond by noting that *when the imagination trumps the proper use of reason*, then one can easily think that God does not exist because of "universe's great waste of time and space." But, if one recognizes what is being talked about when referring to God, then these objections do not amount to much. Objectors who refer to the size of the universe as an undercutting defeater of theistic belief are assuming that God could have been more "efficient" in creating the universe. However, the term "efficiency" only pertains to human persons who have limited time and resources to perform a given task. In the case of an eternal God, there is "unlimited time" (God is timeless, or eternal) and "resources" (God is omnipotent). God is not constrained or "held accountable" to take the most "efficient" path in creating and developing what was otherwise a good universe. Whether the universe

---

14. Ibid., 97.

15. In the Thomist view, divine goodness is not to be understood as moral goodness, but as a convertible category with existence itself.

is fourteen thousand years, fourteen million years, or fourteen billion years, all of these numbers are equally "comprehensible" to an eternal God.

As in the case of the development of the universe, one may be easily misled in thinking that inculpable ignorance counts against the established tenets involved with Christ's uniqueness. At best, the skeptic under the influence of modern theism—whose questions go unanswered about Christ's uniqueness in the face of inculpable ignorance—might be tempted to endorse an unwarranted version of pluralism.[16] As a case in point, John Hick was a salient exponent of the use of theodicies to "justify God's ways to man." Later on in his career, he became a leading proponent of religious pluralism.

Atheists who are arguing against proponents of modern theism might reject the validity of all religions. It is not insignificant that some of the new atheists have referred to the multitude of incompatible truth claims in the religions as an excuse to reject all of them.[17] Unfortunately Hick and many of the new atheists did not adequately understand the Thomist approach to God and natural evil before they each went on to reject the uniqueness of Christ.

Here the skeptics may again ask: "Why aren't there many divine disclosures?" In response to these questions theologians must not lose sight of the fact of that God is not a "moral agent." With this realization in mind, the question is not difficult to answer. But it can become difficult to answer when it is coupled with unwarranted assumptions that have not been addressed by the theologian. One example of an "unwarranted assumption" is that "it is unfair that every person does not have the opportunity to hear the message of the gospel."

Second, no matter where God chooses to reveal himself, the revelatory event and message will be limited by time and space. The same goes for all other divine disclosures. Thirdly, many Catholic theologians (O'Collins, Dupuis) have argued that revelation can be found outside of Christianity. These theologians have argued convincingly that Jesus is working in and through all the religions of the world to bring individuals to himself.[18] Norman Anderson once argued: Christianity "is distinguished from other religions by the event which gave it birth; and it is itself continually corrected and purified in so far as Christians go back to that event—and its

---

16. See Hick, *Evil and the God of Love*. For his views on religious pluralism, see *An Interpretation of Religion*.

17. See Dennett, *Breaking the Spell*, 100–101, 217. Also see Dawkins, *The God Delusion*, 340.

18. Avery Dulles outlined different models of revelation in his book *Models of Revelation*. Revelation outside Christianity includes some of the models. But the revelation given in Jesus Christ encompasses all the models.

necessary implications—as their starting-point, their touchstone and their inspiration."[19]

Quite naturally, the next question might be "why not many incarnations of Jesus over a period of time, all over the world?" From the outset, a Catholic theologian might pause and ask the critic why he or she would pose such a question. If the concern of the skeptic shows any underlying signs that he or she believes that God could have been "fairer" or "more efficient" by incarnating himself in Jesus over and over again, then the skeptic is obviously working with a set of problematic presuppositions that need to be kindly challenged.

Second, it should be stressed that the idea of many incarnations is more at home in pantheism, not in theistic worldviews. When speaking of an incarnation, the assumption is that a theistic God transcends the world and then becomes part of it.

Thirdly, the world's other religions do not claim that God has reincarnated himself again and again. Even though the Catholic Church says that God the Son became incarnate in Jesus of Nazareth, the other religions do not claim as much. Catholicism also says it happened once. Hence, the contention that there could have been many incarnations sees something in the religions–including Christianity–that they do not claim for themselves.

The traditional Christian claim is that God revealed himself fully in Jesus. Since God revealed himself fully in Jesus, then all that can be given has been given in him. Since God is one, God the Son reveals himself as one person. But, in Catholicism, Christ's revelation was provided *once,* but it is preserved *infallibly* through *many persons.* God not only reveals himself decisively in the person of Jesus, he also provides some means of transmission for that revelation in the Church. To conclude: multiple incarnations would seem to trivialize Christ's *perfectly lived life.*

A final question that might be asked is: "Why, then, did the God-man appear at the time and place where he did?" Again, there is nothing wrong with asking the question and expecting a compelling answer, but some illicit assumptions may prevent the questioner from accepting a traditional answer. Those "assumptions" need to be brought onto the table and exposed. Second, the answer is that God revealed himself in Jesus so that persons might come to know him explicitly. As the apostle Paul wrote (Gal 4:4–5): "when the fullness of time had come, God sent his Son, born of a woman, born under the law, to ransom those under the law, so that we might receive adoption." God revealed himself fully in Jesus, but this does not mean that "outsiders" cannot be saved. In some cases the "formal outsiders" may be

---

19. Norman Anderson, *Christianity and the World Religions,* 47–48.

closer to Christ and to God than the "formal insiders." The exposure and formal acceptance of Christ does not necessarily make one's salvation more likely. Salvation becomes more demanding for the informed Catholic.

To conclude: one of the mysteries of the Catholic faith is that God became a human and revealed his inner-life to a limited group of persons at a certain point in time and space. Why would God allow such a small proportion of the planet to have formal access to the Christ? Why didn't God reveal himself fully in all times and places? Why hasn't the explicit message of salvation reached every human person? The assumptions undergirding these critics' questions may serve as a primary example of natural evil. In this particular case, the natural evil is that many individuals and entire groups have been precluded from hearing the gospel due to different circumstances.

Further, human beings are made for the truth. It is better to hear, understand and live out the gospel than to be inculpably ignorant of it. Not to hear and respond to the gospel would count as a prime example of natural evil. If the critic assumes that God could have done a "better job" in making Christ and his Church available to everyone at least once during their lives, then these questions are incapable of being meaningfully asked or even answered.

Conclusion

Notwithstanding the continuity and discontinuity of the Church's teaching on "outside the Church, no salvation," many skeptics have posed objections to Church's teaching. It should be noted that the challenge is directly linked to the "problem of evil." But there is no such problem according to Thomas Aquinas. For, God is not a moral agent. If we understand what is meant by God, then we would not impose or project moral characteristics onto him. This realization should help Catholics to remain confident in holding to the uniqueness of Christ and his Church. On a Thomistic philosophical premise, the so-called "unfairness of God" for revealing himself once in Jesus in the face of inculpable ignorance is a pseudo-problem.

In many cases, the reason why some accept (or reject) the doctrine *extra ecclesiam nulla sallus*, ("outside the Church, no salvation") is predicated upon one's philosophical conception of God.[20] In classical Thomist theology, God is not a "moral agent" (on a footing similar to that of humans). Therefore, it would not make sense for skeptics to fault God for being "unfair" or "supremely fair" in deciding who hears the message and who does

20. Cf. Paul VI, *Ecclesiam Suam*, 95.

not. The "playing field" of who can be saved and who cannot is rendered equal for everyone.

Paul VI also recognized that one's acceptance of the uniqueness of Jesus seems to be predicated upon one's philosophical conception of the nature of God:

> It [that is, the Catholic Church] realizes only too well the enormous difficulties of such a mission. It is well aware of the numerical disproportion between itself and the rest of the human race. It knows its own limitations, its own shortcomings and the failings of its own members. It realizes too that the acceptance of the gospel does not depend on any apostolic endeavors of its own, nor on the existence of the right temporal conditions. Faith is a gift of God. *He alone determines in the world the order and the time of salvation.* The Church does, however, realize that it is the seed, as it were, the leaven, the salt and the light of the world. Fully conscious of all that is new and remarkable in this modern age, it nevertheless holds its place in a changing world with sincere confidence, and says to men: "Here in my possession is what you are looking for, what you need." (italics mine).[21]

The pope rightly observed that God is above human categories, and cannot be understood as a moral agent.

21. Ibid., 95.

— 15 —

Knitter's Pluralism and Christian Orthodoxy

UNDOUBTEDLY, THE UNIQUE MEDIATORIAL role that Jesus has for salvation has been defended by Christians from the earliest days of the Church. In recent years some theologians have tried to reverse the Church's traditional understandings of Jesus for the sake of reinterpreting Catholic doctrine in more defensible terms in the modern world. Sometimes these revised understandings of Christ's uniqueness result in unacceptable versions of "religious pluralism." In essence, these religious pluralists deny the unique salvific role of Jesus Christ.

One of the most provocative theologians of pluralism and dialogue is theologian Paul Knitter. Because Knitter has listened and adapted his theology in response to many criticisms over the years, this chapters comprehensively engages Knitter's pluralism in the light of Catholic teaching.

An assessment of Knitter's most up-to-date pluralist theology reveals that he continues to be mistaken in holding to certain teachings about Jesus and the Church. Conversely, one might affirm the uniqueness of Jesus and the Church in the face of Knitter's most recent challenges.

Paul Knitter on Jesus, the Fullness of Revelation

Catholic teaching holds that Jesus Christ is the one redeeming mediator between God and the human race. It follows that Christ's revelation is true, unique, full, and ultimate. Paul Knitter, by contrast, argued that the doctrine of Christ's fullness precludes the need for additional theological understandings.

He asks: "how can any one of the partners really be open to growing in the truth when they believe that they have the fullness of God's truth?"[1]

One point that Knitter needs to seriously consider is that the term "fullness" should be interpreted as an ontological category, not an epistemological one. For instance, Catholic teaching holds that believers may continuously gain a more comprehensive understanding (epistemology) of God's revelation in Jesus (ontology). Jesus is the one mediator (ontology) between God and humanity, regardless of whether anybody is aware (epistemology) of this fact or not.

Unfortunately, when it comes to understanding the distinction between ontological truth and theological epistemology, Knitter sometimes conflates them together: "Truth is not dished out (even by God) in any one, unchanging package. Nor is it found in any one place, unchanging, for all times."[2] What Knitter should have said is that "one's understanding of the truth can-not (or rather, should not) be unchanging." For example, the Council of Chalcedon taught that Christ was/is true God and true man (and that he is the image of the living God). These descriptions of Christ fall within the realm of propositional statements that correspond to reality. In saying that Jesus is the fullness of God's revelation to humanity, this would not mean that there is no room for further exploration and a more profound understanding of the incarnation itself.

As a result, Knitter refuses to accept any declaration that the Church is the "one true religion," and the Catholic belief that "God has dealt [the Catholic Church] all the aces." Here he seems to be quite confused. For Catholic faith holds that God revealed himself decisively and fully in Jesus, and believers can continuously explicate and live out that truth in a variety of ways in different cultural contexts.

So although Knitter correctly speaks of Christians as "growing in the truth," and as "being open" to the truth, he should remember that both of these notions pertain to one's epistemology, not to ontological truth. Curiously, Knitter has elsewhere observed that no one could ever fully grasp (epistemology) the truth given in Jesus: "I'm not against making truth claims in the dialogue. And I don't think that that's an impediment to dialogue at all. But I fear that it is an impediment to dialogue if I make truth claims that I *think* I have fully and finally *understood*. . . . No one can *understand* God's

1. Knitter, "Can Only One Religion Be True?" in *Can Only One Religion Be True?* 29–30.

2. Hill, Knitter, and Madges, *Faith, Religion, and Theology*, 193.

revealed truth *fully and finally*" (italics mine).[3] Knitter's statement should henceforth be welcomed and reinforced by Catholics and other Christians.

Second, Knitter utilizes the distinction between kataphatic and apophatic theology to argue that God's revelatory disclosures can occur outside of Jesus himself. Because there is "always more to be known about God's revelation" (read: because of "apophatic theology"), he says, it follows that God probably revealed himself in and through the other religions and religious founders.[4] Jesus, then, must be considered one of many true saviors. Knitter, then, introduces the "unknowable aspect of Christological revelation" to dislodge any restraint on God's revelation to humanity.

When addressing the question on whether the religious others are saved in and through Jesus without knowing it explicitly, Knitter affirms that such a proposition is "imperialistic."[5] But a few things can be said in response to his contention. For one thing, to pronounce a truth claim does not automatically make one an imperialist. An imperialist takes truth claims and uses them against those (in an abusive way) who are ignorant of the truths being made. For example, Catholic teaching claims that Jesus is the full and true revelation of God. It follows that Catholics can understand something about the religious others that the latter do not know about themselves. Knitter himself once captured this insight: "we believe that where we stand gives us the ability to see elsewhere; it enables us to understand others. Even more, religious beliefs lead us to suspect or even assert, that if the others stood where we stand, they would understand themselves better!"[6]

Be that as it may, the more important issue to note is whether Jesus is the one true savior of the world, even for those who are unaware of him, not whether this notion is "imperialistic." Perhaps Knitter should be sympathetic to those who disagree with him and use another word to label or describe them. For, the fundamental question has to do with whether Jesus is the one and only savior or not. Is he one of many saviors? Knitter opts for the latter position, but with more nuance.

Therefore, Knitter's comment about labeling certain Catholic theologians as "imperialists" is unhelpful. It smacks of a soft *ad hominem* attack.

3. Knitter, "Can Only One Religion Be True?" 50.

4. Knitter, "The Meeting of Religions," in D'Costa, Knitter, and Strange, eds., *Only One Way?* 49–50, 67–68.

5. Hill, Knitter, and Madges, *Faith, Religion, and Theology*, 198. Elsewhere Knitter recognizes that there is some type of common ground between the religions which makes interreligious dialogue and understanding possible. See Knitter's *One Earth, Many Religions*, 41.

6. Knitter, "Is the Pluralist Model a Western Imposition?" in Knitter, ed., *The Myth of Religious Superiority*, 31–32.

Nevertheless, Knitter's allegation against particularism is self-defeating. Indeed he seems to recognize this problem for his own version of pluralism. In Knitter's words: "This is the caveat of the that proponents of a pluralistic-liberative approach to dialogue must bear in mind—that because they are not sufficiently aware of how all truth claims are political and 'power-full,' their program for plurality and dialogue can become, whether they are aware of it or not, oppressive of others."[7] As long as truth claims are involved, there is always the possibility that someone will be ignorant of those claims. For it can easily be asked: is Knitter an imperialist with respect to those who are ignorant of his writings? The answer, per Knitter's logic, would have to be "yes." Surely Knitter does not consider himself an imperialist.

Another point to consider is that Catholic theology says that evangelists and apologists are not always called to evangelize the religious others at all times and places. Perhaps Knitter thinks that most Catholics believe that there is no room for dialogue, but only for evangelization. Such a view is not defended by responsible Catholic theologians. Sometimes dialogue is necessary without Catholics having to sense the immediate need to evangelize the formal outsiders. This is a point that I shall address later in this chapter.

In Catholic theology, the apophatic is, in a certain sense, "restrained" by the kataphatic—by the propositional content derived from the experience of divine revelation. Catholic theology affirms that there is "always more" to discover about *Jesus* within the parameters defined by orthodoxy. Of course there is nothing wrong in thinking there is "more" to God's revelation than what can be articulated about Jesus, but in Catholic theology the "more" of apophatic theology is always "more" about Jesus. Here many theologians will ask whether Knitter thinks there are contradictions between Christianity and the other religions. For if the distinctive teachings in religions all come from God (ontological truths), then we would not expect them to contradict one another (for these purported truths claim to represent reality). But they do, in part, contradict one another. Therefore, Knitter's specific version of pluralism cannot be true.

However, when Knitter addresses the challenge of some incompatible truth claims, however, he affirms that they are basically saying the same thing in their own unique ways.[8] Such a contention expresses some truth that can be embraced and defended by Catholics. Catholic theologians can hold that there is some room for reconciling the different claims in the religions and Christological truth (because the different claims in the religions and in Christianity can have an analogous relationship with one another

7. Knitter, *One Earth, Many Religions*, 49. Also see 49–53.
8. Knitter, "Can Only One Religion Be True?" 40.

at times), but Catholics will insist that there must be some contradictions between the religions as well. For if there were no contradictions between the religions, then Christ's revelation would have to be reduced to one among many equal divine revelations. In other words, the full-fledged compatibility of all religions would only make sense if the critic has already denied the traditional understanding of Jesus' uniqueness. Inclusivism is a much more subtle position: it recognizes some similarities and continuities between Catholic faith and the world's religions, but it also affirms the dissimilarities and discontinuities between them.

Not to be overlooked, Knitter affirms that God's revelation in Jesus is a true revelation, but is not the only revelation.[9] Here again one might notice some truth and significant ambiguity. The Scriptures and tradition teach that God revealed himself in the person of Jesus Christ. Here there is agreement between Knitter and the Catholic faith. But Knitter goes much further: the Church expresses her belief in a true revelation, but there are complementary revelations to be found alongside of Jesus. After all, he affirms, there is "more to God's revelation" than what was given in Jesus.

Now, to say that there are other saviors who are complementary to Jesus Christ is not inherently problematic, but to say that Jesus is not working in and through the other religions or religious founders is a problematic position. Unfortunately Knitter holds unwaveringly to the latter perspective: Jesus is not working in and/or through the other saviors, but is out of the picture altogether. Knitter distances himself from all versions of inclusivism.

According to Catholic teaching, the risen Christ makes himself present to everyone in their unique circumstances, including those who are inculpably ignorant of him. Here Catholic theologians would want to emphasize that the word "inculpable" is paramount for understanding Catholic teaching. If one is inculpable with respect to accepting Christ as a member of the Church, then that person can be saved. But for the person who can overcome their ignorance of salvific truth, he or she is held accountable for accepting it. Some individuals may be culpable for accepting truths in their own religions, still refuse to abide by those truths, and not be saved.

In summary, Knitter argues that belief in Jesus is one of many ways to God. If one holds to Christian uniqueness, then she or he is being unfaithful to what God is revealing in Jesus and in the world today. In contrast, one must assess why Knitter maintains that revelations that go beyond Jesus should be interpreted as revelations that fundamentally exclude Jesus.

9. Knitter, "The Meeting of Religions," 72, 76.

Are There Scriptural Arguments for Pluralism?

In order to respond adequately to Knitter's pluralism, apologists must inquire about the authoritative sources that Knitter uses for his theology. Given the mere fact that "there is more to revelation than what was given in Jesus," it is at least a logical possibility that there are other saviors who formally exclude Jesus. This is why the issue of theological sources is so crucial in the dialogue with pluralists such as Knitter. Who gets to decide whether God will make himself known in some other historical, concrete form—alongside of the incarnate Christ?

Like most Catholic theologians, Knitter refers to the Scripture and official Catholic teaching to support his views. But Knitter's understanding of these sources is dubious. For instance, he holds that the biblical passages that are traditionally used to demonstrate the notion of Christian uniqueness can also be used in support of his version of pluralism:

> But what about all the language in the Bible that *does* place Jesus in the center, to the apparent exclusion of any possibility of truth in other religions? "No other name . . . One mediator . . . Only begotten Son . . . No one comes to the Father except by me." We're biblical people. We have to take this language seriously. That means we have to ask not only what it meant but also what it means. The New Testament scholar who has helped me most to figure out what it means is Krister Stendahl. He points out that all this talk about Jesus as "one and only" is essentially confessional language, not philosophical or ontological language. Or more personally, he calls it love language. The early Jesus followers were speaking about the Jesus with whom they were in love, who had transformed their lives, whom they wanted others to know about. . . . The primary intent is to be superlative, not exclusive. The intent is to say something positive about Jesus, not something negative about Buddha. We misuse this language when we use it to degrade or exclude the Buddha or Muhammad.[10]

Scripture is indeed normative for Catholics and all other Christians. But, according to Knitter, our interpretations of Scripture do not teach Christ's uniqueness in the way that has been proposed. Rather, the Scriptures reinforce Knitter's version of pluralism.

We can set aside the allegation that inclusivism entails "a degradation of other religions." Instead let us turn to Knitter's biblical case in support

10. Knitter, "Can Only One Religion Be True?" 34. Also see Hill, Knitter, and Madges, *Faith, Religion and Theology*, 216–217.

of his pluralism. Knitter merely appeals to the insights of Krister Stendahl which is disputable. Knitter should also appeal to the history of biblical interpretation in arriving at a doctrinal position that is well established, not merely appeal to one contemporary exegete (who already distances himself from Catholic tradition).

Consequently, Knitter's interpretations of the Scriptures flatly contradict the longstanding tradition of how these passages have been almost unanimously understood by Catholics, Orthodox, and Protestant Christians, let alone how the magisterium plainly understands God's revelation in Jesus. The Church's doctrinal stance of Christ's uniqueness, which is based on sound biblical exegesis, is that every saved formal outsider is saved through Jesus Christ.[11]

Knitter's also articulates an analogy for supporting the relevant biblical passages on Catholic uniqueness: "I commit myself to my wife because I feel certain that she is person she has shown herself to be, not because I am certain that there is no other woman whom I could possibly marry."[12] Although his point is well taken, this analogy does not succeed as an argument in support of Knitter's pluralism, simply because there are considerable differences between the love that two people have for one another, and the love that persons should have in response to the love of an infinite God who reveals himself concretely in Jesus. Analogies can be presented to *illustrate* one's theological stance, but they do not provide *arguments* for those views. Knitter's analogy succeeds in illustrating his pluralism, but this is no substitute for argument. The central question has to do with whether God saves the formal outsiders through Jesus or not.

Now, although Knitter formulates an biblically based case, he also recognizes the importance of tradition for doing theology:

11. Many interpreters would gainsay the expressivist speech perspective, especially in light of the proper methods of Catholic biblical interpretation. Relevant is John Paul II, *Fides et Ratio*, 82: "A radically phenomenalist or relativist philosophy would be ill-adapted to help in the deeper exploration of the riches found in the word of God. Sacred Scripture always assumes that the individual, even if guilty of duplicity and mendacity, can know and grasp the clear and simple truth. The Bible, and the New Testament in particular, contains texts and statements which have a genuinely ontological content. The inspired authors intended to formulate true statements, capable, that is, of expressing objective reality. It cannot be said that the Catholic tradition erred when it took certain texts of Saint John and Saint Paul to be statements about the very being of Christ. In seeking to understand and explain these statements, theology needs therefore the contribution of a philosophy which does not disavow the possibility of a knowledge which is objectively true, even if not perfect. This applies equally to the judgements of moral conscience, which Sacred Scripture considers capable of being objectively true." Also see paragraphs 83–84.

12. Knitter, *Introducing Theologies of Religions*, 105. Also see 133–34.

Therefore, in order to determine what makes up the "unique-ness of the Christian message," we have to turn to *both* the data on the historical Jesus that is found in scripture *and* the guidance found in the pneumatic working of the Spirit of the absent but risen Christ in the church. If we appeal only to the data of the scriptures, we end up with a type of Biblicism; if we are guided only by the Spirit, that Spirit can easily become the spirit of subjectivism.[13]

Catholic theology holds that Scripture and tradition provide a frame-work for interpreting one's Christian experience in the world. Knitter seems to agree. Moreover, these sources unequivocally affirm that God's full revela-tion is in Jesus. Here one cannot help but wonder if Knitter believes that the Church has changed her mind on the uniqueness of Jesus. More precisely stated, although Knitter takes the Scriptures and tradition seriously when it comes to formulating his ecclesiology and soteriology (as we will soon discover, Knitter believes that the magisterium changed her mind on the possibility of salvation outside the Church), he never comments on whether the magisterium has revised her understanding of Jesus.

Yet it is Knitter who formulates an exclusive biblically based case in support of his specific version of pluralism. Surely this can count as a "biblicist" position. This noticeable omission (on whether the magisterium has changed her mind on the fullness of revelation that was given in Jesus) makes Knitter's case for a revised understanding of Christology and plu-ralism vulnerable to serious criticisms. For the Church has taught that no other special revelation, strictly speaking, will complement or run parallel to Christ's revelation. The Church also teaches that if one is saved outside the Catholic Church, then she or he is still saved through Christ.

This brings us to the magisterium, the authoritative body of interpret-ers for understanding Scripture. Interreligious misunderstanding is some-times due to the impediments caused by sin. This is precisely one of the reasons why God revealed himself in the person of Jesus. In Jesus we have a revelatory disclosure which is normative and different in kind from all the distinctive teachings of the world's religions.[14] Further, the problem of sin cries out for an authoritative voice to interpret Jesus in the contemporary world. The significance of the magisterium for doing theology should not be all that controversial for Catholic theologians. For the magisterium is

13. Knitter, *Jesus and the Other Names*, 88.

14. By contrast, Knitter, *Jesus and the Other Names*, 169, says "I would endorse an understanding of Jesus as a *norma normans et normata*—a norm that norms others but can also be normed itself."

seen as the authoritative interpreter of Scripture and Sacred Tradition for contemporary contexts.

"Unaware of the Savior:"
Knitter and the Magisterium

It should come as no surprise that Knitter believes that the Church changed her mind on the possibility of salvation outside the Church: "My Roman Catholic community is an example of a major Christian denomination that, as it were, has changed its mind (although, when my church changes its mind or teachings, it never admits of doing so)."[15] He concludes that "Such a model [religious pluralism], which no longer insists on the superiority of the 'finality' of Jesus, is indeed quite new for Christian consciousness."[16] Since the Church has redefined her teachings and now holds the belief that outsiders can be saved, Knitter says that there are "other revelations" that exclude the risen Jesus. Let us now turn to Knitter's interpretations of the magisterium's teaching.

As we have already seen, Catholic teaching consistently holds that other religions are not as objectively salvific as Catholicism. Knitter, however, seems to have a confused perspective about the objectivity of truth and the culpability levels of different individuals in response to the truth of Christ: "In other words, with a correlational theology, Christians insist on the *possibility*, and urge the *probability*, that the Source of truth and transformation that they have called the God of Jesus Christ may have more truth and other forms of transformation to reveal than have been made manifest in Jesus."[17]

Catholic theologians will have some problems with Knitter's aforesaid contentions. Catholics want to argue that it is not possible to find more "truth" outside of the spiritual encounter (subjective pole) and verbal proclamation of the message of Jesus (objective pole). But it is possible to find

---

15. Knitter, "Can Only One Religion Be True?" 28. Also see Hill, Knitter, and Madges, *Faith, Religion, and Theology*, 212–13. Part of the reason for the change on who can be saved is due to the intellectual and cultural situation that we find ourselves in today. See Knitter, "Can Only One Religion Be True?" 27–28: "We are in a very different context than that in which our Christian ancestors formulated their first confessions of faith, which became our New Testament. Yes, there was religious pluralism at the time. But I believe it was felt, perceived, reacted to in a very different way than is the case for us today. At that time, for the minority Christian community, the other religions were primarily a threat. Today, as I will contend, the others are our fellow citizens, our fellow collaborators in promoting the well-being of this world."

16. Hill, Knitter, and Madges, *Faith, Religion, and Theology*, 213.

17. Knitter, *One Earth, Many Religions*, 30.

more transformation in those individuals and groups who have not been exposed to the proclamation of Jesus. When the religious others subjectively respond to the "divine light" that has been given to them, it is indeed possible for these individuals to be "closer to Christ and to God" than many Catholics who are explicitly aware of gospel truth. It is possible that many Catholics are not living out the truth that was objectively revealed to them through the verbal proclamation and spiritual encounter with Jesus.

The erroneous teachings of the world's other religions (i.e., those teachings which contradict basic Catholic truths) indicates that they cannot be total vehicles of divine grace. When theologians argue that the other religions are not complete or total vehicles of divine grace, many pluralists (such as Knitter) respond that there is also corruption and sinful structures in the Catholic Church.[18]

But here one needs to carefully delineate the differences and similarities between problematic teachings in the Church and in the other religions. As long as Christ is the one savior of humanity, it follows that, objectively speaking, Catholicism can promise its adherent the greatest potential for spiritual transformation. The Church can articulate some truth that no other religion can express as true. The Church is allowed to make this claim because of the external preaching, sacraments, and ministries which have been entrusted to her from Jesus himself.

Although some false doctrines or disciplines might be found inside the Church, these sinful doctrines and practices are not found at the foundational level in the hierarchy of truths, which are preserved unfailingly by the Church (teaching, sacraments, etc.). The errors in the other religions prevent these groups from the fullness of truth that can only be found in Jesus as a member of the Catholic Church.

Next, Knitter adds additional evidence for his pluralism when he refers to *Redemptor Hominis*: "the Holy Spirit can be found in the other religions."[19] However, the pope's claim does not contradict any of his other authoritative statements on the uniqueness of Jesus, and it does not mean that the other religions express divine revelations that are, strictly speaking, "outside of the saving work of Jesus Christ himself." If one wants to understand the pope's statement, then one should take all of John Paul II's theology into serious consideration, interpreting the pope's statement in the light of his overall theology of Christ and the religions. Other religions can

18. Knitter, "Paul Knitter Responds to Gavin D'Costa and Daniel Strange," in *Only One Way?* 157.

19. Ibid., 156.

take on a sacramental shape, but this would not mean that Jesus Christ is absent from those religions.

Christian Uniqueness and the Possibility of Dialogue

Another argument that Knitter mentions is that Christian uniqueness prevents Catholic inclusivists from dialoguing authentically with members from the other religions:

> Here I would contend respectfully but straightforwardly, that not just the exclusivist but also the inclusivist understandings of the uniqueness of Jesus are impediments to real dialogue. My inclusivist friends insist that this is not true. If we understand dialogue as an open-ended conversation in which all partners have equal rights, then we have to *listen* as genuinely as they witness, and all have to be ready to follow the truth wherever it may lead. But just such a process of dialogue, it seems to me, is hamstrung from the start if one of the partners insists that he or she has the God-given full, final, and unsurpassable vision of truth. Dialogue requires conviction, surely; but when those convictions are held to be divinely sealed as the "last word" or the "total word," then the dialogue cannot take place, as they say, on a level playing field.
>
> If Christians think they are in possession of the "fullness" of revelation and the norm for all truth, then no matter how much they might call for a dialogue "among equals" they retain the position of advantage. It is from *their* vantage point that any conflict of truth claims must be decided. If Christians have the norm, then they are not really able to recognize any truth or value in other religions that is genuinely from what they have; whatever truth or good may be found in other traditions has to be fulfilled or included within the final Christian truth. Such an attitude seems to me to be opposed to the nature and requirements of dialogue.[20]

Notice that Knitter forgets that *everyone* is coming at the world "from somewhere." Nobody—not even Knitter or the magisterium—can temporarily set aside their religious convictions without introducing another set of presuppositions. There is no such thing as a "presuppositionless" standpoint.

---

20. Knitter, "Five These on the Uniqueness of Jesus," in Knitter, Mojzes, and Swidler, eds., *The Uniqueness of Jesus*, 6–7.

If Catholics are to dialogue with the religious others, then everyone in the dialogue must hold to their convictions and speak and defend the truth when the circumstances allow for it, even if those truths are inconvenient and/or resisted by their interlocutors. Although love is unconditional and should be extended to everyone, regardless of one's religious convictions, truth claims are, by definition, exclusive. Love is related to the practical side of dialogue and mission; truth is directed to the theoretical side.

Knitter wants to uphold the universal imperative to love, but he sometimes forgets the importance of Catholic doctrine. Here it should be remembered that love speaks the truth in dialogue. Christianity is indeed "the way that is open to other ways" (to use Knitter's words) but this does not mean that objective truth has no role to play in dialogue. Of course, speaking and defending Christian truth is not always necessary in dialogue, but when the proper circumstances allow for it, it is imperative that Catholics speak the truth and attempt to evangelize the religious others.

Without seeming to recognize it, Knitter smuggled in the inevitability of speaking the truth to our dialogue partners, even when it is resisted: "What, after all, does love mean? To love others means to respect them, to honor them, to listen to them with an authentic openness to what they are saying. . . . Yes, this means that I have to confront them when I think they have gone wrong, but I have to be authentically ready to be so confronted by them. In other words, to love my neighbors I must be able truly to dialogue with them."[21] Surely Knitter cares enough about his readers to help them realize that what he is saying is considered "objectively true."

Here one might hearken back the analogous relationship between evangelization and apologetics on the one hand, and interreligious dialogue on the other. An individual Catholic is within his rights to engage in apologetics when the circumstances allow for it. On the other hand, that same believer can and must engage in dialogue when different circumstances arise.

But Knitter wants to know how it is possible for Catholics, who claim to have the fullness of truth, can learn anything new from the religious others through dialogue. Here too Knitter has answered his own questions in other places in his writings. His dialogue with Buddhists has pushed him "to explore . . . a more unitive and mystical understanding of God in which God is no longer an entity outside of me, but a power that has its very being within."[22] Such an exploration is compatible with a Catholic theology of God. Buddhism has also improved Knitter's prayer life. "My prayer

21. Knitter, *Jesus and the Other Names*, 39. Also see 65, 77, 122.

22. Knitter, "Can Only One Religion Be True? A Dialogue," 44.

life, thanks to Buddhism, has improved."[23] His dialogue with Hinduism has helped him to re-appropriate new understandings of the New Testament.[24] He recognizes that interreligious dialogue can "clarify, deepen, and correct"[25] his Christian beliefs. Knitter explains the possibility of engaging in dialogue *and* experiencing transformation in a way that is also congruent with Catholic teaching:

> Correlationalists believe that even in the case of apparently incommensurable differences between religions, if these differences are transformative and life-giving for their practitioners, then the differences cannot be totally alien to each other. If the Buddhist is transformed into a person more at peace with himself and others through the image of the *no-self*, and if the Christian is similarly transformed through her experience of being a *new-self* in Christ Jesus, the evident contradiction between no-self and new-self in Christ Jesus, in some way, be complementary; the Buddhist and Christian can speak and share, and be better off for doing so.[26]

Simply put, interreligious dialogue can clarify, refine, and transform one's Christian faith. For there is overlap and a shared experience that Catholics might have with the religious others. Dialogue might also result in conversions (either a conversion to one's own faith, or to another religion) when authentic understandings of different religions are kindly presented and defended.

Again Knitter asks: "If one has the fullness of truth already, what is there, really, to learn? At the most, one can clarify what one already knows. . . . One community will have to win out over the others. I prefer to understand dialogue as conversations between *collaborative* communities. That doesn't rule out disagreements and challenges. But it's a conversation where no religion has 'the fullness of truth' and is a final winner."[27] No responsible Catholic theologian would want to deny that Catholics, Christians and all other religionists should collaborate together in renewing and healing the people of this world, regardless of anyone's religious convictions.

But it must be remembered that truth claims exclude statements and practices that oppose them. Objectively speaking, there has to be a "winner" because truth is better than error. Here one might want to ask Knitter and

23. Ibid., 45.

24. Ibid., 41.

25. Ibid., 50.

26. Knitter, *Jesus and the Other Names*, 25.

27. Knitter, "Paul Knitter Responds to Gavin D'Costa and Daniel Strange," 157.

his fellow pluralists: Is his version of pluralism "the winner" over a bare exclusivism? Of course Knitter would say "yes" in response to this question.

It should also be noted that, subjectively speaking, all people have the opportunity to experience spiritual transformation in Christ and be saved (2 Pet 3:9). One can be saved within his or her own religion or within Christianity itself. Some of the outsiders might be closer to Christ and to God than those who know Jesus explicitly.

Historic Christianity claims to be true at its very core. Notice above that Knitter says there are "disagreements" and "challenges" between the religions, even when they collaborate in healing the world. When the earliest Christians were evangelizing the Mediterranean world, they opposed the beliefs of Roman religions. Knitter notes: "that is, the gods of a religious system that was that was part of an imperial oppressive system. Such gods had to be rejected not because they were 'other' but because they were contrary to Jesus' notion of the Reign of God."[28] Knitter rightly distinguishes between rejecting someone's teaching or beliefs, and rejecting the person himself.

Conclusion

Paul Knitter does not think that the Church's teaching on Jesus is defensible in the modern world. His revised interpretation of Jesus is predicated on the following sub-arguments. First, the undeniable reality of the apophatic exceeds what can be known (kataphatically) about Jesus. Therefore, God is probably revealing himself in some way outside of Christianity. Although the notion of "God's revelation outside of Christianity" is not an inherently problematic, it can be interpreted in a way that Scripture, Sacred Tradition, and the magisterium would not find acceptable. Second, Knitter maintains the Scriptures allow for interpretations that affirm Jesus as one of many different saviors; therefore the Scriptures allow Christians to be pluralists. Thirdly, traditional views of Jesus' uniqueness preclude one from engaging in interreligious dialogue.

These arguments, albeit they are interconnected throughout Knitter's writings, are severely flawed for a variety of reasons. For instance, apophatic theology stresses that there is always more to know about Jesus, not that there are other saviors that exclude Jesus. Scripture, tradition, and the magisterium ensure the traditional understanding of Jesus' uniqueness for salvation. In order to understand the relevant biblical passages one must appeal to some teaching authority. These authorities include an analysis of the

28. Paul Knitter, "Paul Knitter Re-Responds to Gavin D'Costa and Daniel Strange," in *Only One Way?* 211–12.

history of biblical interpretation for understanding the relevant Scriptural texts (John 14:6; 1 Tim 2:5; 1 John 2:2), and the magisterium itself. Indeed, Knitter's biblical argument for pluralism is susceptible to "biblicism" and is fallacious. By definition, Catholic understandings of biblical interpretation consider tradition as a binding source for doing theology. His argument from "the impossibility of reconciling the notion of interreligious dialogue and the uniqueness of Jesus" seems to forget that there is no such thing as a neutral standpoint from which to dialogue with the religious others. Everyone interprets the world with a certain set of presuppositions. In sum, Catholics should remain confident in holding to the uniqueness of Christ in the face of Knitter's challenges.

Conclusion

THROUGHOUT THIS BOOK WE have examined many arguments in support of the historic Christian faith. One of my major contentions is that the Church can and should challenge the problem of unbelief and indifference by doing apologetics.

Like so many of the Church's other concerns, the discipline of apologetics needs to be shaped under the larger umbrella of Scripture, tradition, and magisterial teaching. From the time of the Patristics to the decrees of Vatican I to Pope John Paul II's encyclical *Fides et Ratio* (1998), the Catholic Church and her most eminent theologians and philosophers have defended Church teaching. Vatican II and recent papal encyclicals continue to be written with an apologetic spirit.

In this book I discussed and defended the First Vatican Council's teaching on God's existence. This is one of the first steps that need to be taken in classical apologetic approaches. For, unless theism is accepted by the critical historian, it is difficult to see how she, or anyone else who endeavors to investigate miracle claims from the past, could make a responsible inference to the divinity and resurrection of Jesus (although I am willing to grant in some cases that some individuals may see the historical evidence as so compelling that it may in fact change their background theories about God and the material world). Joseph Ratzinger contended:

> It is not a case of exegesis providing evidence that supports a philosophy; rather, it is a matter of a philosophy that produces the exegesis. If (to speak in Kant's terms) I know *a priori* that Jesus cannot be God, that miracles, mysteries, and means of grace are three things it would be crazy to believe in, then I cannot discover in Holy Scriptures any fact that cannot exist as a fact. I

can only then discover why and how people came to make such assertions, how these gradually came about.[1]

Simply put, it does not make sense to speak about a special act of God unless there is a God who can act.

If God exists, it is very likely that he will reveal a message to humanity. Given the assumption of a theistic God, it is reasonable to maintain that he has brought the universe into being for some greater purpose. It will be natural to try to find some evidence of what that purpose is in all of human history. Further, it makes sense that there could be at least one public, divine revelation.

Human reason can only prove some things about God: that he exists, that he is one, unchanging, eternal, and so on. But it cannot tell us everything about him (for example, that God is triune). Human reason can prove that God exists; but it cannot convince anyone to trust in God. As such, knowledge of God's existence is not salvific. But believing in God's revelation brings one to salvation. As an indirect result of the dogmatic declaration of Vatican I, the bishops also saw the need to condemn materialism, pantheism, fideism, and rationalism. All of these worldviews are shown to be fallacious; for God's existence can be known with certainty.

With the assumption that God exists, it makes sense to look for clues in human history to find answers to the deepest questions about human life: Why is there suffering? What lies beyond the grave? By the time the Catholic philosopher has finished arguing successfully for the existence of God, he must lateral the ball to the professional historian. Here too we have seen that there is some remarkable evidence for the central claims and acts of Jesus. In the words of Catholic apologist Hugo Meynell:

> Christians have always presupposed that the picture of Jesus which we get from the gospels is at least roughly accurate; and it is difficult to see how Christianity could survive abandonment of this assumption except in a radically attenuated form. Now a very wide range of opinions as to the historical reliability of the gospels are held by serious scholars. Yet I think it can safely be said that the tide of scholarship, quite apart from the *Zeitgeist*, has set pretty heavily in opposition to the second position which I have called the "liberal Protestant view of Jesus." Subsequent research has on the whole confirmed the point forcefully argued by Albert Schweitzer at the beginning of the present century, that there are no consistent and objective principles of criticism, where the desired conclusions are not allowed more or less

---

1. Ratzinger, (Pope Benedict XVI), *Truth and Tolerance*, 132–33; cf. 186.

surreptitiously to dictate the method, whereby one can extract
the liberal Protestant view of Jesus from the gospel narratives.[2]

One does not have to believe everything in the New Testament writings is
historical in order to conclude that they offer some reliable historical information about Jesus. The relevant evidence is unanimously in favor of the
historicity of the resurrection of Jesus, despite the different ways in which the
New Testament writers describe what actually happened after the crucifixion.

God's vindication of Jesus and his teachings provides human beings
with the answers that they might have about death and eternal life. Believing
in the risen Lord ought to make a positive difference in human life, given
the needs that human beings have. When the foundational questions about
human existence are answered in the light of God's revelation, humans will
know how to organize their lives in harmony with one another, putting
them on the proper paths toward their final end.

Hence we should be able to perceive a positive difference in the lives of
those who believe in Jesus. For, he is the "way, the truth and the life." One of
the great themes of *Gaudium et Spes* has to do with "reading the signs of the
times." By reading the signs of the times, the Church will be able to answer the
deepest questions about humanity, God, and the cosmos. Despite the winding
turns of history and the various challenges that have been raised throughout
the centuries, the gospel is the answer to human suffering and longing.

By seeing the positive difference that Christianity makes for human
life, outsiders and other doubters sometimes may suspect that human life
is supposed to be lived—as a believing Catholic. I provided some philosophical arguments to illustrate how Catholic beliefs are positioned in such
a way that seems to foster moral motivation and right relationships. Many
sociological studies strongly suggest that the Catholic Christian faith has
had positively impacted many of the established structures of the West.

Quite naturally, the next question that skeptics might ask is the following: If Jesus is God's answer for the human race, then how is it that not
everyone has the opportunity to hear the good news? If human beings have
a need to hear from God to answer their most vexing, troubling questions,
then why hasn't this God enabled everyone to hear the gospel and be saved?

Down through the ages of Church history, this challenge was known
as the "scandal of particularity." Why would an all loving God reveal himself
uniquely in Jesus alone? After reviewing Catholic teaching on the unique
mediatorship of Jesus, I have argued that many challenges to the Catholic
doctrine of non-Christian religions stem from having an inadequate understanding of God's nature in the face of natural evil. The evil, in this specific

2. Meynell, *Is Christianity True?* 67.

case, is that many individuals have been unable to overcome their ignorance of the gospel. Sometimes the failures of missionaries and other Christians can solidify the invincible ignorance of the religious others. Thus many people are deprived of knowing the truth of Jesus in an explicit way.

Theologians might prevent outsiders from rejecting the particularity of Jesus by accurately defining what is meant by God. The God of Christianity is not one of many beings within the universe, but is the Creator of the universe. Catholics should distance themselves from modern theism and the theodicy that almost always accompanies it. Certain philosophical formulations of God's nature has something to do with accepting the particularity of God's revelation in Jesus. Correlatively, many atheist arguments can help theologians to strip away idolatrous conceptions of God. Stephen Bullivant has keenly observed: "It is surely true that positive atheists often reject specific conceptions of God that, frankly, do not pass muster in classical Christian theology . . . . To a certain degree, this helps us to see some of the points of constructive contact between faith and unbelief. For example, atheists' critiques can indeed aid us in purifying our ever faulty notions of 'the God who is not a god.'"[3] God is not a moral agent who can be morally praised by theists, or blamed by atheists for behaving badly. Morality only applies to humans beings, not to a timeless, infinite, and unchanging God.

Classical Christian theology holds that the Christian God is a God of universal love; he wills the salvation of every person in his or her unique circumstances. God wants all human beings to be saved through Jesus Christ in the power of the Holy Spirit, regardless if the redeemed are aware of this fact or not.

---

3. Bullivant, *Faith and Unbelief*, 16, 23.

Bibliography

Allison, Dale C. "Rational Apologetics and the Resurrection of Jesus." *Philosophia Christi* 10 (2008) 315–35.

———. *Resurrecting Jesus: The Earliest Christian Tradition and Its Interpreters.* London: T. & T .Clark, 2005.

Amundsen, Darrel W., Ronald L. Numbers, and Martin E. Marty, eds. *Caring and Curing: Health and Medicine in the Western Religious Traditions.* Baltimore: Johns Hopkins University Press, 1997.

Anderson, Norman. *Christianity and the World Religions.* Downer's Grove, IL: IVP, 1984.

Angeles, Peter. *The Problem of God.* Columbus: Merrill, 1974.

Anscombe, Elizabeth. "Modern Moral Philosophy." *Philosophy* 33 (1958) 1–19.

Aquinas, Thomas. *Compendium of Theology.* Translated by C. Vollert. St. Louis: Herder, 1947.

———. *Summa Theologiae.* Translated by the Fathers of the English Dominican Province. Westminster, MD: Christian Classics, 1981.

———. *Summa Contra Gentiles.* Translated by A. C. Pegis. 4 vols. Notre Dame, IN: University of Notre Dame Press, 1991.

Ashley, Benedict M. *Choosing a World-View and Value System: An Ecumenical Apologetics.* New York: Alba House, 2000.

———. *The Way Toward Wisdom: An Interdisciplinary and Intercultural Introduction to Metaphysics.* Notre Dame, IN: University of Notre Dame Press, 2009.

Baldwin, John W. *The Scholastic Culture of the Middle Ages, 1000–1300.* Lexington, KY: Heath, 1971.

Balthasar, Hans Urs von. *Love Alone is Credible.* San Francisco: Ignatius, 2005.

Barbour, Ian. *Religion and Science: Historical and Contemporary Perspectives.* Rev. ed. New York: HarperOne, 1997.

Bauckham, Richard. *Jesus and the Eyewitnesses: The Gospels as Eyewitness Testimony.* Grand Rapids: Eerdmans, 2006.

———. *Jesus and the God of Israel: God Crucified and Other Studies on the New Testament's Christology of Divine Identity.* Milton Keynes, UK: Paternoster, 2008.

Benedict XVI. *Caritas in Veritate.*

———. *Deus Caritas Est.*

———. *Spe Salvi.*

Bird, Michael F., and James G. Crossley. *How Did Christianity Begin?: A Believer and Non-believer Examine the Evidence.* London: SPCK, 2008.

Blau, Joseph L. *Modern Varieties of Judaism.* New York: Columbia University Press, 1966.

Blehl, V. F. *The Essential Newman.* New York: Mentor Omega, 1963.

Blondel, Maurice. *Action (1893): Essay on a Critique of Life and a Science of Practice.* Notre Dame, IN: University of Notre Dame Press, 1984.

―――. *The Letter on Apologetics and History and Dogma.* Translated by A. Dru and I. Trethowan. Grand Rapids: Eerdmans, 1995.

Bloom, Allan. *The Closing of the American Mind.* New York: Simon & Schuster, 1987.

Bode, E. L. *The First Easter Morning: The Gospel Accounts of the Women's Visit to the Tomb of Jesus.* Rome: Biblical Institute, 1970.

Borg, Marcus. *Jesus: Uncovering the Life, Teachings, and Relevance of a Religious Revolutionary.* San Francisco: HarperCollins, 2006.

Borg, Marcus J., and N. T. Wright. *The Meaning of Jesus.* San Francisco: HarperCollins, 1999.

Boyd, Craig A. *A Shared Morality: A Narrative Defense of Natural Law Ethics.* Grand Rapids: Baker Academic, 2007.

Boyd, Gregory A., and Paul R. Eddy. *The Jesus Legend: A Case for the Historical Reliability of the Synoptic Jesus Traditions.* Grand Rapids: Baker Academic, 2007.

Brady, Baruch A., ed. *Readings in the Philosophy of Religion.* Englewood Cliffs, NJ: Prentice-Hall, 1974.

Brown, Raymond E. *The Death of the Messiah.* 2 vols. Garden City, NY: Doubleday, 1994.

―――. *An Introduction to New Testament Christology.* Mahwah, NJ: Paulist, 1994.

―――. *The Virginal Conception and Bodily Resurrection of Jesus.* New York: Paulist, 1973.

Buckley, Michael J. *At the Origins of Modern Atheism.* Reprint. New Haven, CT: Yale University Press, 1990.

―――. *Denying and Disclosing God: The Ambiguous Progress of Modern Atheism.* New Haven, CT: Yale University Press, 2004.

Bullivant, Stephen. *Faith and Unbelief.* Norwich, UK: Canterbury, 2013.

Burridge, Richard A. *What are the Gospels? A Comparison with Graeco-Roman Biography.* 2nd ed. Grand Rapids: Eerdmans, 2004.

Byrskog, Samuel. *Story as History―History as Story: The Gospel Tradition in the Context of Ancient Oral History.* Leiden: Brill Academic, 2002.

Casey, Maurice. *Jesus of Nazareth: An Independent Historian's Account of His Life and Teaching.* London: T. & T. Clark, 2010.

―――. *Jesus: Evidence and Argument or Mythicist Myths?* London: T. & T. Clark, 2014.

Catholic Church. *Catechism of the Catholic Church: Revised in Accordance with the Official Latin Text Promulgated by Pope John Paul II.* Vatican City: Libreria Editrice Vaticana, 1997.

Chilton, Bruce, and Craig A. Evans, eds. *Studying the Historical Jesus: Evaluations of the State of Current Research.* Leiden: Brill Academic, 1994.

Bryan, Christopher. *The Resurrection of the Messiah.* Oxford: Oxford University Press, 2011.

Clooney, Francis X. *Hindu God-Christian God: How Reason Helps Break Down the Boundaries between Religions.* Oxford: Oxford University Press, 2010.

Clarke, W. Norris. *The One and the Many: A Contemporary Thomistic Metaphysics.* Notre Dame, IN: University of Notre Dame Press, 2001.

Clayton, Philip, and Jeffrey Schloss, eds. *Evolution and Ethics: Human Morality in Biological and Religious Perspective.* Grand Rapids: Eerdmans, 2004.

Cohen, Harvey J., and Harold G. Koening. *The Link between Religion and Health: Psychoneuroimmunology and the Faith Factor.* Oxford: Oxford University Press, 2005.

Congar, Yves. *The Wide World, My Parish: Salvation and Its Problems.* Translated by D. Attwater. London: Darton, Longman, & Todd, 1961.

Congregation for the Doctrine of the Faith. *Dominus Iesus.*

Copan, Paul, ed. *Will the Real Jesus Please Stand Up?: A Debate between William Lane Craig and John Dominic Crossan.* Grand Rapids: Baker Academic, 1998.

Cornille, Catherine. *The Im-Possibility of Interreligious Dialogue.* New York: Herder & Herder, 2008.

Craig, William L. *Reasonable Faith: Christian Truth and Apologetics.* 3rd ed. Wheaton, IL: Crossway, 2008.

Craig, William L., and J. P. Moreland. *Philosophical Foundations for a Christian Worldview.* Downer's Grove, IL: IVP, 2003.

Crean, Thomas. *God is No Delusion.* San Francisco: Ignatius, 2007.

Davies, Brian. *An Introduction to the Philosophy of Religion.* 3rd ed. Oxford: Oxford University Press, 2004.

———. *The Reality of God and the Problem of Evil.* New York: Continuum, 2006.

———. *Thomas Aquinas on God and Evil.* Oxford: Oxford University Press, 2011.

Davies, Paul. *The Cosmic Jackpot.* New York: Houghton Mifflin, 2007.

———. *The Mind of God.* New York: Simon & Schuster, 2002.

Davis, Leo D. *The First Seven Ecumenical Councils (325–787): Their History and Theology.* Collegeville, MN: Liturgical, 1987.

Davis, Steven, Daniel Kendall, and Gerald O'Collins, eds. *The Resurrection: An Interdisciplinary Symposium on the Resurrection of Jesus.* Oxford: Oxford University Press, 1999.

Davison, Andrew, ed. *Imaginative Apologetics: Theology, Philosophy, and the Catholic Tradition.* Grand Rapids: Baker Academic, 2012.

Dawkins, Richard. *The God Delusion.* New York: Houghton Mifflin, 2006.

———. *River Out of Eden: A Darwinian View of Life.* New York: HarperCollins, 1995.

———. *The Selfish Gene.* 2nd ed. Oxford: Oxford University Press, 2006.

Dawson, Christopher. *Religion and the Rise of Western Culture.* New York: Doubleday, 1991.

D'Costa, Gavin, Paul Knitter, and Daniel A. Strange, eds. *Only One Way? Three Christian Responses on the Uniqueness of Christ in a Religiously Plural World.* London: SCM, 2012.

D'Costa, Gavin. *Vatican II: Catholic Doctrines on Jews and Muslims.* Oxford: Oxford University Press, 2014.

Dennett, Daniel C. *Breaking the Spell: Religion as a Natural Phenomenon.* New York: Viking Penguin, 2006.

Derrida, Jacques. "Limited, Inc. abc . . ." In *Glyph 2*, 162–254. Baltimore: Johns Hopkins University Press, 1977.

Dulles, Avery. *Apologetics and the Biblical Christ.* New York: Newman, 1971.

————. *The Assurance of Things Hoped For: A Christian Theology of Faith.* Oxford: Oxford University Press, 1994.

————. *The Catholicity of the Church.* Oxford: Oxford University Press, 1987.

————. "The Church as 'One, Holy, Catholic, and Apostolic.'" *Evangelical Review of Theology* 23 (1999) 14–28.

————. *A Church to Believe In: Discipleship and the Dynamics of Freedom.* New York: Crossroad, 1983.

————. "Historians and the Reality of Christ." *First Things,* December 1992, 20–25.

————. *A History of Apologetics.* Rev. ed. San Francisco: Ignatius, 2005.

————. *Magisterium: Teacher and Guardian of the Faith.* Naples, FL: Sapientia Press of Ave Maria University, 2007.

————. *Models of Revelation.* Reprint. Maryknoll, NY: Orbis, 1992.

————. "The Population of Hell." *First Things,* May 2003, 36–41.

————. "The Rebirth of Apologetics." *First Things,* May 2004, 18–23.

Dunn, James D. G. *Did the First Christians Worship Jesus? The New Testament Evidence.* Louisville: Westminster John Knox, 2010.

————. *The Evidence for Jesus.* Louisville, KY: Westminster, 1985.

————. *Jesus Paul, and the Gospels.* Grand Rapids: Eerdmans, 2011.

————. *Jesus Remembered.* Grand Rapids: Eerdmans, 2003.

————. *The Oral Gospel Tradition.* Grand Rapids: Eerdmans, 2013.

Dupuis, Jacques. *Christianity and the Religions: From Confrontation to Dialogue.* Maryknoll, NY: Orbis, 2002.

————. *Toward a Christian Theology of Religious Pluralism.* Maryknoll, NY: Orbis, 1997.

Dyson, Freeman. "Energy in the Universe." *Scientific American* 225 (1971) 50–59.

Ehrman, Bart D. *Did Jesus Exist? The Historical Argument for Jesus of Nazareth.* New York: HarperCollins, 2013.

————. *How Jesus Became God: The Exaltation of a Jewish Preacher from Galilee.* New York: HarperCollins, 2014.

————. *Jesus, Interrupted: Revealing the Hidden Contradictions in the Bible (And Why We Don't Know about Them).* New York: HarperOne, 2010.

————. *The New Testament: A Historical Introduction to the New Testament Writings.* 3rd ed. Oxford: Oxford University Press, 2004.

Englehart, H. Tristam, Richard M. McMillan, and Stuart F. Spiker, eds. *Euthanasia and the Newborn: Conflicts Regarding Saving Lives.* Dortrecht: Reidel, 1987.

Everitt, Nicholas. *The Non-Existence of God.* New York: Routledge, 2004.

Farrelly, M. John. *Belief in God in Our Time.* Collegeville, MN: Liturgical, 1992.

Fenton, Joseph C. *The Catholic Church and Salvation: In Light of the Recent Pronouncements of the Holy See.* Westminster, MD: Newman, 1958.

————. "The True Church and the Notes of the Church." *The American Ecclesiastical Review* 114 (1943) 282–97.

Ferngren, Gary B. "Medicine and Compassion in Early Christianity." *Theology Digest* 46 (1999) 1–12.

————. *Medicine and Health Care in Early Christianity.* Baltimore: Johns Hopkins University Press, 2009.

Feser, Edward. *Aquinas.* Oxford: Oneworld, 2009.

————. "Teleology: A Shopper's Guide." *Philosophia Christi* 12 (2010) 142–59.

Fisichella, Rino. *The New Evangelization: Responding to the Challenge of Indifference.* Leominster, UK: Gracewing, 2012.

Fisichella, Rino, and René Latourelle, eds. *Dictionary of Fundamental Theology.* New York: Crossroad, 2000.

Flew, Antony. *God and Philosophy.* London: Hutchinson, 1966.

———. *God and Philosophy.* Amherst, NY: Prometheus, 2005.

———. *There is a God: How the World's Most Notorious Atheist Changed His Mind.* New York: HarperCollins, 2007.

Flew, Antony, and Gary R. Habermas. *Did Jesus Rise from the Dead? The Resurrection Debate.* San Francisco: Harper & Row, 1987.

Foucault, Michel. *Discipline and Punish: The Birth of the Prison.* Translated by A. Sheridan. New York: Pantheon, 1978.

———. "Nietzsche, Genealogy, History." In *Language, Counter-Memory, Practice: Selected Essays and Articles,* 139–65, translated by D. F. Bouchard and S. Simon. Ithaca, NY: Cornell University Press, 1977.

Foster, Daniel R., and Joseph W. Koterski, eds. *The Two Wings of Catholic Thought: Essays on Fides et Ratio.* Washington, DC: The Catholic University of America Press, 2003.

Francis. *Lumen Fidei.*

Freud, Ernst L., and Heinrich Meng, eds. *Psychoanalysis and Faith: The Letters of Sigmund Freud and Oscar Pfister.* Translated by E. Mosbacher. New York: Basic, 1962.

Fuller, Reginald. *The Formation of the Resurrection Narratives.* New York: Macmillan, 1971.

Gaca, Kathy L. *The Making of Fornication: Eros, Ethics, and Political Reform in Greek Philosophy and Early Christianity.* Berkeley, CA: University of California Press, 2003.

Gaillardetz, Richard. "Apologetics, Evangelization, and Ecumenism Today." *Origins* 35 (2005) 9–15.

———. "Do We Need a New(er) Apologetics?" *America* 190 (2004) 26–33.

Gale, Richard M. *On the Nature and Existence of God.* Cambridge: Cambridge University Press, 1993.

Garcia, Robert K., and Nathan L. King, eds. *Is Goodness Without God Good Enough? A Debate on Faith, Secularism and Ethics.* Lanham, MD: Rowman & Littlefield, 2009.

Garrigou-Lagrange, Reginald. *God: His Existence and His Nature.* 2 vols, 5th ed. St. Louis: Herder & Herder, 1955.

Gathercole, Simon J. *The Preexistent Son: The Earliest Christologies of Matthew, Mark and Luke.* Grand Rapids: Eerdmans, 2006.

Gaukroger, Stephen. *The Emergence of a Scientific Culture: Science and the Shaping of Modernity 1210–1685.* Oxford: Oxford University Press, 2009.

Gauld, Alan. *The Founders of Psychical Research.* New York: Schoken, 1968.

Gies, Frances, and Joseph Gies. *Cathedral, Forge and Waterwheel: Technology and Invention in the Middle Ages.* New York: HarperCollins, 1995.

Gilson, Etienne. *The Christian Philosophy of Saint Thomas Aquinas.* Notre Dame, IN: University of Notre Dame Press, 1994.

Gimpel, Jean. *The Medieval Machine: The Industrial Revolution of the Middle Ages.* New York: Penguin, 1976.

Giola, Francisco, ed. *Interreligious Dialogue: The Official Teaching of the Catholic Church from the Second Vatican Council to John Paul II: 1963–2005.* Boston: Pauline, 2005.

Gordon, Colin, ed. *Power/Knowledge.* New York: Pantheon, 1980.

Goyette, John, Mark S. Latcovic, and Richard S. Myers, eds. *St. Thomas Aquinas and the Natural Law Tradition.* Washington, DC: The Catholic University of America Press, 2004.

Grant, Edward. *The Foundations of Modern Science in the Middle Ages: Their Religious, Institutional, and Intellectual Contexts.* Cambridge: Cambridge University Press, 1996.

Green, Celia, and Charles McCreery. *Apparitions.* London: Hamilton, 1975.

Griffiths, Paul J. *An Apology for Apologetics: A Study in the Logic of Interreligious Dialogue.* Eugene, OR: Wipf & Stock, 2008.

———. "Why We Need Interreligious Polemics." *First Things* (June/July 1994) 31–37.

Grigsby, Bryon L., and Stephen Harris. *Misconceptions About the Middle Ages.* New York: Routledge, 2007.

Grindheim, Sigurd. *God's Equal: What We Can Know about Jesus' Self-Understanding in the Synoptic Gospels.* London: T. & T. Clark, 2011.

Guinness, Ivor-Grattan, ed. *Psychical Research: A Guide to its History, Principles and Practices: In Celebration of 100 Years of the Society for Psychical Research.* Wellingborough, UK: Aquarian, 1982.

Habermas, Gary. "Resurrection Claims in Non-Christian Religions." *Religious Studies* 25 (1989) 167–77.

———. "Resurrection Research from 1975 to the Present: What are Critical Scholars Saying?" *Journal for the Study of the Historical Jesus*, 3 (2005) 135–53.

Haight, Roger. *Dynamics of Theology.* Maryknoll, NY: Orbis, 2001.

Haldane, John, and J. J. C. Smart. *Atheism and Theism.* 2nd ed. Cambridge: Blackwell, 2003.

Haraldsson, Erlunder. *The Departed Among the Living: An Investigative Study of Afterlife Encounters.* Guildford, UK: White Crow, 2012.

Haught, John F. *Is Nature Enough? Meaning and Truth in the Age of Science.* Cambridge: Cambridge University Press, 2006.

———. *Science and Religion: From Conflict to Conversation.* Mahwah, NJ: Paulist, 1995.

Hardon, John A. *The Catholic Catechism.* New York: Doubleday, 1975.

Hart, David Bentley *Atheist Delusions: The Christian Revolution and Its Fashionable Enemies.* New Haven, CT: Yale University Press, 2009.

Hebblethwaite, Brian. *In Defence of Christianity.* Oxford: Oxford University Press, 2005.

Hefling, Charles, and Stephen J. Pope, eds. *Sic et Non: Encountering Dominus Iesus.* Maryknoll, NY: Orbis, 2002.

Heim, S. Mark. *The Depth of the Riches: A Trinitarian Theology of Religious Ends.* Grand Rapids: Eerdmans, 2001.

Henry, Jane, ed. *Parapsychology: Research and Exceptional Experiences.* New York: Routledge, 2004.

Hick, John. *Evil and the God of Love.* 2nd ed. London: Palgrave Macmillan, 1977.

———. *An Interpretation of Religion: Human Responses to the Transcendent.* 2nd ed. New Haven, CT: Yale University Press, 2005.

Hill, Brennan, Paul Knitter, and William Madges. *Faith, Religion, and Theology: A Contemporary Introduction.* Mystic, CT: Twenty Third, 1990.

Hodgson, Peter E. *Theology and Modern Physics.* Burlington, VT: Ashgate, 2005.

Holder, Rodney D. *God, the Universe and Everything: Modern Cosmology and the Argument from Design*. Farnham, UK: Ashgate, 2004.

Hooykaas, Reijer. *Religion and the Rise of Modern Science*. New York: Regent College, 2000.

Houran, James, and Rense Lange. *Hauntings and Poltergeists: Multidisciplinary Perspectives*. Jefferson, MO: McFarland & Company, 2001.

Hünermann, Peter, ed. Heinrich Denzinger, *Enchiridion symbolorum definitionum et declarationum*. 43rd ed. San Francisco: Ignatius, 2012.

Hurtado, Larry W. *At the Origins of Christian Worship: The Context and Character of Earliest Christian Devotion*. Carlisle, UK: Paternoster, 2000.

———. *How on Earth Did Jesus Become a God? Historical Questions about Earliest Devotion to Jesus*. Grand Rapids: Eerdmans, 2005.

———. *Lord Jesus Christ: Devotion to Jesus in Earliest Christianity*. Grand Rapids: Eerdmans, 2003.

———. *One God, One Lord: Early Christian Devotion and Ancient Jewish Monotheism*. 2nd ed. London: T. & T. Clark, 2003.

Hyman, Gavin. *A Short History of Atheism*. London: I. B. Tauris, 2010.

International Theological Commission. *Christianity and the World Religions*.

———. *Select Themes of Ecclesiology on the Occasion of the Twentieth Anniversary of the Closing of the Second Vatican Council*.

Irwin, Harvey J., and Caroline A. Watt, *An Introduction to Parapsychology*. 5th ed. Jefferson, MO: McFarland, 2007.

Jansen, J. H. *Militant Islam*. New York: Harper & Row, 1979.

Jaki, Stanley. *Science and Creation: From Eternal Cycles to an Oscillating Universe*. New York: University Press of America, 1974.

John XXIII. *Ad Petri Cathedram*.

———. *Mater et Magistra*.

———. *Pacem in Terris*.

———. *Princeps Pastorum*.

John Paul II. *Centesimus Annus*.

———. *Crossing the Threshold of Hope*. New York: Knopf, 2005.

———. *Dives in Misericordia*.

———. *Dominum et Vivificantem*.

———. *Ecclesia de Eucharistia*.

———. *Evangelium Vitae*.

———. *Fides et Ratio*.

———. *Letter to Artists*.

———. *Redemptoris Mater*.

———. *Redemptoris Missio*.

———. *Tertio Millennio Adveniente*.

———. *Ut Unum Sint*.

———. *Veritatis Splendor*.

Johnson, B. C. *The Atheist Debator's Handbook*. Buffalo, NY: Prometheus, 1981.

Johnson, Paul. *Art: A New History*. New York: HarperCollins, 2003.

Johnson, Luke T. *The Real Jesus*. San Francisco: HarperCollins, 1996.

Journet, Charles. *The Meaning of Evil*. Translated by M. Barry. New York: Kenedy, 1963.

Kamen, Henry. *The Spanish Inquisition: A Historical Revision*. New Haven, CT: Yale University Press, 1997.

Kasper, Walter. *The God of Jesus Christ*. Translated by M. J. O'Connell. New York: Crossroad, 1984.

———. *Jesus the Christ*. Translated by V. Green. Mahwah, NJ: Paulist, 1976.

———. *Theology and Church*. New York: Crossroad, 1989.

Kaufman, Walter, ed. *The Portable Nietzsche*. New York: Viking Penguin, 1968.

Keener, Craig S. *The Historical Jesus of the Gospels*. Grand Rapids: Eerdmans, 2009.

———. *Miracles: The Credibility of the New Testament Accounts*. 2 vols. Grand Rapids: Baker Academic, 2011.

Kenny, Anthony. *The Five Ways*. New York: Routlege, 1969.

Kereszty, Roch. A. *Christianity Among Other Religions: Apologetics in a Contemporary Context*. New York: Alba House, 2006.

Kimball, Charles. *When Religion Becomes Evil*. New York: HarperCollins, 2003.

Knitter, Paul. *Introducing Theologies of Religions*. Maryknoll, NY: Orbis, 2002.

———. *Jesus and the Other Names*. Maryknoll, NY: Orbis, 1996.

———. ed. *The Myth of Religious Superiority*. Maryknoll, NY: Orbis, 2005.

———. *One Earth, Many Religions*. Maryknoll, NY: Orbis, 1995.

Kreeft, Peter. *Heaven: The Heart's Deepest Longing*. Exp. ed. San Francisco: Ignatius, 1989.

Kreeft, Peter, and Ronald Tacelli. *Handbook of Catholic Apologetics: Reasoned Answers to Questions of Faith*. San Francisco: Ignatius, 2009.

Krueger, Douglas. *What is Atheism?* Buffalo, NY: Prometheus, 1998.

Küng, Hans. *Does God Exist? An Answer for Today*. New York: Doubleday, 1980.

Kurtz, Paul. *Forbidden Fruit*. Buffalo, NY: Prometheus, 1988.

Lapide, Pinchas. *The Resurrection of Jesus: A Jewish Perspective*. Translated by W. C. Linss. Reprint. Eugene, OR: Wipf & Stock, 2002.

Latourelle, René. *Christ and the Church: Signs of Salvation*. Translated by D. Parker. New York: Alba House, 1972.

———. *Finding Jesus Through the Gospels: History and Hermeneutics*. New York: Alba House, 1979.

———. *The Miracles of Jesus and the Theology of Miracles*. Mahwah, NJ: Paulist, 1988.

———. *Theology of Revelation*. New York: Alba House, 1966.

Latourelle, René, and Gerald O'Collins, eds. *Problems and Perspectives of Fundamental Theology*. Translated by M. J. O'Connell. Ramsey, NJ: Paulist, 1982.

Leclercq, Jean. *The Love of Learning and The Desire for God: A Study of Monastic Culture*. New York: Fordham University Press, 1982.

Levada, William. "Giving Reasons for Our Hope: A New Apologetics for the New Evangelization." *Origins* 43 (2013) 33–42.

———. "A New Apologetics for the Church in the 21st Century." *Origins* 35 (2005) 7–15.

———. "Toward a New Apologetics." *Origins* 31 (2002) 661–67.

Levenson, Jon. *Resurrection and the Restoration of Israel: The Ultimate Victory of the God of Life*. New Haven, CT: Yale University Press, 2008.

Levering, Matthew. *Scripture and Metaphysics: Aquinas and the Renewal of Trinitarian Theology*. Oxford: Blackwell, 2004.

Lewis, C. S. *God in the Dock: Essays in Theology and Ethics*, Grand Rapids: Eerdmans, 1970.

———. "Is Theology Poetry?" In *Essay Collection and Other Short Pieces*, 1–21. London: HarperCollins, 2000.

————. *The Screwtape Letters*. Rev ed. New York: Palgrave Macmillan, 1961.

Lindberg, David C. *The Beginnings of Western Science: The European Scientific Tradition in Philosophical, Religious, and Institutional Contexts, Prehistory to A.D. 1450*. 2nd ed. Chicago: University of Chicago Press, 2008.

Lüdemann, Gerd. *The Resurrection of Christ: A Historical Inquiry*. Amherst, NY: Prometheus, 2004.

————. *The Resurrection of Jesus: History, Experience, Theology*. Translated by J. Bowden. Minneapolis: Fortress, 1994.

————. *What Really Happened to Jesus? A Historical Approach to the Resurrection*. Louisville, KY: Westminster John Knox, 1995.

Lyotard, Jean-François. *The Postmodern Condition*. Minneapolis: University of Minnesota Press, 1979.

Mackie, J. L. *The Miracle of Theism*. Oxford: Oxford University Press, 1982.

Manson, Neil. *God and Design*. New York: Routledge, 2003.

Maritain, Jacques. *Approaches to God*. Translated by P. O'Reilly. New York: Harper, 1954.

Marshall, I. Howard. *I Believe in the Historical Jesus*. Grand Rapids: Eerdmans, 1977.

Martin, David. *Does Christianity Cause War?* Oxford: Oxford University Press, 1997.

Martin, Michael, ed. *The Cambridge Companion to Atheism*. Cambridge: Cambridge University Press, 2006.

McGrath, Alsiter E. *The Open Secret: A New Vision for Natural Theology*. Oxford: Blackwell, 2008.

McGrath, Alister E., and Joanna C. McGrath. *The Dawkins Delusion?* Downer's Grove, IL: IVP, 2007.

McInerney, Ralph. *Characters in Search of Their Author*. Notre Dame, IN: University of Notre Dame Press, 2001.

McIntyre, Alisdair. "Which God Ought We to Obey and Why." *Faith and Philosophy* 3 (1986) 359–71.

McKnight, Scot, and Joseph B. Modica, eds. *Who Do My Opponents Say I Am? An Investigation of the Accusations against the Historical Jesus*. London: T. & T. Clark, 2008.

McMullin, Ernan, ed. *Evolution and Creation*. Notre Dame, IN: University of Notre Dame Press, 1985.

Meier, John P. *A Marginal Jew: Rethinking the Historical Jesus, Vol. 1, The Roots of the Problem and Person*. New York: Doubleday, 1991.

————. *A Marginal Jew: Rethinking the Historical Jesus, Vol. 2: Mentor, Message, and Miracles*. New York: Doubleday, 1994.

————. *The Vision of Matthew: Christ, Church, and Morality in the First Gospel*. Mahwah, NJ: Paulist, 1979.

Meynell, Hugo A. *Is Christianity True?* Washington, DC: The Catholic University of America Press, 1994.

Miller, William R., and Carl E. Thoreson. "Spirituality, Religion, and Health: An Emerging Research Field." *American Psychologist* 58 (2003) 24–35.

Mitchell, Edgar D., and John White, eds. *Psychic Exploration: A Challenge for Science*. New York: Putnam's, 1974.

Moreland, J. P. *Scaling the Secular City: A Defense of Christianity*. Grand Rapids: Baker Academic, 1987.

Morerod, Charles. *The Church and the Human Quest For Truth.* Naples, FL: Sapientia Press of Ave Maria University, 2008.

Morrison, Frank. *Who Moved the Stone?* Grand Rapids: Zondervan, 1987.

Morris, J. D. et al., eds. *Research in Parapsychology.* Metuchen, NJ: Scarecrow, 1977.

Murphy, John P. *Pragmatism: From Pierce to Davidson.* Boulder, CO: Westview, 1990.

Neusner, Jacob. *A Rabbi Talks with Jesus.* New York: Doubleday, 1993.

Nielson, Kai. *Ethics Without God.* Rev. ed. Amherst, NY: Prometheus, 1990.

Nietzsche, Friedrich. *The Will to Power.* Translated by W. Kaufmann and R. Hollingdale. New York: Random, 1968.

Newman, John H. *An Essay in Aid of a Grammar of Assent.* Notre Dame, IN: University of Notre Dame Press, 1992.

Nichols, Aidan. *The Shape of Catholic Theology.* Collegeville, MN: Liturgical, 1991.

O'Collins, Gerald. *Believing in the Resurrection: The Meaning and Promise of the Risen Jesus.* Mahwah, NJ: Paulist, 2012.

———. *Christology: A Biblical, Historical, and Systematic Study of Jesus.* 2nd ed. Oxford: Oxford University Press, 2009.

———. *Easter Faith: Believing in the Risen Jesus.* Mahwah, NJ: Paulist, 2003.

———. "Fundamental Theology: The Continuing Debate." *Pacifica* 27 (2014) 97–110.

———. *Interpreting Jesus.* London: Chapman, 1983.

———. *Jesus Risen: An Historical, Fundamental and Systematic Examination of Christ's Resurrection.* New York: Paulist, 1987.

———. "The Resurrection and Bereavement Experiences." *Irish Theological Quarterly.* 76 (2011) 224–37.

———. *Rethinking Fundamental Theology.* Oxford: Oxford University Press, 2011.

———. *The Second Vatican Council on Other Religions.* Oxford: Oxford University Press, 2013.

———. *The Tripersonal God: Understanding and Interpreting the Trinity.* 2nd ed. Mahwah, NJ: Paulist, 2014.

Oppy, Graham. *Arguing About Gods.* Cambridge: Cambridge University Press, 2006.

Osler, Margaret J. *Reconfiguring the World: Nature, God, and Human Understanding from the Middle Ages to Early Modern Europe.* Baltimore: Johns Hopkins University Press, 2010.

Palmer, John. "A Community Mail Survey of Psychic Experiences." *Journal of American Society of Psychical Research* 69 (1979) 226–39.

Pannenberg, Wolfhart. *Jesus—God and Man.* Translated by L. L. Wilkens and D. A. Priebe. London: SCM, 1968.

Pargament, Kenneth I. *The Psychology of Religion and Coping: Theory, Research Practice.* New York: Guilford, 2001.

Paul VI. *Christi Matri.*

———. *Ecclesiam Suam.*

———. *Humanae Vitae.*

———. *Mysterium Fidei.*

———. *Populorum Progressio.*

———. *Sacerdotalis Caelibatus.*

Peacocke, Arthur. *Theology for a Scientific Age: Being and Becoming—Natural, Divine.* Minneapolis: Fortress, 1993.

Peters, Ted, ed. *Science and Theology: The New Consonance.* Boulder, CO: Westview, 1998.

Peterson, John. *Aquinas: A New Introduction.* Lanham, MD: University Press of America, 2008.

Phan, Peter C., ed. *The Gift of the Church.* Collegeville, MN: Liturgical, 2000.

Pinckaers, Servais. *The Sources of Christian Ethics.* Translated by M. T. Noble. Washington, DC: The Catholic University of America Press, 1995.

Pinker, Steven. *The Blank Slate.* New York: Penguin, 2002.

————. *How the Mind Works.* New York: Norton, 1997.

Polkinghorne, John. *Belief in God in an Age of Science.* New Haven, CT: Yale University Press, 2003.

————. *Serious Talk.* London: SCM, 1996.

Pontifical Biblical Commission. *The Historicity of the Gospels.*

————. *The Interpretation of the Bible in the Church.*

Pontifical Council for Interreligious Dialogue. *Dialogue and Proclamation.*

Porter, Jean. *Nature as Reason: A Thomistic Theory of the Natural Law.* Grand Rapids: Eerdmans, 2004.

Porterfield, Amanda. *Healing in the History of Christianity.* Oxford: Oxford University Press, 2005.

Rahner, Karl. *Foundations of Christian Faith.* Translated by W. V. Dych. New York: Seabury, 1978.

————. *Theological Investigations,* vol. 3. New York: Crossroad, 1975.

Ratzinger, Joseph. "Relativism: The Central Problem for Faith Today." *Origins* 26 (1996) 309–16.

————. *Truth and Tolerance: Christian Belief and World Religions.* San Francisco: Ignatius, 2004.

Riche, Pierre. *Education and Culture in the Barbarian West: From the Sixth through the Eighth Century.* Translated by J. Contreni. Columbia, SC: University of South Carolina Press, 1976.

Rorty, Richard. *Consequences of Pragmatism.* Minneapolis: University of Minnesota Press, 1982.

————. "Solidarity or Objectivity?" In *Objectivity, Relativism, and Truth.* New York: Cambridge University Press, 1991.

Rowe, William L. *The Cosmological Argument.* Princeton, NJ: Princeton University Press, 1975.

Ruokanen, Miika. *The Catholic Doctrine of Non-Christian Religions: According to the Second Vatican Council.* Leiden: Brill Academic, 1992.

Russell, Bertrand. *Human Society in Ethics and Politics.* London: George Allen & Unwin, 1954.

————. *Why I Am Not A Christian.* New York: Simon & Schuster, 1957.

Rziha, John. *Perfecting Human Actions: St. Thomas Aquinas on Human Participation in Eternal Law.* Washington, DC: The Catholic University of America Press, 2009.

Sanders, E. P. *The Historical Figure of Jesus.* New York: Penguin, 1993.

————. *Jesus and Judaism.* Philadelphia: Fortress, 1985.

Saward, John. *The Beauty of Holiness and the Holiness of Beauty: Art, Sanctity, and the Truth of Catholicism.* San Francisco: Ignatius, 1997.

Scholem, Gershom. *Major Trends in Jewish Mysticism.* 3rd ed. New York: Schoken, 1954.

Scott, Robert A. *The Gothic Enterprise.* Berkeley, CA: University of California Press, 2003.

Searle, John. *The Construction of Social Reality*. New York: Free, 1995.

Shermer, Michael. *How We Believe*. New York: Freeman, 2000.

Shook, John R. *The God Debates: A 21st Century Guide for Atheists and Believers (and Everyone in Between)*. Oxford: Blackwell, 2010.

Sidgwick, Henry, et. al. "Report on the Census of Hallucinations." *Proceedings for the Society of Psychical Research* 10 (1894) 25–422.

Sinnott-Armstrong, Walter. *Morality Without God?*. Oxford: Oxford University Press, 2011.

Smith, George H. *Atheism: The Case against God*. Amherst, NY: Prometheus, 1989.

Stark, Rodney. *For the Glory of God: How Monotheism Led to Reformations, Science, Witch-Hunts, and the End of Slavery*. Princeton, NJ: Princeton University Press, 2003.

———. *The Rise of Christianity*. Princeton, NJ: Princeton University Press, 1996.

———. *The Triumph of Christianity: How the Jesus Movement Became the World's Largest Religion*. New York: HarperOne, 2011.

———. *The Victory of Reason: How Christianity Led to Freedom, Capitalism, and Western Success*. New York: Random, 2006.

Stewart, Robert B., ed. *Can Only One Religion Be True? Paul Knitter and Harold Netland in Dialogue*. Minneapolis: Fortress, 2013.

———, ed. *The Resurrection of Jesus: John Dominic Crossan and N. T. Wright in Dialogue*. Minneapolis: Fortress, 2006.

Stump Donald, et al. *Harmartia: The Concept of Error in the Western Tradition*. New York: Mellon, 1983.

Sullivan, Francis A. *The Church We Believe In: One, Holy, Catholic and Apostolic*. Mahwah, NJ: Paulist, 1988.

———. *Salvation Outside the Church? Tracing the History of the Catholic Response*. Mahwah, NJ: Paulist, 1992.

Swinburne, Richard. *Providence and the Problem of Evil*. Oxford: Oxford University Press, 1998.

———. *The Resurrection of God Incarnate*. Oxford: Oxford University Press, 2003.

———. *Revelation: From Metaphor to Analogy*. 2nd ed. Oxford: Oxford University Press, 2007.

———. *Was Jesus God?* Oxford: Oxford University Press, 2009.

Templeton, John M., ed. *Evidence of Purpose*. New York: Continuum, 1994.

Thiselton, Anthony. *The First Epistle to the Corinthians: A Commentary on the Greek Text*. Grand Rapids: Eerdmans, 2000.

Turner, Denys. *Faith, Reason and the Existence of God*. Cambridge: Cambridge University Press, 2004.

Tyrrell, G. N. M. *Apparitions*. New York: Collier, 1963.

Van Voorst, Robert E. *Jesus Outside the New Testament: An Introduction to the Ancient Evidence*. Grand Rapids: Eerdmans, 2000.

Vatican II. *Ad Gentes*.

———. *Dei Verbum*.

———. *Dignitatis Humanae*.

———. *Gaudium et Spes*.

———. *Lumen Gentium*.

———. *Nostra Aetate*.

———. *Optatium Totius*.

————. *Sacrosanctum Concilium.*

————. *Unitatis Redintegratio.*

Vermes, Geza. *The Resurrection of Jesus: History and Myth.* New York: Doubleday, 2008.

Vitz, Paul C. *The Faith of the Fatherless: The Psychology of Atheism.* Dallas: Spence, 2000.

Ward, Keith. *Is Religion Dangerous?* Grand Rapids: Eerdmans, 2007.

Waterman, Mark. *The Empty Tomb Tradition of Mark: Text, History and Theological Struggles.* Los Angeles: Agathos, 2006.

Weaver, Andrew J., et al. "A Systematic Review of Research on Religion and Spirituality in the *Journal of Traumatic Stress*, 1990–1999." *Mental Health, Religion, and Culture* (2003) 215–28.

Weisel, Elie. *Souls on Fire: Portraits and Legends of Hasidic Leaders.* New York: Vintage, 1973.

White, Lynn. *Medieval Religion and Technology.* Berkeley, CA: University of California Press, 1978.

Wielenberg, Erik J. "In Defense of Non-Natural, Non-Theistic Moral Realism." *Faith and Philosophy* 26 (2009) 23–41.

————. *Value and Virtue in a Godless Universe.* Cambridge: Cambridge University Press, 2005.

Weinberg, Steven. "A Designer Universe?" *The New York Review of Books* 46, 1999.

————. *Dreams of a Final Theory: The Scientist's Search for the Ultimate Laws of Nature.* New York: Vintage, 1993.

Wippel, John. *The Metaphysical Thought of Thomas Aquinas: From Finite Being to Uncreated Being.* Washington, DC: The Catholic University of America Press, 2000.

Wright, N. T. *The Resurrection of the Son of God.* London: SPCK, 2003.

Zuckerman, Phil. *Society Without God.* New York: New York University Press, 2010.